Reading Together, Reading Apart

THE ASIAN AMERICAN EXPERIENCE

Series Editors
Eiichiro Azuma
Jigna Desai
Martin F. Manalansan IV
Lisa Sun-Hee Park
David K. Yoo

Roger Daniels, Founding Series Editor

A list of books in the series appears at the end of this book.

READING TOGETHER, READING APART

Identity, Belonging, and South Asian American Community

TAMARA BHALLA

UNIVERSITY OF ILLINOIS PRESS
Urbana, Chicago, and Springfield

1 2 3 4 5 C P 5 4 3 2 1
∞ This book is printed on acid-free paper.

Library of Congress Control Number: 2016950833
ISBN 978-0-252-04048-1 (hardcover)
ISBN 978-0-252-08195-8 (paperback)
ISBN 978-0-252-09892-5 (e-book)

For Asha, my hope, and Kiran, my light.

CONTENTS

ACKNOWLEDGMENTS

Right now, my five-year-old daughter, Asha, is learning how to read. Reading to her, hearing her put new sounds together, seeing her determinedly page through books, and watching her teach her little sister, Kiran, to do all these same things comprise some of my most precious daily pleasures. Among my many hopes for my daughters is that reading becomes a central, treasured practice in their lives—a practice of empathy, solace, learning, imagination, solitude, and community—as it is for so many of us who love to read. I am grateful for the opportunity to watch this burgeoning literacy developing in my own home. It is a very personal and literal example of the practices and privileges of reading that reminds me of the fellowship and family of readers who have enabled me to complete this book.

I give my most heartfelt thanks first to the generous, insightful group of readers in the Network of South Asian Americans book club in Washington, DC, who took time out of their busy schedules, let me into their homes, agreed to have coffee or lunch with me, all in the service of helping me, a stranger, to complete this research. I especially want to thank the two leaders of the book club at the time that I was completing this ethnography for their unwavering support and interest in this research. I felt so fortunate to be working on a project that allowed me to discuss books with all of you.

My memories of the University of Michigan, where this project began, are particularly fond because of the excellent mentorship, guidance, and support I received, particularly from Sarita See, June Howard, and Meg Sweeney. Sarita, you remain for me a model of integrity, intellectual generosity, and compassion. I'll never forget your encouragement and your reminders to focus on the things that matter most to me. June, without you, I would have never been able to imagine this project into being. You've never failed to help me make sense of things. And Meg, I thank you for your inspiring work on readership and for helping me so graciously and with such close attention to improve an early draft of the introduction.

I also want to thank my colleagues at the University of Maryland Baltimore County. In the American Studies department, Nicole King, Theo Gonzalves, and Michelle Stefano have read various proposals and drafts and offered their guidance and support all the way. They also happen to be incredibly fun people to hang out with. I'm also grateful to Warren Belasco, Pat McDermott, Kimberly Moffitt, and Ed Orser for their advice and collegiality over the years. Nicoleta Bazgan, my kindred spirit, thank you for always celebrating and commiserating as need be. Jason Loviglio, your guidance was invaluable to me as I made the transition from graduate student to assistant professor. Rebecca Adelman, you are an inspiring scholar and good friend—so glad we're in this together.

My colleagues in Asian American studies have provided an outstanding network of friendship, mentorship, and readership. Crystal Parikh, Pam Thoma, and Daniel Y. Kim, —in addition to sharing some wonderful meals and drinks—you all have helped me to begin and finish this book, talking through the major concepts, reading chapters, explaining the publication process, and introducing me to new ideas and wonderful people. Crystal and Pam, I do not know how I would have finished this book without your support and I hope you know that I am ever grateful to you both. In myriad official and unofficial ways I have benefited from the mentoring and comradery of my colleagues in the field of Asian American studies; thank you Anita Mannur, Pawan Dhingra, Cathy Schlund-Vials, Anupama Jain, Yoonmee Chang, Min Hyoung Song, Bakirathi Mani, Nitasha Sharma, Lavina Dhingra, Rajini Srikanth, and Rani Neutill for your advice, for leading by example, and for your excellent contributions to the field. I was also fortunate to attend the inaugural East of California Junior Faculty Mentoring Workshop sponsored by the Association for Asian American Studies early on in my career as an assistant professor and benefited there from the wise guidance of Tina Chen, Sue Kim, Miliann Kang, Judy T. Wu, and Eric Hung.

Jigna Desai, when I wanted to give up, you helped me figure out how to keep going, as I know you have done for so many people. Your incisive comments on this book allowed me to see its potential and I feel truly grateful to count you as a friend, colleague, and mentor. Vanita Reddy, I feel like you've been next to me every step of the way. You have sustained me throughout this process, reading drafts, offering insight, and just talking through ideas. I feel so lucky to know that I have a friend as supportive and brilliant as you on my side. Anantha Sudhakar, the time we have spent together has had a huge impact on me: you have taught me so much, not only about South Asian American studies, but also about compassion and facing life's challenges with grace. Manan Desai, thank you for reading messy, early drafts of various chapters for me, and thank you for being a supportive and skeptical companion in this whole academic enterprise, from our days as graduate students to the present. Ji-Hyae Park, I am so lucky to have a friend who is such a brilliant and voracious interpreter of all kinds of texts as you are.

Dawn Durante, my editor at the University of Illinois press, I thank you for making this whole daunting process feel manageable. I have felt since I first met you that you have been an enthusiastic advocate for this project, and I am so grateful for your support and the support of the series editors as well as the editorial team at the press. I owe a particular debt of gratitude to Anita Mannur and Martin Manalansan for helping me to find a name for this book when I was at an impasse. I also give thanks to *MELUS* for allowing me to reprint in chapter 5 a portion of my essay "'Being (and Feeling) Gogol': Reading and Recognition in Jhumpa Lahiri's *The Namesake*," which was first published in *MELUS* 37.1 (2012): 105–29.

And finally, I give thanks to my friends and family:

Thanks to Jaime Pseres who not only listens patiently to my worries about work but who is my daily confidante on just about everything else.

Thank you to my inspiring mother, Ann Bhalla, an autodidact, a woman who has written two novels. You were the very first person to teach me the pleasures of reading.

Thank you to my father, Subhash Bhalla. I hope now you see what I've been working on for years. Thank you for your support, your kindness, and most of all, for your love, even when the whole enterprise seemed questionable.

Thank you to my sister, Natasha Bhalla, best friend since birth, *didi* and *maasi* extraordinaire. Thank you for sharing the problems and thinking up the solutions; it's an amazing gift to know I have someone who is always in my corner (no matter how wrong or right I am).

Thank you to my mother-in-law and father-in-law, Maggie and Nick Cords—two voracious readers who have always shared that love with friends, family, and each other. I wish you had been here to see this to the end, Nick; I think you had more faith I would get here than I did.

Thank you to my daughters, Asha and Kiran, I'll never be able to do as much for you two as you have done for me, but I promise I will try. You brighten each day and make even the mundane wondrous.

And, finally, thank you to my husband, John Cords, my in-house editor who helped with every word of this book, my partner in raising the little ladies, my absolute favorite person to talk to, my biggest source of support in all endeavors, my love.

Reading Together, Reading Apart

INTRODUCTION

MAD FOR DIFFERENCE

Authenticity, Ambivalence, and the Cosmopolitan South Asian American Reader

Though we often think of reading as a solitary activity, histories of reading demonstrate that it is in fact a deeply communal practice—structured and encouraged interpersonally by family and friends and fostered institutionally through formal education.[1] In the twenty-first century, the practice of reading continues to be an expression of our associations and of our desire to forge particular communities, both imagined and real—communities of fellow feminists, foodies, literary connoisseurs, history buffs, fantasy fans, and romance readers to name a few. Of course, this is not to say that the simple act of reading is always an explicit or even conscious act of identification with a particular community but rather to emphasize that just as readers derive complex meaning from the literature they choose, that meaning can in turn be circumscribed by readers' aspirations for particular forms of affiliation.

Taking a highly literary population of South Asian Americans as a case study, *Reading Together, Reading Apart* offers a sustained examination of the precise ways in which the practice of reading can encode the complex politics of community formation in the United States. As several scholars have pointed out, engagement with literary culture has been an integral facet of South Asian diasporic identity formation.[2] In this book, I chart how South Asians in the United States employ transnational South Asian literature to forge a dynamic, interactive practice of reading that serves as a complex expression of their sense of belonging in the United States.[3] Drawing on institutions (such as the literary marketplace, the nonprofit sector, and the industry of literary review), technology (such as blogs,

Listservs, and social media), and traditional forms of literary discussion (such as book clubs and academic literary criticism) the members of this reading group actively tussle with questions of representation, community formation, and ethnic American identity formation.[4]

While attentive to the ideals of community formation, *Reading Together, Reading Apart* is not a mere celebration of the unifying potential of communal forms of reading and readership; rather, it is an in-depth investigation of the types of identity, community, and belonging that are engendered and obscured though practices of reading. This book questions how the positive values we commonly ascribe to reading can be limited by the circumstances in which we read and by the desires that we bring to our practices of reading. Just as reading can be an empathic, imaginative, and transformative practice, I argue that it can also be shaped by the ideologies that circulate around a particular body of literature or among a self-selected, imagined community of readers. In the chapters that comprise this book, I trace how practices of reading among South Asian Americans reveal unease about and acquiescence to the conditions of neoliberal multiculturalism.[5] For these cosmopolitan readers, pervasive and contradictory cultural ideologies of authenticity produce ambivalence as a structuring feature of South Asian belonging in the United States.

Ideologies of Authenticity and Neoliberal Multiculturalism

The discourse of authenticity is one of the most pervasive themes in South Asian American cultural politics, diasporic literary production, and identity formation in the United States. Scholars observe that anxieties about being authentically ethnic among South Asian Americans subsume issues of cultural ownership, appropriation, commodification, and desires for belonging (Das Gupta, *Unruly* 61; Maira, "Ideologies" 142; Rudrappa 136–37). The relationship of South Asians in the United States to ideals of cultural authenticity is powerful and contradictory because of how this discourse mediates their belonging and ethnic American identity formation. Among second- and third-generation South Asians in the United States, claiming norms of ethnic authenticity as their own requires knowledge of and adherence to particular kinds of cultural traditions; as Sunaina Maira explains, they are expected to have familiarity with classical arts and religion (particularly Hinduism), be fluent in South Asian languages, participate in South Asian social circles, engage in heterosexual relationships with other South Asians, and preserve chastity ("Ideologies"

141). The attachment to the authentic thus emerges as a tacit expression of guilt and nostalgia for declining tradition in the diaspora (Bakrania 167). Relatedly, South Asian Americans' preoccupations with cultural authenticity not only express a nostalgic desire for a culture of origin but also constitute a response to feelings of exclusion in the diaspora. Claims to authentic ethnic heritage thereby become a means by which South Asians can validate their own belonging under the conditions of neoliberal multiculturalism—a market-based ideology prevalent in twenty-first century that governs which forms of racial difference are valuable, assimilable, and palatable in America (Melamed 138).[6]

In order to fully elucidate the complex and contradictory ways in which authenticity shapes belonging for South Asian Americans, I want to situate this paradoxical discourse in a context of readership that is integral to this project. One of the most crucial primary sources in *Reading Together, Reading Apart* is an extensive ethnography of the members of the Network of South Asian Professionals (NetSAP) book club in Washington, DC, which is a regional chapter of a national nonprofit organization known as the Network for Indian Professionals (NetIP). The ethnography includes thirty extensive individual interviews with NetSAP book club participants, as well as participant-observation work I conducted, attending, participating in, and recording thirteen book club meetings, from 2005 through 2010. Members of the book club are generally of South Asian descent and gather together monthly to read fiction and nonfiction that deals primarily in South Asian themes. Participants are generally second-generation, postcollegiate, highly educated South Asians of the upper-middle class.[7]

Because of the high levels of education and general economic affluence of the book club's membership, participants' discussions of transnational South Asian literature often entailed a certain amount of gatekeeping regarding issues of representation and authenticity.[8] These concerns were particularly at issue during a book club meeting in March 2010 in the Columbia Heights neighborhood of Washington, DC. Compared to other meetings, which eight to ten people attended on average, this particular book had attracted a smaller group of five participants, myself included (see appendix 2).[9] The meeting, held in the apartment of one of the book club regulars, felt more like an intimate dinner party than a bookish gathering of acquaintances. The hostess, Afrah, had cooked an Indian meal for the small group and encouraged us to continue refilling our plates.

The book under discussion was Michelle de Kretser's novel *The Hamilton Case* (2003), a mystery set in colonial Ceylon that follows the story of

Sam Obeysekere, a Sinhalese lawyer and member of the native elite.[10] As often occurred in these meetings, the convivial, social setting contrasted with the seriousness of the conversation, which centered on questions of how transnational South Asian literature reflects the complexities of South Asian American identity formation.[11] In this discussion, the conversation focused on a particularly self-reflexive moment in de Kretser's novel. The story intertwines Sri Lanka's colonial past and its unsettled postcolonial present with the decline of the once-affluent Anglophilic Obeysekere family. The central mystery of the narrative is the murder of British planter Hamilton on his way home from delivering wages to plantation workers. The novel takes a decidedly postmodern turn at the end, when it shifts focus to John Shivanathan, a lawyer and Sam's former school friend through whom Sam originally became involved with the Hamilton case. We learn that Shivanathan has become a successful writer, fictionalizing the events of the Hamilton case for Western consumption.

Shivanathan reflects on the popularity of his stories in the United States and Europe, describing how his work was lauded for its presumed authenticity, its presentation of a "life uncorrupted by the West" (303). Shivanathan responds wryly to the praise:

> An ash-smeared sadhu. The fragrance of cumin. I pulled them from my hat in earnest good faith when I first ventured into fiction. And my stories proved very popular with readers in the West. They wrote to tell me so. *Your work is so exotic. So marvelously authentic.* [. . .] The colonizer returns as tourist, you see. And he is mad for difference. That is the luxury commodity we now supply, as we once kept him in cinnamon and sapphires. The prose may be as insipid as rice cooked without salt. No matter: call up a monsoon or the rustle of a sari, and watch him salivate. (303)

Shivanathan, who might stand in for the author of the novel, admits his own complicity in peddling "traditional" images of South Asia to Western literary audiences. But he also excuses this complicity by framing it as a reversal, his own attempt as a South Asian writer to capitalize on the Orientalist tendencies of modern-day literary tourists. Like the colonizers of the past, he simplifies South Asian cultures, reducing them to a "luxury commodity," a series of exotic clichés, ripe for consumption. In ventriloquizing this moment through Shivanathan's jaded narration, de Kretser introduces yet another level of signification, enabling her, a writer of South Asian origin just like Shivanathan, to produce a South Asian novel for a

Western audience while also indirectly critiquing her own complicity in exporting South Asian otherness to the West.

Homing in on this passage, NetSAP book club readers debated whether only non–South Asian audiences strategically exploit the idea of South Asia as a land of the exotic, the authentic, and the ethnic or if exoticism and authenticity also inform how South Asians understand and categorize themselves in the United States.

> **RAJ:** I think India is exotic. Authentic India is totally exotic, right?
> **GAYATRI:** But what is authentic? And exotic to whom?
> **RAJ:** I mean everyone except the people who actually live there.
> **AFRAH:** What normal white person would not find India exotic? It is exotic.
> **SNEHA:** Or even a normal brown person who's not poor. Even our families in India, my dad loves going to the village. [. . .] He's taking photographs. He loves it. (NetSAP book club meeting, *The Hamilton Case*)

NetSAP book club participants' responses to this passage mirror its ironic humor and self-conscious tone. More importantly, however, their discussion of it demonstrates that a desire for exoticism and authenticity, the strange and the familiar, drive the interests of Westerners, non-South Asians, *and* South Asians, all of whom are "mad for difference" in their interactions with South Asian literature and culture.[12]

Further, their literary interpretations expose a desire within the group to align themselves with forms of South Asian identity that are at once familiar, like ethnic kinship, and different, along axes of race, location, class, and migration.[13] Indeed, the group's discussion of how ideologies of authenticity and exoticism structure the literary interests of South Asians and non-South Asians alike spurred one Punjabi-American reader, Gayatri, to interrogate how she constructs and understands her own South Asian identity in the United States through literary culture. Asking if the discussion exposed a sense of "threat" and insecurity among South Asian Americans, Gayatri answered her own question:

> I feel a threat to our identity. It's a threat to who we are, so why do we want to hold onto that identity in the first place? I mean, I think it's a very interesting question that's been defining for me: to what extent am I on the spectrum of Indianness and what does that mean about me? (NetSAP book club meeting, *The Hamilton Case*)

The responses of NetSAP book club members to *The Hamilton Case* illuminate three of the most salient elements of readership in the group—elements that more generally reveal how practices of reading serve the dynamic, complex processes of community formation. First, this scene of readership exemplifies the heuristic structure of reading in communal settings such as the book club. NetSAP participants triangulate their personal experiences, the text, and the dynamics of conversation in order to build meaning from the selected work of transnational South Asia literature. Second, Gayatri's uncertainty regarding her place on the "spectrum of Indianness" demonstrates that South Asian ethnic identity in the United States, particularly among the more affluent classes, is a dynamic performance of cultural authenticity that intensifies and diminishes situationally.[14] This is particularly evident when she, like other readers in the group, unconsciously exposes the hegemony of India on the subcontinent and in the diaspora by using the term "Indianness" to describe the shared ethnic identity of readers in the group. Here, she and her fellow readers inaccurately use the term "Indian" to refer to something more general, like "South Asian," or specific, like "Sri Lankan."[15] The reversion to the paradigm of Indianness in this case, makes manifest the habit or compulsion among South Asians American readers in this group to embrace ideas about ethnic difference that are legible and common in the United States. Finally, in a related vein, NetSAP book club members' responses to this description of commodified South Asian culture in literature embody the contradictory relationship that they have with ideologies of authenticity. Shivanathan's sardonic account of peddling cliché images of South Asian culture for the entertainment of Western audiences offers a critique of the elite cosmopolitan South Asian writer. As he tells it, cosmopolitan South Asian writers objectify and exoticize South Asian culture for non–South Asian audiences through an authenticating discourse figured frequently for Western audiences as Indian, premodern, rural, and poor.[16] But the response of the book club members to this passage demonstrates that it is not just the elite cosmopolitan South Asian writer who might understand South Asian culture through tropes of authenticity and exoticism but also the elite cosmopolitan South Asian reader.

In one sense, these readers relate to the exotic, Orientalist versions of South Asian ethnic authenticity that Shivanathan narrates. They recognize that in some ways, as ethnic American subjects, they are hailed by these discourses and thus examine their own complicity in perpetuating these narrow conceptions of authentic South Asian identity within the reading group. Given the stakes of cultural and ethnic authenticity within the South Asian American community, it is no surprise that it is a discourse that, no matter how fraught, tense, and contradictory it is, is difficult to shake off. After all, claims to ethnic authenticity offer a powerful point of commonality for South Asian Americans who may feel racially or economically displaced in the United States.[17] And yet, readers' dissatisfaction with authenticity as a marker of South Asian American identity pervades this conversation as well. Their frustration with exotic and authentic performances of ethnicity—and their acknowledgment that these categories are not just imposed but also adopted by South Asians in the United States—equally demonstrates an overall discomfort with monolithic, constructions of South Asian identity. Their responses reveal a savvy awareness that such ideologies of authenticity can become an abstract, exclusive means of negotiating South Asian belonging in the United States (Radhakrishnan 210).[18]

Reading Together, Reading Apart traces how literary scholars, reviewers, and especially NetSAP book club members ambivalently shift among various models of what constitutes South Asian authenticity in the United States. In these chapters, I examine how ideologies of authenticity shape communal practices of reading among South Asian American readers. Such ideologies can serve to reinforce gender inequality in the construction of transnational South Asian literary culture, promote ethnic homogeneity, and encourage complacency around their own privilege, even as South Asian American readers, particularly in their individual reflections on transnational South Asian literature and in institutional settings like that of the NetSAP book club, envision the terms of South Asian belonging in the United States as based in ideals of gender equality, ethnic heterogeneity, secularism, and class and caste consciousness.

In this way, ideologies of authenticity, as they operate in transnational South Asian literary culture, produce ambivalence as a structuring feature of South Asian belonging in the United States. Readers accede to paradigms of tradition and ethnic homogeneity even while they aspire to build a progressive and inclusive sense of South Asian American identity and community, and thus practices of reading include complex acts of identification and disidentification with the common, popular themes of transnational South Asian literature. Such practices, in turn, allow readers to construct an ambivalent sense of belonging and community in the

United States. Whether relating to ideologies of authenticity or rejecting them, the cosmopolitan South Asian readers that populate this study always retain a certain amount of distance from this discourse—an effect, in part, of their social and class privilege. They critique the stereotypes and clichés that abound in popular examples of transnational South Asian literature even while sustaining a vested interest in the importance of writing and reading as a representational practice for South Asians in the United States.

The ambivalence of their position toward ideologies of authenticity is a crucial element in the production of South Asian forms of community and belonging in the United States. Throughout this book, I argue that such ambivalence is an affective response to the stronghold of neoliberal multicultural ideology in U.S. culture. As Jodi Melamed argues, under regimes of neoliberal multiculturalism, literature has served as a "privileged apparatus for knowing difference," often in its most essentialized, tokenistic forms (xvi).[19] Melamed explains that in the late twentieth and early twenty-first centuries, the appreciation of literary culture by "enlightened multicultural global citizens" constitutes an act of self-improvement and consciousness-raising that also obscures the "racial procedures that continue to structure global capitalism" (145).

In other words, even though literature can provide a legitimate education in antiracism, this education is frequently valued in various contexts (such as the university, media, etc.) for the advantages it provides individuals who seek to fashion themselves as agents within the global capitalist economy. As such, ethnic literatures in the United States are often used as a technology of neoliberalism, a cultural domain through which to negotiate and manage racialized forms of difference (Melamed 140–41).[20] This process of managing racialized difference through literary culture on the part of NetSAP book club participants, global elites who also happen to be marked by racialized difference in the United States, produces ambivalence as an overriding structure of feeling and affective mode of analysis in their own reception of transnational South Asian literary culture. At the same time that South Asian American readers celebrate the prestige and popularity of transnational South Asian literature—realizing that it affords the ethnic community an elite, respected representational platform under the auspices of neoliberal multiculturalism—they are aware that the price of such inclusion within American culture involves a certain amount of complicity with narrowly authentic, marketable representations of South Asian identity.

Practice Makes Culture: NetSAP Book Club's Cosmopolitan Membership

The concept of practice that I use to study South Asian American reading culture encompasses the act of reading itself as well as the participatory elements of it such as the methods, institutions, and procedures that enable reading as a social practice and the more individual or private registers of reading as a repeated activity, ritual, or habit. My use of the term "practice" builds on Michel de Certeau's well-known theorization of the term. De Certeau is one of many theorists of reading who emphasize that the meaning of a text is not created solely, or even mainly, in the act of production (writing) but perhaps more fully in the act of reception (reading). De Certeau's model of reading as practice argues that a given text produces a "plurality of readings" among its various audiences and endorses a kind of democratization of reading in which professional and lay interpretations are equally significant (169–70). More importantly, de Certeau argues that reading can become a type of "poaching," serving as a "tactics" with which to resist "strategies" of elite, institutional domination (35–37). Although NetSAP book club members are well-educated and economically successful cultural elites—not likely part of de Certeau's "art of the weak" (37)—de Certeau says that readers may be drawn toward a text's cultural orthodoxies and at the same time focus on and augment the "cracks" in these hegemonies through their own "inventiveness" in reading (169).

Building on but departing from de Certeau, I theorize the practice of reading as an activity that is defined by more than just literary reception. In this study, I understand the practice of reading to be constituted by three key, interrelated elements: first, institutional structures such as social relationships, family structures, classrooms, and universities (Long 11); second, the interactive discourses and discussions that arise from the activity of reading; and third, the individual act of reading a book. These structural, communal, and individual registers of reading, or in other words, the range of settings and discourses that constitute the practice of reading, are evident in NetSAP's book club culture and consequently in the ethnography of the NetSAP book club that informs this book.

At the structural level, the NetSAP book club has over the course of its nearly twenty-year existence institutionally connected the practice of reading and South Asian American identity formation to governmental institutions in two ways: through its association with NetIP and as the annual cosponsor and main organizer of the South Asian Literary and Theater Arts Festival (SALTAF) in coordination with the Smithsonian Institution's Asian Pacific American Center from 2000 to 2011.[21] The NetSAP book club's connection to the federally funded nonprofit NetIP directly links its practices of reading to issues of cultural citizenship. As stated on the organization's website, NetIP's overall purpose is to "serve as the unequivocal voice for the South Asian Diaspora by developing and engaging a cohesive network of professionals to benefit the community."[22] NetIP's philosophy is based on promoting South Asian community in the United States through the "four pillars" of professional development, cultural awareness, community service, and political awareness.[23] The book club seeks to fulfill this mission by raising cultural awareness of the significant population of South Asians in the Washington, DC, metro area.[24] Additionally, the long-standing association between the book club and SALTAF, a major literature and arts festival at the Smithsonian, not only has afforded the reading group a kind of unusual public presence but has also helped integrate NetSAP's literary culture with the cultural agendas of the largest state-administered complex of research centers and museums in the world.[25]

Arguably, through these connections the NetSAP book club exposes the tacit ways in which practices of reading more generally have always been connected to the state through discourses of citizenship. In 2004 and 2008, for example, the National Endowment for the Arts (NEA) issued two survey reports that explicitly articulated reading as an agent of citizen subject formation. The surveys were intended to gauge national interest in literary reading among adults of all educational levels. The first report, *Reading at Risk,* notes a decline in interest while the second, *Reading on the Rise,* contradicts those results, demonstrating a rise in literary reading for the first time in twenty-six years. Dana Gioia, the former NEA chairperson, argues that the results of the 2004 report indicate that the importance of literary reading goes beyond "intellectual capability" and that its decline reflects more than just "cultural impoverishment":

> More than reading is at stake. As this report unambiguously demonstrates, readers play a more active and involved role in their communities. The decline in reading, therefore, parallels a larger retreat from participation in civic and cultural life. The long-term implications of this study not only affect literature but all the arts—as well as social activities such as volunteerism, philanthropy, and even political engagement. (vii)

Throughout the report, Gioia emphasizes that literature and reading are tied to civic, cultural, and political participation: "Anyone who loves literature or values the cultural, intellectual, and political importance of active and engaged literacy in American society will respond to this report with grave concern" (vii). Here we see reading overtly linked to its social benefits and defined as a practice that supports the development and maintenance of community life and engaged citizenship in the United States.

"More than reading" is at stake as well for NetSAP book club participants—and thus the activities of the book club cannot be defined solely in terms of reading literature but must also be understood through the practices that make reading a discursive, communal, dialogic practice. The NetSAP book club brings South Asian readers together in a highly motivated way each month to discuss, debate, and interpret transnational South Asian literature with the explicit aim of constructing a sense of South Asian identity in the United States. That is, in the NetSAP book club, transnational South Asian literature is not only an object of interpretation or a body of literature organized around a shared interest or hobby. These texts also come to stand in for the South Asian experience and, to some degree, the South Asian family and friends from which these readers may feel isolated as a result of their diasporic position. They use these texts and this body of literature to forge and debate a shared sense of South Asian American identity and to nurture connections to their countries and cultures of origin.

Within the NetSAP book club, reading is a complex practice of community formation defined by the policies and procedures that guide NetSAP book club's membership, literary selections, and interpretations of transnational South Asian literature. It is also a practice that is shaped by the members' shared race and class status. In this way, NetSAP represents a departure from dominant perceptions of book club culture in the United States. Reading groups are often organized around location (a neighborhood or local library), acquaintance (friends or colleagues), or interest (a love, say, for Charles Dickens, gardening, or mystery novels) (see Long 59).[26] As Janice Radway's and Elizabeth Long's foundational work on book clubs attests, book clubs are generally thought of as an easy-to-dismiss, feminized cultural form and even more specifically as the almost exclusive purview of white, middle-class, female readers—an image compounded by recent popular cultural representations such as the novel-turned-movie *The Jane Austen Book Club.*[27]

In contrast to general versions of book club culture wherein shared gender, race, or class is a tacit or incidental feature of the club's origin and development, in the NetSAP book club this commonality is an intentional and explicit part of the group's formation. *Reading Together, Reading Apart* offers the first book-length study of this phenomenon in a contemporary reading group. Over time, scholarship on readership has sought to recover reading practices that are institutionally obscured (such as Megan Sweeney's *Reading is My Window: Books and the Art of Reading in Women's Prisons* [2010], which examines the reading practices of incarcerated African American women), historically invisible (such as Elizabeth McHenry's *Forgotten Readers: Recovering the Lost History of African American Literary Societies* (2002), an investigation of nineteenth-century African American literary societies), or ostensibly representative (such as Long's *Book Clubs: Women and the Uses of Reading in Everyday Life* [2003] and Radway's *Reading the Romance: Women, Patriarchy, and Popular Culture* [1984], which explore the reading practices of white, middle-class women). This project investigates the reading practices of a group that is neither invisible nor typical and that has very purposefully constructed a communal culture of reading around shared ethnicity and class.

The procedures that guide the book club's membership and process of literary selection and that shape discussions about literature at the meetings are informed by a desire to bring together a community of readers purposefully defined as coeducational, South Asian, and professional. Literature in the book club is self-selected: at the beginning of each year, the book club leader sends out a call for members to email him or her their top book selections for the year. He or she then distributes a ballot for all members to vote on and collates the members' top picks. This process is designed to cater to the interests and composition of current regular members who cycle through the book club over time. The books must deal in South Asian themes, but they do not need to be written by authors of South Asian descent. The only voting and nomination rule is that the book club will not repeat a book that has already been read. Generally, participants are keen to read newer fiction and nonfiction (see appendix 3). There is an even distribution of best-sellers in Western markets among the books the members choose, but works that are more popular on the subcontinent, as well as more obscure transnational literary fiction, are also represented.[28] Meetings are scheduled for the second Thursday of each month and usually take place at a volunteer member's house. The book club holds its meetings at different locations in order to encourage both new and old participants to attend. Further, unlike a regular book club there is no expectation that participation will be ongoing, nor is there a requirement that participants attend any particular number of meetings a year, which results in a diversity among participants.

In general, the group is very open to accepting new members—and in fact relies on the rotation of old and new members for its continuance. Anyone (whether or not they are officially members of NetSAP DC) who has signed up for the NetSAP DC Yahoo group Listserv can join the book club, which as of October 2016 had 593 members—about the number of members that the group has had since I began this research.[29] Even though participation is open to non-South Asians, book club meetings tend to almost exclusively attract people of South Asian descent. Readers in the book club are mainly second-generation South Asian Americans; however, there are a considerable number of South Asians born and raised in South Asia in the group as well. While most participants are of Indian descent, meetings attract attendees with a wide range of ethnic, linguistic, regional, national, and diasporic affiliations. Readers who identify as Indian American, Pakistani American, Sri Lankan, Indian, South Indian, Indo-Caribbean, Indo-African, Bangladeshi American, Punjabi American, and Bengali American were present at the meetings included in this study.[30]

The book club tends to appeal to the same demographic as NetIP in terms of age, educational level, and professional and class status, even if not all of its members are members of the larger organization. The NetIP website reports that the median age of members is twenty-seven to twenty-eight, 60 percent of whom have a graduate degree, and that the average salary level is $75,000 to $150,000.[31] Clearly, NetSAP book club members are South Asian Americans who are economically and legally secure. Their incomes and educations put them in the upper-middle class, and for those who were not born here, their class position also enables their permanent residency as naturalized citizens, green card holders, or long-term visa recipients. For these individuals, communal reading is a practice that offers an expression and consolidation of their social class, bolstering their economic security through the cultural capital that habitual reading affords and indicates.

Scholars of readership note that the pleasures of reading have long been associated with a certain amount of class privilege: generally, only individuals in the middle and upper-middle classes would have time for the leisure of reading. Furthermore, the activity of reading itself is tethered to values typically associated with the middle classes, such as self-improvement, a focus on education, delayed gratification, and the budgeting of both time and money (Long 14–15; Radway, *A Feeling* 15). In this way, reading is a practice that reflects aspirations to upward mobility and a desire to consolidate economic and cultural capital through education and taste acquisition.[32] Practices of reading, thus, cannot be disarticulated from questions of literary taste and cultural capital, particularly as these values are inflected by issues of class, race, and gender.

Oprah Winfrey's popular 1996 televised book club is one oft-cited context in which questions of taste, communal practices of reading, and issues race, class, and gender emerge in popular culture. While there were multiple controversies associated with the book club, the disagreement between Winfrey and critically acclaimed novelist Jonathan Franzen provides a particularly lively example of this cluster of issues. In 2002, Winfrey selected Franzen's *The Corrections* (2002) for the book club, catapulting the novel to best-seller status. But when Franzen publicly expressed hesitation about the impact that this selection might have on his book, his literary career, and his self-avowed reputation as an author in "the high-art literary tradition," he was disinvited from appearing on the program, at which point the story became the subject of much media speculation and editorializing (qtd. in Collins 105). As Jim Collins succinctly puts it, Winfrey and Franzen quickly became representatives of two opposing cultural positions: "the librarian, who brings knowledge to the people, and the modernist artist, who creates genuine art and therefore must avoid the taint of anything that smacks of mass culture" (105). The debate as it played out in the media raised the broader question of with whom literary authority—in terms of tastemaking and interpretation—rightfully rests, of whether Oprah was commercializing literature or performing a vital social role by promoting literacy and readership in America.[33] But even more importantly, this literary drama unfolded, as Kathleen Fitzpatrick observes, as a battle between "the white male literary humanist" and "the black female producer of mass media, each vying for control of the cultural arena" (205). Thus, this literary controversy demonstrated that readers' preferences are not just expressions of one's personal inclinations but are also shaped by various influences on taste—ranging from *New York Times* book reviews, Amazon book lists, friends' recommendations on Facebook, and famous tastemakers like Winfrey. More accurately, readers' tastes are an expression of their inclinations as they are mediated through structures of class, race, gender, and the literary marketplace.

Among readers in the NetSAP book club, questions of taste and judgments about transnational South Asian literature are refracted through key contradictions in their cosmopolitan subjectivity. Cosmopolitanism is a discourse that has been defined and redefined through its relationship to forms of privilege and subject to a spate of condemnations and recuperations. Bishnupriya Ghosh explains that postcolonial scholars regard cosmopolitanism with suspicion because although it is historically associated with a sense of "belonging to the world," it in fact seems to reflect the cultural production and consumption of only the most elite migrants (19). In *At Home in the World: Cosmopolitanism Now*, Timothy Brennan offers a sustained critique of cosmopolitanism in its modern incarnations, arguing that structures such as the media and academia enable cosmopolitan celebrity writers to pander to the global literary consumer by appropriating the language of displacement and wandering and capitalizing on their own native cultures. He contends that cosmopolitanism is a postnational form of belonging that obscures the influence and contributions of radical nationalist narratives written by "third world" authors who live and work in their countries of origin (36).[34] In response there has been considerable scholarly revision of the concept of cosmopolitanism that aims to acknowledge the role of privilege in constructing the cosmopolitan subject and at the same time to root literary cosmopolitanism in the development of local political engagements and the building of class solidarities. Recent articulations of cosmopolitanism seek to reconceptualize the place of privilege within this discourse (Rajan and Sharma 18). Scholars have arrived at a renewed sense of the possibilities of cosmopolitan discourse tempered by distinctions between cosmopolitanism in its elite, global form and its more class-conscious, locally committed versions.[35]

This study of readership charts a middle ground between the critiques of cosmopolitanism that condemn the appropriation and commodification of third world culture by global elites and the recuperations of the term that ground its politicization in a radical dissociation from elite cultures. NetSAP book club members' engagement with transnational South Asian literature within the setting of the book club is a dynamic process of taste formation and acquisition of cultural capital screened through their cosmopolitan subjectivity. Their process of taste formation is of course shaped by their class status, age, ethnicity, and gender—the features that place them in what Pierre Bourdieu identifies as an objective social order—but their interaction with this body of literature also provides opportunities for reading to be a highly subjective and contradictory process of cultural engagement, complacency, and transformation.[36]

At times, in their discussions in the book club, South Asian American readers act as typical cosmopolitan subjects in the sense that they reinforce their belonging in the United States through the fetishization of tradition and cultural authenticity as it is represented in literature. In this facet of their practice of reading, NetSAP book club participants display a strong sense of kinship and familiarity with the hegemonic ideologies of authenticity, figured through Indian cultural tradition, ethnic homogeneity, masculinity, Hinduism, class and caste taboos, and rural settings. However, in other facets of their practice of reading, such as the organizational procedures of the book club and their individual perspectives on transnational South Asian literature, they aspire to more heterogeneous, inclusive forms of South Asian belonging. In these settings, readers emphasize the importance of intraethnic diversity, class consciousness, and feminism. If there is one unifying element that defines practices of reading among these South Asian American subjects, it is an overriding ambivalence about the cohesion of South Asian American identity and forms of community.

The Defining Discourse of Ambivalence in South Asian American Literary Culture

Ambivalence has arguably been one of the most integral elements of middle- and upper-middle-class South Asian American community formations. As several scholars observe, South Asians in the United States are a group caught between paradigms of nation and diaspora (Jain 20–21), purity and mixing (Maira, *Desis* 194), and the local and global (Mani, *Aspiring* 14). All the while, neoliberal multiculturalist ideologies converge to delimit the ways that South Asians in the United States are perceived by non-South Asians, but equally, to shape how South Asians in the United States see themselves and their fellow coethnics.[37] In the most general sense, ambivalence is a state of contradiction and mixed feelings; it is the experience of holding conflicting or opposing views simultaneously. It is a term that can denote the negative feeling of being torn between two positions, but it can also imply a kind of equilibrium in this opposition, the feeling that these two opposing sides or viewpoints have commensurate value.

Ambivalence in the context of this study is defined as a dynamic feeling, as the process of choosing between two opposing views or ideas situationally, depending on context, desires, and needs. Ambivalence is a concept that has been tied to the central questions and processes of immigration; as Jim Cullen puts it, the United States has long had an ambivalent relationship to immigration, and uncertainty about whether to stay or return to their homelands has been a defining experience for immigrants (188). Conceptually, ambivalence lends itself easily to poststructural critique, and it pervades postcolonial studies by providing what Anupama Jain terms "a vehicle for deconstructing binaries [. . .] and examining active interconnections between supposedly oppositional processes and realities" (25). Homi Bhabha, for example, famously states in *The Location of Culture* that "the conceptual ambivalence of modern society becomes the site of *writing the nation*" (209). Here Bhabha refers to a split between the idealization of national communities as they are produced through narrative and how the people who populate the nation use these narratives to ambivalently perform their relationship to it (209–11).

In my analysis, I want to shift the examination of ambivalence and national belonging away from the study of writing that has by and large been the object of poststructuralist scholarship and toward the practice of reading. In the chapters that follow, I deconstruct practices of reading as a means of illuminating why ambivalence, as a response to neoliberal conditions of racial inclusion and exclusion, has become such a structuring affective feature of South Asian American community formation and literary culture.[38] The first half of the book focuses on the contradictory practices of reading within the South Asian American community formation of the NetSAP book club. In these two chapters, I examine ambivalence through the contradiction that inheres between the NetSAP book club's ideals of progressive, heterogeneous community (reflected in what I call the infrastructures or institutional effects of the book club) and its reversion to norms of cultural conformity and privilege within the community-based interpretive practice of reading in book club meetings themselves. In the second half of the book, I broaden my focus on the situated, localized practice of reading in the NetSAP book club to forge larger connections to practices of reading among nonacademic and academic South Asian American reading audiences and literary discourses. In these latter chapters, I examine how interpretative variation and the pressures of disciplinary formation on transnational South Asian literature encode ambivalence as an affective response to paradigms of South Asian belonging in the United States.

Through my analysis of the practices of reading in the book club, I have found that the ambivalence that structures South Asian American community formation cannot be separated from the ambivalence of South Asian as an identity category itself (Koshy, *Transnational South Asians*, 12). Almost every major work of South Asian American and diasporic cultural criticism devotes some attention to defining its relationship to the term "South Asian."[39] As an ethnic category, South Asian has taken on a particular relevance in the United States, where more affluent, educated immigrants from the various nations comprising the region use the term as a coalitional, politicized construct (Mani, *Aspiring* 14). Jigna Desai succinctly explains, however, that while strategically identifying oneself with the term can create alliance, it does not ensure it and can authorize inclusions as well as exclusions: "It is important to recognize the ambivalent function of the term; although South Asia provides opportunity to analyze the region because of its interconnected history, politics, and economics, it is also imagined as a homogenous community from an 'external' (often Western) point of view" (5). To summarize, the overall ambivalence about the term "South Asian" balances on the question of whether its homogenizing and marginalizing effects outweigh its potential to provide a unifying racial construct for people originating from the subcontinent.[40]

Like the broader discipline of Asian American studies, South Asian American studies has wrestled with the binaries of resistance and accommodation in the field's development.[41] Scholars such as Rey Chow, Kandice Chuh, Laura Kang, and Viet Nguyen have addressed the shortcomings of the models of resistance and accommodation that dominate the field, arguing that these models limit Asian American literary representation in general. Reducing Asian American literature to paradigms of resistance or accommodation leads critics to simplistically condemn allegedly "negative" depictions of Asian American subjectivity and naively embrace seemingly "positive" representations.[42] Nguyen in particular argues that this model wherein a text is seen as either resisting or accommodating the structures of racism and capitalism does not account for the set of "flexible strategies" that Asian American producers and consumers use to negotiate social conditions of consumer capitalism and its commodification of difference (144–45).

The overarching rejection of such binary frameworks within South Asian American studies illustrates how ambivalence can be a compelling and productive position for South Asian Americans subjects.[43] In *How to Be South Asian in America: Narratives of Ambivalence and Belonging* (2011), Anupama Jain offers an analysis of how ambivalence in South Asian American narratives serves to show that the process of "becoming American" involves "some aspect of volition, adaptation to the country combined with the maintenance of ethnic or other identifications predating immigration, and inevitable ambivalence about transformations that are engendered by migration" (20). In *Aspiring to Home: South Asians in America* (2012) Bakirathi Mani offers yet another, more implicit, example of how ambivalence is a defining positionality for South Asian American communities through her theorization of locality as a means of belonging for South Asians in the United States who are contending with processes of globalization (4). In direct engagement with Nguyen's work, she emphasizes that the middle-class South Asian immigrants who abound in the interview, literary, and cinematic texts she explores "are at once complicit with normative frameworks of citizenship in the United States and generate notions of selfhood and community that question these same frameworks" (15).

Even though it is a concept that has been taken up explicitly in this recent scholarship, ambivalence is not a new analytical framework for South Asian American studies; it is, in fact, evident in the field's conception and in the perpetual unease that scholars express regarding the homogenizing effects of the term "South Asian" itself. This disciplinary legacy is particularly evident in the title and introduction of Rajini Srikanth and Lavina Dhingra Shankar's landmark anthology on the complex situation of South Asian American culture within the broader structure of Asian American studies, *A Part, Yet Apart* (1998). The title of the anthology points to the incomplete, binaristic, and ambivalent relationship that South Asians in the United States had at the time to Asian American culture and studies; as the editors explain, "South Asians ask why are they a part, yet apart, admitted, yet not acknowledged?" (x). While South Asian American studies is by now a recognized subfield of Asian American studies, I contend that it has retained its original, ambivalent status as "a part, yet apart" of Asian American studies. Shortly after this anthology was published, major scholars in the field of South Asian American studies began recognizing ambivalence as a persistent and descriptive position for South Asian Americans.

In 2000, seven leading scholars in the field of South Asian American studies cowrote an essay about the state of the field titled "De-Privileging

Positions: Indian-Americans, South Asian Americans, and the Politics of Asian American Studies" in which they conjectured about future directions for South Asian American studies.[44] The authors posit that ambivalence among South Asian Americans results from the strain of fitting their identities into nationalist models of belonging and suggest that this ambivalence could be addressed through a "deeper understanding of transnationalism and its implications for ethnicization, racialization, material status, and gendered experiences" (81). In other accounts, scholars suggest that the field's ambivalent relation to Asian American studies can be traced to the absence of U.S. colonial ties to South Asia (Mani, *Aspiring* 10).[45] In either case, it seems that rather than seek a way to resolve this ambivalence, scholars have, in different ways, instead embraced it as an ongoing, primary theme in South Asian American cultural studies—one that is produced as a response to these negotiations and omissions.

Chapter Summaries

In chapters 1 and 2 I examine how the shifting relationship of NetSAP book club participants to the ideologies of authenticity that define South Asian identity in the diaspora produces contradictions in their practices of reading in the book club. In these chapters, I consider ambivalence an effect of the dissonance between the NetSAP book club's aspirational ideals of South Asian American community formation and its actualization of that sense of community in the interpretive practice and discussions of the book club meetings. Taken together, these chapters trace how readers show interest in the experiences of South Asian individuals who are not of their social class or who live and work in South Asia but with whom they identify to an extent through a sense of ethnic kinship. The pedagogical function of literature in their practice of reading entails antiracist, coalition-building agendas across class and location, as well as a desire to manage their experience of cosmopolitan South Asianness against other, perceivably more "authentic" South Asian identities. In chapter 1, I analyze how the NetSAP book club's practices of reading expose the various inclusions and exclusions of South Asian American identity and community formation and how NetSAP book club participants forge a conflicted and ambivalent sense of South Asian American community in the formation of the book club culture itself. When readers use the organizational structures and regulations of the book club to project South Asian heterogeneity, they counter hegemonic constructions of South Asian identity in literature as primarily Indian, privileged, and male. In contrast, when they discuss the parameters of South Asian identity in literature within the coethnic space of the book club, the endogamous process of community formation often flattens South Asian heterogeneity.

In chapter 2, I examine how discussions of class as well as its more tacit effects in NetSAP book club meetings reveal the ambivalent effects of economic privilege among members as they construct a sense of South Asian American identity in the group. On the one hand, NetSAP participants challenge the representative dominance of economically affluent South Asians in the United States. On the other hand, members' shared privilege makes them both nostalgic and uncomfortable when they broach issues of economic inequality that reveal the persistent effects of class privilege in the book club. In conversations about the book club and within the meetings themselves, readers reflect on the terms of their own privilege particularly through an engagement with ethnically authenticating discourses like that of the model minority paradigm and caste consciousness.

In chapters 4 and 5, I broaden the scope of readership in the project by focusing on ambivalent, shifting practices of reading among a variety of groups salient to the formation of South Asian American and diasporic literary studies, such as literary academics, reviewers of transnational South Asian fiction, and lay readers who participate in the NetSAP book club. These two chapters incorporate the ethnography of readership on the NetSAP book club but that is not their primary or sole focus.

In chapter 3, I look specifically at how gender in the form of the gendered design of book covers, the construction of the authorial persona of Arundhati Roy and Salman Rushdie, and the gendered disciplinary formations of South Asian diasporic literary studies shapes ideologies of authenticity across readerships, erecting regimes of value that minoritize women's writing. I suggest that the gendered minoritization of South Asian literary culture influences how South Asians in the United States define their own sense of belonging via oppositional and ambivalent models of cosmopolitanism or ethnicity, postcolonialism or nationalism, and history or identity. I conclude this chapter by positing that transnational South Asian literature links minority literatures and female authors—an association that has in turn unwittingly devalued the literary contributions of South Asian female writers within U.S. contexts and created a problematic discourse of feminized minoritization with South Asian American culture.

In chapter 4, I continue the examination of how discourses of authenticity in transnational South Asian literary culture produce ambivalence about belonging by exploring how these discourses function specifically in the field of interpretation, shifting from a focus on the disciplinary effects of ideologies of authenticity to an exploration of the ambivalent field of interpretation around a touchstone text of South Asian American experience, *The Namesake. The Namesake* has become an oversignified text for nonacademic readers of South Asian descent and academics alike, both of whom bring overlapping, authenticating, representational desires to their interpretations of this novel, and I argue that the ambivalent field of interpretation around this novel signals a broader ambivalence about South Asian belonging in the United States across a variety of reading audiences.

A Method Born of Ambivalence: Ethnography, Affect, and Identification

The interdisciplinary method that I employ throughout this study incorporates an ethnography of readership, textual analysis, and a study of the literary critical reception of popular South Asian American and diasporic texts. It is a method born in part out of ambivalence about the types of analytical tools available to scholars who are interested in studying how literature impacts and shapes the communities of readers that it purportedly represents. In its attention to reading as a practice of community formation, the ethnographic component of this project cannot be overstated—my involvement with the NetSAP book club is at the heart of this study and has shaped its central concerns regarding South Asian American belonging, identity, and representation as they are mediated through literary culture.

When I started this project, I was quite simply seeking the tools to learn about how this set of South Asian American readers, with whom I identify in many ways, used the everyday practice of reading and their insatiable love of literature to understand their ethnic origins, their families, their community, and themselves. Ethnographic methods of participant observation and interviewing seemed the most evident way to capture the connections between reading, literature, and lived experience among this group of readers, and more importantly, to enter into a dialogic process of studying the personal and communal meanings that transnational South Asian literature takes on for South Asians in the United States. In conducting this ethnography, I was fortunate to be able to participate in some lively, sometimes heated, and frequently passionate discussions about the representational and personal significance of practices of reading within this community. Each of my interview subjects agreed to an in-depth interview that would often last for two hours or more. These interviews, in which we discussed ethnic background and self-identification, reading preferences, opinions of transnational South Asian literature, and involvement in the NetSAP book club, felt more like conversations (see appendix 4). They were often held in locations that the readers chose, intimate spaces, such as local coffee shops, restaurants, or their homes. In both interviews and book club meetings, my role as a researcher was impacted by my enthusiastic participation in the discussions at hand.

Overall, the methods that I employ throughout this project have come to mirror its primary concerns. That is, even while the ethnographic elements are a crucial component of my study of readers' lived experiences and social worlds, the ethnography I have built throughout this project is heavily invested in and informed by the techniques of literary study—such as textual exegesis and thematic analysis—rather than more traditional qualitative techniques alone. As Jain explains in constructing a similar ethnographic method to study Indo-Guyanese narratives of Americanization in New York, the hybridized scholarly approach of combining ethnography and literary interpretive tools accommodates the partialities, ambiguities, and ambivalences of personal narratives (87). It is an approach that generalizes from the particularity of a set of South Asian American experiences, providing "an entry point for expanded thinking" about the relationship between this specific community of South Asian American readers and larger questions of how literature mediates belonging and representation among South Asians in the United States more broadly (87).

I believe that such an approach is particularly useful not only for this interdisciplinary study of practices of reading but also as a way to think through and perhaps bridge the salient differences between sociological and literary approaches to the study of race and ethnicity. In "Why the Humanities Matters for Race Study Today," Susan Koshy contends that sociological methods of studying race and ethnicity are limited by analytic tools that restrict the study of racial formation to an examination of "desires, anxieties, memories, and dispositions"—the elements that "lie beneath the threshold of rational consciousness" (1545). The humanities, and particularly the literary humanities, she argues, are more "receptive to the contingencies of racial formation," the murkiness of personal narrative, representations of otherness, "the temptations and perils of authenticity and full description" than the social sciences (1545). In the version of ethnographic cultural studies that I employ in this book sociological and literary techniques feed into one another: readers' descriptions of their literary experiences, their desire for realism in narrative, and their perceptions of the lived realities of South Asian American subject formation fashion a rich, complex text that requires both *belief in* and *skepticism about* the agency and self-knowledge of racialized subjects.

Ironically, this blending of ethnographic and literary techniques speaks to an abiding suspicion in minority literatures, and Asian American literatures more specifically, regarding ethnographic methods of reading. Literary critics such as Sau-ling Cynthia Wong, Laura Kang, and Kandice Chuh, to name just a few, explain that ethnographic and sociological readings of Asian American fiction have the potential to discredit the literary merit of such texts, subjecting these works to the representational demands of identity politics, historical veracity, and linguistic fidelity (Kang 33; Chuh 18; Wong 181). Ethnographic inclinations in reading Asian American fiction have come to signal a contraction of interpretive meaning and limitations on the kinds of texts that are published, circulated, and promoted. However, I have found that even when critics worry that a work of minority literature capitulates to mainstream ethnographic desires or plays into a homogenizing identity politics, the reception of realist accounts among actual readers, especially those who might be most likely to see themselves reflected in a particular text, is never straightforward, singular, or homogenous. In other words, ethnographic approaches to reading Asian American literature, of the kind that Asian American critics caution against, can be as useful in unearthing complex subjectivities, narrative meaning, and social heterogeneity in a given text as literary critical methods of close reading and formal analysis.

Rather than seeking a singular or monolithic version of South Asian American identity, the members of the NetSAP book club engage in practices of reading that are affective and identificatory. Readers offer qualitative judgments on the characters, the writing, and the writers: they love, they hate, they like, they dislike, they identify, they don't relate. All of these affective responses blend into their analyses of whether or not they feel the literature represents an authentic version of South Asian identity and shape their debates on whether the literature is pedagogically instructive or politically stereotypical, progressive, or retrograde. Similarly, in literary academia, critics increasingly value affective forms of interpretation and modes of literary identification.[46] Michael Warner, Rita Felski, Kimberly

DeFazio, and Carla Kaplan explain that there is a long history of literary interpretation that presumes divides between forms of readings that they respectively refer to as uncritical and critical, theological and ideological, spontaneous and contrived, based in identification or critical distance, creating powerful and misleading binaries.[47]

Commenting on the tacit function of affect in practices of reading in literary academia, Eve Sedgwick cautions against a reliance on the hermeneutics of suspicion—what she deems a particularly paranoid style of reading—as standard practice in literary criticism and theory (2). She argues that reading in this way produces literary interpretations that endow a work with the agency to "subvert, interrogate, or disrupt that mirrors" the critic's own theoretical bent. Additionally, this style of reading decontextualizes how various audiences respond to a given literary text, making it "less rather than more possible to unpack the local, contingent relations between any given piece of knowledge and its narrative/epistemological entailments for the seeker, knower, or teller" (Sedgwick 4). Each of these scholars argues that presumed binaries between affective and critical modes of literary analysis and reading, while powerful, are ultimately false, and have made the case that both approaches to reading are in fact equally systemic, deliberate, and informed by ethical projects.

Indeed, as these scholars point out, affective and identificatory modes of literary analysis have always shaped the institutionalization of literary studies, particularly in terms of the pedagogical practices of literary academia. Warner, for example, asserts that in teaching we often encourage our students to move away from identification in reading—in these settings identification and affective responses to literature can be configured as naïve, as an early developmental stage in becoming a good reader (15). Affective and experience-based modes of analysis tend to emerge institutionally and in pedagogy in some arenas more than in others: for example, in the teaching of minority literatures. In these fields, academics are subject to tacit pressures to teach topics that conform to one's subject position and to make use of first-hand experience, emotion, and identity to authenticate their interpretive practice. While NetSAP book club members' explicit and open adoption of affect and identification may seem to contrast with the more tenuous role of affective, identificatory forms of analysis in literary academia that Warner and Sedgwick expose, I emphasize throughout this book that they share a salient commonality: in both contexts of readership, affect and identification demonstrate a powerful shared concern for structures of representation and the conditions of inclusion for South Asian Americans within neoliberal U.S. culture and its institutions.

The forms of affect, identification, and ambivalence in academic and nonacademic practices of reading that pervade this book have not only been objects of study but elements of my own personal experience. From its inception, this project has been deeply personal. My interest in this body of literature began in college, when I sought out South Asian diasporic literature for the same reasons that many South Asian American subjects do: I was seeking a sense of kinship, familiarity, and above all, identification with the characters and even at times with the authors of these literary texts. When I first read Jhumpa Lahiri's *Interpreter of Maladies,* for example, I profoundly identified with the experiences and descriptions of the South Asian characters in several of the stories; many of the feelings of confusion, displacement, and guilt that I had experienced after my family immigrated to the United States from New Delhi in the early 1980s had been described and represented and, as a bonus, by an accomplished, critically acclaimed South Asian American woman.

My shared professional and ethnic background with NetSAP book club participants largely enabled my study of the practices of reading in the book club. Additionally, as I have worked to complete this project, I have over time become professionalized and incorporated into the readership of South Asian American literary academics, many of whom are, like me, South Asian in origin. My membership in both groups offers me a view into the overlapping contexts, institutions, and desires that shape practices of reading in nonacademic and academic settings. However, I want to note that my own analyses of reading within these communities are delimited just as much as they are facilitated by my ethnic and professional subject position. That is, I find myself, as a South Asian American reader, mired in the same ideologies of authenticity and ambivalence that I seek to analyze—I identify and disidentify with hegemonic and progressive forms of South Asian belonging through my engagement with this literature. Furthermore, like the readers in my study, I invest in the practice reading regardless of its limitations, hoping that it will help me to imagine a form of South Asian belonging in the United States beyond ambivalence.

1

THE GLUE THAT KEEPS US TOGETHER

Constructing Ethnic Community in the NetSAP Book Club

"I have this need to identify with my culture, and I have this need to talk to people who I don't have to give South Asian 101 to, who can identify with the same things," says Ajay, a medical school student, during an interview, midday on a weekend at busy coffee shop in suburban Maryland. Ajay and I spent the better part of his interview discussing why he initially joined the NetSAP book club. He emphasized that the shared practice of reading in the club fulfilled his longing to be part of a local, coethnic community and explained that literature with South Asian themes provided a common denominator capable of bringing young, professional South Asians in the DC area together in a setting where they were able to identify with each other. Similarly, during another interview, when Arya, a Punjabi-American woman, began explaining why transnational South Asian literature brought NetSAP book club members together—and more generally why this literature might offer such a compelling site of community formation for South Asians in the United States—she noted, "I think for South Asians, there's a very strong and passionate identification: this is who I am. It's really personal. [. . .] We're just very sensitive to how we're portrayed." Members reflected on their participation in the group in interviews and book club meetings. In one such circumstance, when the discussion came around to the topic of why South Asian Americans are so invested in positive literary representations, Maya offered, "I feel like I very rarely meet a South Asian who doesn't take criticisms of the country personally. And I really do wonder, are people from Mexico, [for example], that way?" (NetSAP book club meeting, *The Marriage Bureau for Rich People*). As is evident in all of these comments, NetSAP book club participants' practices of reading are self-consciously mediated by their shared ethnic identity and cluster around issues of identification, representation, and community formation.[1]

At the most basic level, Ajay, Arya, and Maya characterize their investment in transnational South Asian literary culture in terms of affiliation—both kinship with particular kinds of literary representations and with other South Asians. They seek out fellow readers who are ethnically and culturally similar, slip between "I" and "we" to explain South Asian diasporic sensitivities, and question why representational concerns are so prevalent among members of the ethnic community. Their comments attest to an overall sensitivity in the group to the representational stakes of transnational South Asian literature. However, rather than denying the representational quandaries that this literature might present, NetSAP book club members engage with them by explicitly framing their practice of reading through both individual and collective language. That is, they generalize about their personal experiences of reading in order to connect their own responses to those of a broader South Asian American community of readers. Their comments open a view into the central question of this chapter: what do practices of reading in the NetSAP book club tell us about the possibilities and limitations of constructing South Asian American community as an expression of shared ethnicity?

Like the practice of reading, the formation of community is almost always evoked as an undeniable good. As Miranda Joseph explains, the concept of community is idealized as "an indicator of a high quality of life, a life of human understanding, caring, selflessness, belonging" (vii)—qualities that are, notably, also associated with the practice of reading. And yet, as with reading, the values that drive the formation of community only become visible when we begin to examine the circumstances that allow for the production of particular communities.[2] A shared identity is often thought to be the bond that unites members of a community. But studying the practices of reading in the NetSAP book club demonstrates that, in keeping with Joseph's arguments, communities are constituted not solely through celebratory notions of shared identity but also through various acts of production and consumption (viii). In the communal reading culture of the NetSAP book club, shared South Asian ethnic identity may ostensibly function as the primary and most obvious criterion for membership (aside from professional status which, as I discuss in chapter 2, works as a more tacit bonding mechanism in this group). And yet through their practices of reading, which involve, at least partially, their consumption of transnational South Asian literature, members of the book club continually question the cohesion of South Asian ethnic identity in the United States.

Because ambivalence about what constitutes South Asian identity itself prevails among South Asians in the United States, it is unsurprising that South Asian forms of belonging and community provide a compelling object of inquiry in the NetSAP book club. As I discuss in the introduction, the term "South Asian" itself, just like any form of community that it might describe, is itself aspirational (Mani, *Aspiring* 14). One of the most problematic features of the term is that it effaces the particularities of South Asian experience in the United States in order to name and thereby facilitate a unified sense of South Asian American identity and community. This flattening of difference among South Asians in the United States not only tends to cast Indians as the dominant ethnic group but also promotes middle- and upper-middle-class experiences as representative of South Asian American culture. The concept of South Asian American identity thereby takes on an interpellative function: it offers a paradigm of belonging that is primarily appealing to middle- and upper-class South Asians of the second and third generations (Mani, *Aspiring* 14). For these South Asian subjects, the concept of a South Asian panethnic identity is a more legible construct than it is for working-class and first-generation South Asians whose regional, national, religious, or linguistic origins tend to govern their affiliations. And so the conceptualization of South Asian identity in the United States paradoxically encompasses a progressive politics based in a desire for ethnic solidarity *and* an erasure of those South Asians who do not embrace a panethnic identity.

Ideals of community and the parameters of South Asian ethnic identity are thus concepts that are fraught, fluid, and constructed. In this chapter, I argue that the practice of reading in the NetSAP book club embodies the broader ambivalence of South Asian American belonging and community formation under the conditions of neoliberal multiculturalism. South Asian American ethnic identity formation both in the book club and beyond it is bolstered and depoliticized through discourses of community. As a microcosm of the dilemmas of South Asian American community formation, the NetSAP book club encapsulates the contradictions between South Asian Americans' desire for heterogeneous and inclusive forms of ethnic community and their tendency to homogenize South Asian American experience within book club discussions. Bakirathi Mani has noted that middle- and upper-middle-class South Asians tend to be complicit with "nationalist discourses in the United States and the subcontinent" even while resisting such frameworks of belonging. Mani describes this oscillation as central to the formation of South Asian community in the United States (*Aspiring* 15). In this chapter, I study how NetSAP book club participants' practices of reading, communally and individually, exemplify these contradictions of South Asian American community formation.

Specifically, I trace how the NetSAP book club is constituted through the contradictions of community as a site of inclusion and exclusion. It is formed between the aspirational ideals of South Asian American community and belonging as progressive, inclusive, politically engaged and its often depoliticized, homogenizing, and conformist actualization. I argue that the contradictions between NetSAP's structure and practice is indicative of the impact of neoliberal multiculturalist ideologies on South Asian American community formation.

As Jodi Melamed explains, neoliberal multiculturalism unites the free market ideology of neoliberalism with the tokenistic racial pluralism of multiculturalism (138). Although Melamed does not specifically refer to ethnically marked elites as neoliberal multiculturalists, such elites, like the members of the NetSAP book club, may well fall into this category. In fact, Melamed's argument is very instructive for an analysis of how the economic privilege of South Asian readers in this book club ambivalently regulates their reading preferences, drawing them to literature that they deem ethnically authentic. Under the auspices of neoliberal multiculturalism, literature has become a vital tool for the education of a professional-managerial class of transnational elites that influences their "self-making" (141).

In other words, reading together in the NetSAP book club is a cultural practice that allows this set of South Asians in the United States to try on different versions of South Asian identity among fellow South Asians. They use the book club, in both form and practice, not simply to instantiate a simplistic identity politics but also to debate which versions of South Asian identity feel "realistic," authentic, and which versions ease their sense of belonging and cultural citizenship in the United States. Through the organizational, structural features of the book club, members insist on the value of transnational perspectives and project ideals of South Asian heterogeneity and inclusion.[3] These organizational elements, such as the book club's mission statement, its connection to federally funded institutions (like NetIP and the Smithsonian), and the online publication of reading lists provide the reading group with a cohesive public image not only within the South Asian American community but among non-South Asians as well. These governing features of the book club are elements that its participants literally build together, and they function as public expressions of their literary preferences and their desire for a diverse South Asian community; they are the means through which the group establishes a community-based canon that anchors the collective expression of their tastes to ideals of South Asian heterogeneity, progress, and inclusion.

However, when they discuss and debate literature in the coethnic space of the book club, their endogamous process of community formation at times draws on depoliticized, nationalist, and limiting notions of what it means to be South Asian in the diaspora. That is, in the conversational elements of book club culture—such as participants' interpretive practices of reading in the book club meetings themselves—the ideals of the book club's infrastructure are occluded. In interviews, in particular, I found that NetSAP book club participants were reluctant to politicize their membership in it as an act of racial coalition and emphasized instead the value of shared culture, homogenous community, and coethnic familiarity. In this way, their reading practice conforms to Susan Koshy's foundational work on South Asian American constructions of race and ethnicity in which she argues that there is a long history of South Asians in the United States avoiding racial stigma through the assertion of ethnic and cultural difference ("Category" 285).[4] The emphasis on shared ethnicity in the NetSAP book club parallels the construction of South Asian American identity in multicultural American society, allowing for the articulation and suppression of intraethnic differences within the group and functioning as a crucial feature in the dialectic of American identity formation. But at the same time, the emphasis on shared ethnicity and common culture in the book club reveals the autoessentializing effects of neoliberal multiculturalist ideology within this coethnic community. In this vein, the focus on a shared, uniform ethnicity can also emerge as an act of containment, self-management, and limitation.

In the first section of the chapter, I examine how the organizing elements of the NetSAP book club—its mission statement, its connection to governmentally funded structures of NetIP, its decade-long involvement with the Smithsonian Institution through the South Asian Literature and Arts Festival (SALTAF), and the online publication of its community-selected reading lists—project the aspirations of South Asian American community formation through ideals of heterogeneity and inclusion.[5] In the second section of the chapter, I trace how the imagined community of the NetSAP book club calls forth a sense of South Asian community founded primarily in a desire for coethnic familiarity. In this section, I argue that participants' reflections on the importance of coethnic South Asian community complicate the heterogeneous, politicized ideals of the book club's infrastructure. In the final section of the chapter, I examine how this contradiction between aspiration and actuality played out in a book club meeting on Lavanya Sankaran's *The Red Carpet: Bangalore Stories* (2005). In this meeting, readers reconfirmed their ethnic community through representations of South Asian experience with which they were familiar and were collectively confounded by those that did not fit as well into dominant paradigms of South Asian American identity. This discomfort suggests that the intractable discourses of neoliberal multiculturalism—which are generally associated with the management of *inter*ethnic and *inter*racial difference—also regulate how South Asians relate to one another through a desire for both familiarity and otherness even in an *intra*ethnic space such as the NetSAP book club.

Ideals of Organization and the Making of a Community-Based Canon

The NetSAP book club was founded on the belief that its most crucial function was to bring South Asians together to build community around a shared cultural and ethnic heritage. In an extensive interview and over the course of many informal conversations, Sri, the NetSAP book club's founder and leader for a decade, explained to me that the original members of the reading group first met as part of a mentoring program for women called Indus Women Leaders (IWL). IWL, active since 2003, is an organization whose mission is "to create a community of strong South Asian women leaders who are comfortable sharing their challenges and dreams so they can encourage one another."[6] As Sri explains, many of her friends in IWL were also involved in NetSAP and shared an interest in business and professional mentoring. A close friend of hers who was a fellow member of both groups suggested that they start a book club as part of NetSAP's cultural arm. After a few months Sri's friend dropped out, and she took over. As she explains, the book group "evolved" and became a "very consistent" part of NetSAP DC, so much so, that the president of

NetSAP DC asked Sri if the book club should be its own committee rather than remaining part of the cultural committee.

Despite the book club's development in association with organizations that explicitly promote professional advancement, in all of my conversations with Sri, she, like other NetSAP book club participants, emphasized that the most unique and compelling feature of the book club is the shared ethnic background of the participants rather than their shared professional status. She explained that from the start the book club was designed to explicitly promote the ethnic commonality of NetSAP members as a unifying theme of the organization: "Over the years there were always different people that had said, 'Well, you know, we should maybe read these other [non-South Asian] books." And we said, "You know? We're the NetSAP book club—what is it that we have in common? And what we have in common is we're all South Asian." Sri describes ethnic commonality as the "the glue that keeps us all together in the NetSAP book club." In discussions with Sri and other NetSAP book club participants, it's clear that even though NetSAP is a middle- and upper-middle-class institution, grounded as it is in professional networking and mentoring organizations, professional status remains secondary to how the reading group functions and perceives of itself as a group based in a sense of shared South Asian community.

Indeed, NetSAP DC's website emphasizes the importance of establishing a South Asian community above any other shared value or service goal, including the development of a professional network.[7] However, because it is a community built through a nonprofit, the version of South Asian American identity it emphasizes is connected to the bureaucratic, state-regulated apparatus of nonprofit organizations (Joseph 70). In other words, the affiliation between the NetSAP DC book club and the NetSAP DC nonprofit not only determines the class makeup of the organization but also connects its practices of reading to multicultural, neoliberal methods of governance. These strategies of governance rely on the exploitation of community alliance: neoliberalism, as Nikolas Rose explains, "govern[s] through the regulated and accountable choices of autonomous agents—citizens, consumers, parents, employees, managers, investors—and [. . .] through intensifying and acting upon their allegiance to particular 'communities,' such as ethnic and racialized communities (61). The NetSAP book club offers a perfect example of how neoliberal multicultural agendas can impact community formations without completely defining them.

These associations with a federally recognized nonprofit are not overtly or self-consciously at work in the discussions of literature by book club participants, who are not required to be official members of NetSAP itself in order to join the club. Even so, the association with an official nonprofit affects the book club's procedures and public image in two ways. First, it affects practices of reading in the group by encouraging a constant influx of new members. In contrast to more traditional book clubs in which membership tends to be stable (very often consisting of friends), each NetSAP book club meeting is publicized to the entire membership of the local nonprofit chapter via social media and the Yahoo Listserv. Even though the NetSAP book club does tend to attract a set of regular attendees that cycle through over the years, anyone interested in the book under discussion can participate, not only in a book club meeting but also in selecting new literature for the book club to read in upcoming months. In this way, the book club's association with a nonprofit promotes open participation, democratizes the activity of selection, and shapes the community-based canon that NetSAP book club members build and publicize online. Second, the affiliation between NetSAP the nonprofit and NetSAP the book club endorses the latter via the patina of authority that accompanies nonprofit status.

The literature in the book club, as I outline in the introduction, is selected by current participants and chosen by polling them about their preferences. The book club leader is responsible for collating all nominations and distributing them for members to vote on—the top twelve choices make up the reading list for the year. Between 1998 and 2014, the group read 176 works of fiction and nonfiction dealing in South Asian themes by authors who are almost exclusively of South Asian descent but who come from different countries and are of different religion, ethnicities, and nationalities. The reading list through 2014 includes 109 male and 67 female authors, and 127 works of fiction and 49 of nonfiction, including single-authored works, anthologies, and short stories (see appendix 3). Over the years, the literary selections have featured books set in both South Asia and the United States or in both South Asia and the UK, the United States exclusively, Pakistan, Bangladesh, Canada, Ethiopia, Burma, Malaysia, Sri Lanka, Afghanistan, Germany, Kenya, and the Caribbean and authored by writers from a range of countries, although the majority have been set in India and written by Indians (see appendix 3 for further detail). The selections circulate among various national contexts, and book club members strive to include selections that are popular on the subcontinent as well as in transnational contexts. In a similar vein, there has always been a commitment in the group to reading authors of varying prestige, popularity, and success. Although it's not an official rule, the book club generally keeps its reading selections quite contemporary, and in any given year, the majority of the reading selections will have been published within the preceding two years.

The voting process not only accommodates the current preferences of the book club's membership but it also allows new members to curate a reading list of transnational South Asian literature on an ongoing basis that reflects a topical vision of South Asian and South Asian diasporic culture and community. The process of selection itself becomes a democratic, community-building activity, an ideal reflection of NetSAP's community-oriented public profile and nonprofit status. Even as these ideals are impacted by neoliberal ideologies that promote managing difference by containing it in innocuous cultural rather than political sites, the generic, national, religious, and gender diversity of the lists that NetSAP book club members' generated over the years demonstrates an investment in reading a variety of voices and perspectives on South Asia by South Asian and non-South Asian writers.

Furthermore, the annual reading lists produced through this process of selection contribute to the vision of a diverse South Asian American community in the DC area through their online publication on NetSAP DC's main website. Published for more than a decade, these lists are still publicly available on the NetSAP DC book club Facebook page and Yahoo group Listserv.[8] Indeed, book club moderators have explained that their shared commitment to publishing the lists online and the emphasis on reading new transnational South Asian literature endows the book club with a dynamic, current literary authority. At first, the online publication of the book club's reading lists, a practice Sri introduced when she founded the club in 1998, was instrumental in establishing it and helping readers adhere to the rules of book selection, particularly the rule that it would not accept nominations for repeats. Sri explained that this rule initially had a pragmatic function—avoiding redundancy was crucial to generating interest in the newly formed book club.

But as time went on, this rule became integral to the book club's role in the second of NetIP's "four pillars": to promote awareness of South Asian culture in the United States. Once Sri passed on the post of leader to Raj, he maintained this commitment to keeping the book selections fairly contemporary and topical and to avoiding choosing the same book more than once. When I asked him how he felt about posting the reading list on the NetSAP website, he explained its importance for the book club's continuance:

> I think it's very good for the book club. Number one, it makes it seem like a real thing. It makes it look healthy. I think that's something that is attractive to people. Even though there's no overlap between the people attending now and the people who were attending ten years ago, people will suggest books that have been on the list eight years ago. [. . .] Even if we were not in the book club eight years ago reading this book, chances are a lot of us have read this book. And now it's eight years old anyway. And there are just a lot of new books out there. And why not read the things that are new? I think the new books, also, people are more excited about reading.

According to Sri, the online lists provide the book club with institutional history: "It's not only a historical database for what books to recommend, but other people have gone to our book club list to say, what are the other South Asian books out there? What have you read? What's good? What would you recommend? So here's a database of books that are South Asian books that our group has read and could write a review about or have some experience about. Different people have contacted us over the years about it." Sri, Raj, and other regular participants emphasized that the online publication of the book list serves a pedagogical function for South Asian and non-South Asian readers by publicizing the book club's commitment to reading new and diverse transnational South Asian authors. The publication of these reading lists online has also served to connect the club to other book groups, South Asian and non-South Asian alike, and to other NetSAP chapters seeking to start book clubs, to attract the attention of editors of a book club cookbook, and to provide a blueprint for SALTAF, a well-attended annual event at the Smithsonian Institution that was launched in 2001.

SALTAF was, according to the now defunct website, an "annual celebration of South Asian creative talent" that grew out of the NetSAP book club and that was organized largely by NetSAP book club participants, with help from the Smithsonian Institution's Asian Pacific American Center as well other local and national South Asian organizations. There are other organizations, online forums, and festivals that celebrate South Asian culture, literature, and arts, such as the Kriti Festival in Chicago, South Asian Women's Network (SAWNET), the Indo-American Arts Council (IAAC), the South Asian Literature Festival in the UK, or the Jaipur Literature Festival in India. However, SALTAF proved to be unique, initially, because it was the first festival in the United States to emphasize South Asian (rather than Indian) culture, and second, because of how its connection to the federally funded cultural mammoth of the Smithsonian situated the NetSAP book club's literary vision of South Asian identity and community formation in relation to state recognition.

For its first few years, Sri served as chair of both the book club and SALTAF, and she worked to ensure that the goal of heterogeneous representation would be reflected in the festival by giving new, non-Indian authors a chance to showcase their talent alongside more canonical figures. Sri explained that the idea for the festival came from a book club meeting. In 1999 a NetSAP book club member suggested that the group try to contact the authors they had been reading. The reading list that NetSAP participants had been collectively curating became a template for the festival. In 2000, Sri organized the first SALTAF event. The first couple of festivals were mainly funded by ticket sales. But a few years later, Sri and Dr. Franklin Odo, the director of the Smithsonian's Asian Pacific American Center at the time, met at a "DC We Read" public library event and began discussing plans for bringing the festival to the Smithsonian. According to Sri, originally Dr. Odo was interested in an evening event, but Sri had larger ambitions: "Let's partner and do it for a Saturday/Sunday. [. . .] And then I had to convince NetSAP [. . .] to take the South Asian Literary Festival and put it on a mainstream platform [that is] free and open to the public and [. . .] funded by grant sponsors. And talking to the NetSAP president, he said, 'You know, Sri? If you think this can happen, we're the underwriters. We'll support you and go from there.'" The NetSAP book club's associations with the festival, particularly in its affiliation with the Smithsonian, supported its mission as part of the national NetSAP nonprofit: to promote the national, state-sanctioned recognition of South Asian culture among South Asian and non-South Asian audiences in the United States. Furthermore, Raj and Sri's comments demonstrate that the principles that guide the book club's selections are integral in shaping South Asian readers' affinity for a diverse and inclusive transnational South Asian literary culture.

In particular, SALTAF provided a more broadly publicized parallel to the NetSAP book club, emphasizing the dynamism of this literary culture by including newer, less-established South Asian writers alongside more canonical figures. Sri related a conversation she'd had during the 2003 festival with Siddharth Sanghvi, who was twenty-six years old at the time, a budding novelist who would appear on the same stage as established writers like Anita Desai and Bharati Mukherjee: "You know," she said to him, "it's really great to have South Asian writing be on a mainstream platform," to which he replied, "I've always considered South Asian writing to be mainstream." Sri related this anecdote to emphasize the difference in generational perspectives regarding the increasing popularity of transnational South Asian literature—particularly among "mainstream," non-South Asian audiences. The placement of canonical South Asian writers like Mukherjee and Desai next to newer writers such as Sanghvi was central to SALTAF's vision and dovetails with NetSAP's goals to create a space for newer writers. Through its association with the Smithsonian, the festival staged a public, state-recognized performance of South Asian literary culture in the United States that was legible and accessible to mainstream non-South Asian audiences and that was curated by South Asian readers themselves.

The principles of community, democracy, innovation, and heterogeneity that guide NetSAP's process of selecting and promoting transnational South Asian literary culture has established an institutional history and public canon that is rare for contemporary book clubs. However, all canons, whether or not they are community-based, are a function of values, taste, and power. David Palumbo-Liu (*Ethnic* 13–14) and Sau-ling Cynthia Wong ("'Sugar'" 202) have conjectured that within the context of Asian American literary studies, community-based ethnic canons, derived as they are from a different set of governing needs than those of the literary critical establishment, might usefully complicate the literary texts that come to represent Asian American ethnic minorities. There is certainly evidence to support this theory in the construction and promotion of NetSAP's community-based canon (see appendix 3). The book club's literary selections purposefully complicate the various hegemonies of South Asian cultural identity: members chose books written by both men and women, favor new and innovative rather than popular, critically acclaimed authors, and recognize the literary contributions of non-Indian writers.

At the same time, the institutional authority granted to the NetSAP book club through its connection to a national nonprofit and to the Smithsonian offers a view into how ideologies of neoliberal multiculturalism shape the contradictions of South Asian ethnic identity formation in the United States, the subject of the next section. As practices of reading in the NetSAP book club illuminate, ethnic Americans are caught between ideals of American individuality and collectivity: they are expected to display and brandish progressive, heterogeneous forms of ethnic difference through cultural engagement and at the same time to embody and construct a homogenous ethnic authenticity that is legible within multicultural American society.

NetSAP Book Club Participants and the Depoliticized Discourse of Authentic Ethnicity

The demographics of the NetSAP book club itself reveals a gap between the ideal of an intraethnic membership and the reality of a more or less homogenous one. In interviews with Sri and Raj, both leaders emphasized their belief that the NetSAP book club was a relatively heterogeneous space of South Asian American community formation. When I asked Sri specifically about the demographics of the book club, she remarked:

> It always amazes me, I think it's wonderful our book club caters towards first generation, second generation Indians, Sri Lankan, Pakistanis, and the Bangladeshi-Americans, as well as men and women where most book clubs tend to cater towards women.

Sri admitted that there were usually more women than men at meetings, but she did point out that sometimes they had an equal number of male and female participants.

During the period when I studied the book club, its meetings tended, in keeping with trends in mainstream book clubs, to be attended by more women than men; for example, twenty-four of my interviewees were women and only six were men. This gender composition was reflected in each meeting and overall women outnumbered men consistently by a significant majority (see appendix 1). Overall, readers were of similar class and professional backgrounds. As one would expect from a group affiliated with NetIP, they were all college educated, and they mainly worked in the federal government, the nonprofit sector, journalism, development, medicine, and engineering. And there were generally more participants of Hindu Indian background than of any other group: Of the thirty readers that I interviewed, three were Pakistani American, one was a Sikh American, one was a Sri Lankan American, one was an Indo-Ethiopian, and one was of Indian descent but had grown up in the UK and Hong Kong; the remaining thirteen came from Hindu Indian families. At each meeting, there would usually be at most one to two readers who were not of Indian descent.[9] Even so, readers in the book club routinely self-identified as

"South Asian" rather than "Indian" or more specific nationalities, in keeping with the progressive politics of the regional DC chapter that aimed to create an inclusive subcontinental community. The majority of interviewees were second-generation South Asian Americans; nine of them were South Asian immigrants who had emigrated to the United States as adults. In the composition of NetSAP book club meetings, there were often a group of participants who had recently immigrated as well as another set of readers who were second-generation South Asian Americans. The difference between Sri's perception of the book club's diversity and its actual homogeneity demonstrates how strongly the group's aspirations shape members' perceptions of what constitutes South Asian community in the club.

To some degree, the slippage between aspiration and actuality can be understood through Benedict Anderson's well-known concept of imagined communities in which he theorizes the development of national identity through print capitalism (34–36). Here, I expand on Anderson's theorization of the term, drawing on its more colloquial meaning as a community of interest. NetSAP book club members' shared interest is the construction of a sense of South Asian American identity through literary interaction and engagement. But what kinds of shared identity are members building in their discussions about the book club and within it? When asked why they decided to join the book club, participants frequently insisted that they were seeking an apolitical forum in which they could meet other South Asian coethnics and form a cohesive, authentic community. Gayatri, for example, who was a regular book group participant and particularly attuned to issues of authenticity in South Asian literature and culture explained during an interview with her that she was "seeking out South Asian friends and common interests, which was literature." This sentiment was echoed by Arya, an avid Punjabi American reader, who noted that she couldn't "really think of any other organization that brings people of South Asian descent together." She was careful to clarify that while there were organizations geared toward South Asians in particular professions, like the South Asian Journalist Association (SAJA), NetSAP seemed to have the "broadest" reach across professions within the South Asian community in the United States. In response to the same question, Anil matter-of-factly explained that the book club "combined two things: I wanted to socialize with people and then I also wanted to read books about South Asians and South Asian literature." These members were first and foremost seeking out a community of ethnic peers among whom they could work out the parameters of South Asian identity in the United States through the cultural practice of reading.

The politically aware and engaged South Asian American identity projected in the book club's organizational structure potentially stands at odds with members' insistence that the reason they participate in the NetSAP book club is that they desire cultural comradery with other South Asians. Their construction of South Asian identity in the United States is purposefully depoliticized, possibly because the members of the group are, among South Asians in the United States, an elite subset, educationally and economically advantaged, through discourses of community and shared culture. Raj, the book club moderator during the time I was conducting this ethnography, asserted this explicitly:

> I'm not out to actually advance the South Asian people through this book club. I guess it's community building, I think you can legitimately describe it that way. Let's meet other South Asians and let's be friends with other South Asians and let's talk about South Asian things. But doing that just because it's inherently valuable and for personal satisfaction. Not for any political reason.

Here and in other conversations with Raj, he reiterated that he was not concerned with the impact that transnational South Asian literature might have on the recognition of South Asian Americans or their politics or on how they are represented in the United States. He deemed the book club valuable simply because it created a strong social network through shared ethnicity and a common cultural background, not because it might help with coalition building or to advance social justice for South Asians in the United States.

Similarly, Meera, a young Indian American reader, emphasized the cultural and ethnic community that she found in the book club: "I thought it was cool, like it is a taste of home, in a different way than I have at home, so growing up we would do social things with other families. And there, you know, you're Indian on the weekends, that kind of thing. And there are different functions that you go to with your South Asian community, and here, living on my own, I don't have so much, without going to a bar, which isn't what I think is going to make me feel grounded." The NetSAP book group offered "grounding" in the South Asian culture the postcollegiate had been exposed to she was when living at home. This sort of sentiment is common among young South Asian Americans, for whom ethnic identity is often a matter of performance, reliant on social sites of communal ethnic validation to sustain itself (see Maira, *Desis* 88). Meera sought out the book club in order to reinforce her own cultural authenticity within the coethnic culture with which she was raised. Notably, she employs the colloquial expression, "Indian on the weekends," which is popular with second-generation Indian Americans, to explain how her ethnic identity is accentuated with family and friends of Indian descent on the weekends and downplayed at school and work with American friends. The expression is particularly rich for how it implies that there is a perceived flexibility of cultural markers for South Asian Americans—markers, unlike racial ones, that can be slipped on and off. Meera demonstrates how affluent South Asian Americans tend to see racial identification as a choice, a matter of emphasizing shared ethnicity and upward class-mobility to avoid politicizing their identity (Koshy, "Category" 285).

Although the majority of members were inclined to frame their participation in the book club as an act of cultural affiliation, there were readers who were invested in using literature and practices of reading in the club to explore intraethnic diversity among South Asian Americans. For example, as an effect of reading non-Indian South Asian literature in the book club, Arya explained that she was intellectually and emotionally edified. The communal practice of reading in NetSAP book club deepened her knowledge of South Asian culture already familiar to her and exposed her to other narratives of South Asian experience:

> I recognize in reading literature things that I experience and that help me to understand what's going on—or at least come to peace with it a lot of times. It's very comforting to read and realize, I'm not alone going through something or this is a cultural thing. [. . .] Part of it is also just trying to understand, learn more about my culture. I've had my experiences, and my own lifetime narrative of where I've come from, my family, the people I've been exposed to, but through literature, you can be exposed to all sorts of stories and different parts of South Asia. So that's also a part of it. I have a strong fondness for learning more about South Asia and different cultures of South Asian and their ways of life and so literature is a great way to do that.

She explained that she was compelled through this experience of readership, which taught her about other regional, ethnic, and national affiliations that comprise South Asian culture more broadly, to situate her ethnic difference among a range of South Asian experiences.

Meena, a long-time NetSAP book club participant, told me that reading transnational South Asian literature both within and outside of the book club helped validate and expand her own ethnic identity: "I happen to read South Asian literature because it just attracts me. When you go to a bookstore and suddenly you see a South Asian name. Then you want to look at it and you want to read it. And you feel some sort of familiarity because it's set in India, or Pakistan or Bangladesh." Through literary culture, Meena imagines a sense of shared ethnicity among South Asians that would mitigate historically contentious relationships and link the linguistic, religious, and political histories of various South Asian nations to one another. Arya and Meena's comments demonstrate that they seek commonality through South Asian difference, realizing the more inclusive vision of South Asian America integral to the NetSAP book club's ideals. Both use their practices of reading to develop a nuanced construction of South Asian community and identity in the United States. At the same time, their yearning for more complicated narratives of South Asian American experience exposes the dominance of homogenous, nationalistic frameworks of community formation and representation in the diaspora.

This yearning for diverse narratives of South Asian experience in literature was perhaps most explicitly elucidated by Nishi, a Muslim Pakistani American woman. She explained that she was attracted to the NetSAP book club because of its commitment to reading and promoting authors of a variety of South Asian backgrounds. She felt that her personal and literary interactions with the group would help her to better understand why her family decided to emigrate from Pakistan. During our discussion, she explained that she often felt her background was not represented in popular South Asian literature, which is more often concerned with Indian and Hindu experience. Then she read Sara Suleri's memoir *Meatless Days* with the NetSAP book club, which she felt illuminated her parents' experiences of living in Pakistan during General Zia's time, a period that she had heard of through her family but did not experience directly: "Just talking to [my mother] about Pakistan and General Zia's day, you know, that kind of reality, it connected me to my parents and their history as first-generation Pakistani Americans. [. . .] It's not that I don't see myself in literature, it's just that it supplied a lot of other things." Nishi's reading practice animates a familial narrative that is at once personal and historical, offering insight into her own family history but also contextualizing a broader history of Pakistani emigration and first-generation experience.

Arya, Meena, and Nishi's comments expose the partial effects of neoliberal ideology on modern subject formation. All three were motivated to seek out underrepresented, complex, and diverse representations of South Asian identity in the diaspora through shared practices of reading in the NetSAP book club, and all three push back against the monolithic construction of the diasporic South Asian community, challenging neoliberal multiculturalist pressures to totalize South Asian American experience and imagining instead an ethnic identity rooted in an inclusive and heterogeneous vision of the subcontinent. Their practices of reading demonstrate how South Asian American "cultural texts are not [. . .] seamless reflections of neoliberal capitalist rationality" (Thoma 12) particularly when examined in terms of how readers use these texts to understand their ethnic identity. I pause over these readers' remarks as an example of how ideologies of neoliberalism enact, as Aihwa Ong explains, a complex "politics of subjection and subject-making" (*Neoliberalism* 13) capable of producing a depoliticized insularity within South Asian American culture as well as resistance to it.

A Taste for the Familiar in Lavanya Sankaran's *The Red Carpet: Bangalore Stories*

In the final section of this chapter, I depart from my analyses of various individuals' accounts of why they decided to participate in the book club to study how the processes of South Asian American community formation play out in the dynamic contestations and discussions of a book club meeting. Here, I offer an in-depth analysis of the 14 September 2006 book club meeting on Lavanya Sankaran's *The Red Carpet: Bangalore Stories* (2005). This collection is set in urban, upper-class contexts both in India and the United States and unfolds in a cultural milieu familiar to the imagined community of the NetSAP book club. The two stories that I examine in detail in this section, "Alphabet Soup" and "Two Four Six Eight," address second-generation cultural confusion, privilege, the impact of British colonialism on South Asian diasporic culture, and sexual abuse. These themes inspired a lively discussion; they revealed the preferences of members of the book club for narratives that are familiar, representative, and normative among South Asians residing in the United States and illuminated how their investment in ethnic authenticity and their assumption of shared economic privilege shapes group-based practices of reading.

I begin by summarizing the collection's overall theme, which was crucial in governing how participants in the discussion responded to its subject matter, even though they focused only on a handful of stories in it, and on "Alphabet Soup" and "Two Four Six Eight" in particular. I preface this section with a discussion of *Red Carpet*'s reception, particularly in India, where the collection was denigrated for pandering to Western audiences, to examine parallels between its reception in the public media and the NetSAP book club. Finally, I shift to tracing the discussion that the attendees of the book club meeting had about this collection.

Although there were typically never more than ten participants at any given meeting, this one drew a crowd of twenty-six members. The meeting, held in Rockville, Maryland, was hosted by two well-known regular book club participants, Kavita and her brother Vikram. One reason the meeting was so well attended may have been the topic of the collection, which deals in part with the direct and indirect effects of the rapid economic growth of cities such as Bangalore and Hyderabad brought on by the waxing and waning information technology industry that took hold in the '70s and '80 and that was then superseded by the highly profitable business process outsourcing industry, or, as it is better known, the call center or BPO boom.[10] Several book club participants mentioned that they had relatives and friends in India employed in call centers.

Sankaran's stories are populated with characters from a range of class and caste backgrounds. The narratives stage a fascinating connection between India and the United States in their exploration of economic factors that render several characters ambivalent about settling in either country, drawing on pervasive tropes in transnational South Asian literature such as the clash between modernity and tradition as it maps onto Western versus Eastern affiliations.

As is common with transnational South Asian writing, the collection raises questions about South Asian writers' complicity in capitalizing on images of ethnic difference for the consumption of Western audiences. The topics of Sankaran's stories were immediately recognized as having the potential to attract a broad readership not only in India but abroad as well. As S. Bagashree, a reviewer for the popular Indian-based newspaper the *Hindu* explains, the collection was released in fifteen countries simultaneously following a bidding war among international publishing houses based mainly in the United States. Bagashree writes enthusiastically about the collection's international circulation and appeal and praises it for the "nuanced and sensitive" view of the changing "physical and psychological contours" of Bangalore. But having lauded the book for its depiction of the city, he goes on to rhetorically ask, "Why does [the description of the city] tend to be laboured in others, as if the writer is trying to drive home the point about a changing city and changing people in a dogged, self-conscious way, rendering the characters and situations flat in the process? As it happens in even the title story? In fact, the book cover itself seems to spell out the agenda a little too literally for comfort!" Bagashree implies here that in order to earn recognition from Western consumers Sankaran has had to orientalize her own writing by amplifying and exaggerating the clash of modernity and tradition in South Asia. He critiques the touristic gaze of the Western reader and laments that even the imagery of the book cover—which depicts a young South Asian woman slouched over in jeans and a tank top, whose face is partially visible, standing beside a woman wearing a sari whose face is entirely cut off—capitalizes on clichéd tropes of Eastern tradition and Western modernity.

Sankaran, in a response included in Bagashree's review, denies that she compromised her creative process: "I wanted the stories to be true to my experience of contemporary urban Bangalore. Interestingly, when the publishers read them in America, the same thing appealed to them as well!" Sankaran emphasizes the publishers' appreciation of the "literary quality of her writing" and of the glimpse that she provides into an "India that they have not seen captured." And yet Bagashree insists that there were tacit pressures to cater to Western audiences, wryly reporting that even though neither Lane Zachary, Sankaran's literary agent nor her publisher "put her under pressure to write for a western audience," she was told to incorporate "a long description of a *salwar kameez*" even while "they were also gracious enough to let her *chumma* and one-*tharah* be without qualifiers."

The NetSAP book club discussion of Sankaran's short story collection reenacted the debate between the reviewer and the author. At times participants insisted that the narratives present authentic, representative, and "realistic" versions of South Asian identity, and at others they criticized the stories for their cosmopolitan exploitation of stereotypes and clichés. In their discussion of "Alphabet Soup," for example, they took up Sankaran's portrayal of a postcollegiate Indian American woman who struggles to make sense of her bicultural identity by returning to India. In the story, Priya returns to her home in Chicago after attending an "elite East Coast school" (102) armed with a litany of multiculturalist slogans and beliefs. She repeatedly tries to inform her father how he is oppressed as a person of color, telling him that "assimilation is a betrayal of your skin" (103). In turn, he humorously rebukes her with a common-sense approach to her platitudes. He tells her that her pretensions to being an oppressed minority are undercut by the opulence of their five-bedroom home: "It's nice that you have the luxury of your opinions" (103). Priya's journey to ethnic self-discovery contraposed with her parents' reminders not to take for granted the privilege of her upbringing offers an insightful view into issues of class and South Asian American racialization. At one point in the story, Priya meets a young man in India who calls her an "ABCD"—which stands for "American-born confused desi"—a term that has derogatory connotations because of how it implies ethnic inauthenticity and makes light of bicultural confusion. In response, Priya becomes concerned with proving her "Indianness" to this young man and her family. Participants in the meeting picked up on the ABCD trope as a way to characterize the entire story and debated the validity of the use of the epithet:

P1: It was just like every little nuance of an ABCD, you can possibly throw into this one character—[Sankaran] does.

P2: But you know what though? It's different [for] someone to call that character ABCD—it's different than someone calling someone like you or me ABCD, you know?

P3: True.

P4: Exactly.

P2: Which is, I think, something that some [South Asian] people do, and that is not really correct. But the character that she described as ABCD is someone who truly maybe is ABCD though. Rather than someone who really is perhaps in the middle or in tune with his or her culture or cultures. (NetSAP book club meeting, *The Red Carpet*)

In distinguishing between the "real" ABCDs and their own more resolved bicultural position here, the book club discussants reveal (as does the short story itself) the anxiety that they feel as South Asian Americans about their own authenticity as it is assessed by South Asians who were born and raised in South Asia. Overall, they deemed "Alphabet Soup" to be an exaggerated depiction of South Asian American cultural confusion. And yet, ironically, the story seemed to hit a nerve among the second-generation participants who were clearly concerned about how they were perceived by the first-generation participants in the group. These second-generation readers seemed anxious that they might be seen by the "more" authentic,

South Asian readers in the room as exemplifying the ABCD trope. This moment of anxiety among the second-generation readers in the room illuminates, how even among South Asian coethnics, there are pressures to conform to notions of ethnic authenticity.

Unlike "Alphabet Soup," "Two, Four, Six, Eight" is set exclusively in India. The narrative is written as a childhood recollection and tells of the manipulative, troubled relationship between a young middle-class girl and her ayah (or nanny). The young woman, known mainly in the story as "Missy," narrates her experiences growing up in urban Bangalore and attending a strict convent school where the tongue-in-cheek description of the curriculum includes "mathematics, English, geography, history, science, Hindi, a choice of Sanskrit, OR French, OR Kannada, singing, painting, How to Be English, and How to Be Good" (50). The narrative seamlessly integrates Missy's experiences with the forms of discipline she encounters at school under the watchful eye of the school disciplinarian, Mrs. Rafter, and at home, under the care of her sexually abusive ayah, Mary. Indeed, the story begins with the adult Missy hearing, almost simultaneously, the news that both of these women had recently passed away. Parallels between the two women precede their policing of Missy's behavior; they are marked as doubles by their status as cultural outsiders to the middle class Missy belongs to. Mrs. Rafter, who we learn is an Anglo-Indian teacher in charge of home economics and deportment, takes on the stereotypical markers of the Anglo-Indian subculture through her persistent but failed English affectations. Similarly, Mary is depicted as greedy, controlling, and untrustworthy. At home and at school Mary lives under the strict scrutiny of both of these women as she tries to make sense of the contradictions of her colonial education that teaches her to believe in Jesus, to respect Mahatma Gandhi, fantasize about tea with the Queen of England, call the Sepoy Mutiny the First War of Independence, and eat with a fork rather than her fingers.

Sexually abused at home, at school Missy forms a club with three other girls that centers on creating absurd, innocent sexual scenarios involving the characters from Enid Blyton's children's detective novels. In the story's denouement, Mrs. Rafter intercepts a note to Missy from one of her best friends requesting that she prepare a story about "naked boys" to tell later that day during the scheduled club meeting. Mrs. Rafter promptly breaks a ruler on her hands and calls her family. When she arrives home, Mary, who has been sexually abusing Missy in order to discipline her when she misbehaves, informs her parents that Missy has been hiding

Harold Robbins books under her bed and masturbating in the bathroom. In retaliation, Missy threatens Mary's life, thus gaining her independence at home. The story concludes with an account of how Missy, several years later, achieves success as an athlete and top student at school, ultimately winning Mrs. Rafter's approval and admiration.

Class is a salient feature in "Two, Four, Six, Eight" and as such emerged in the group's discussion of the story. All the participants, regardless of whether they were born and raised in South Asia or were second-generation South Asian Americans, identified with the upper-middle-class, convent-educated status of the main character either because they had raised in a similar social setting themselves or had family that had been. For example, everyone in the room either had an ayah as a child or was familiar with the Indian nanny system as a result of taking trips to India to visit relatives. Afrah, a regular and enthusiastic attendee who was born and raised in India and emigrated to the United States after spending time in the UK, identified with the portrayal of the convent school education and related it to her own experiences at a boarding school in Calcutta: "That is absolutely my experience" (NetSAP book club meeting, *The Red Carpet*). This inspired a fair amount of teasing and laughter among group participants as they remembered the sexually explicit stories that the girls in the story tell each other using characters from Blyton's stories, prompting Afrah jokingly to qualify her statement, saying "Well, not exactly like my experiences" (NetSAP book club meeting, *The Red Carpet*).

The shared class background of the book club group was equally evident in their familiarity with the references to Blyton and Robbins, as these are writers whose fiction was very popular throughout the former Commonwealth. Participants born and raised in the United States were acquainted with these authors through their parents or relatives, while those who had spent more time in South Asia had often read the stories themselves. As Sunil Bhatia notes, shared frames of cultural reference among South Asians in the United States serve as a reminder of "the postcolonial hybridity of urban Indianness and leftover colonial Englishness" typical of middle- and upper-middle-class South Asian American professionals (103). Participants' familiarity with Blyton's and Robbins's stories suggest not only their shared cultural context but also their families' privileged origins in South Asia as well as the United States.

The book club subsequently stumbled into a discussion of the less familiar narrative territory of sexual abuse. Initially, the group was uncomfortable acknowledging Missy's sexuality and the narrative of abuse depicted in the story. In one passage, a four-year-old Missy explains how Mary would quiet and control her through sexual manipulation: "Mary took me into the bathroom, raised my frock, removed my underpants, and made me lie down on the floor. Don't tell your mother, she said, and rubbed the palm of her hand between my legs" (67). Raj explained his discomfort with the narrative, noting that Missy was potentially acquiescent: "But that was a weird story. If I'm remembering the story right, the girl is not altogether unhappy with what the ayah does" (NetSAP book club meeting, *The Red Carpet*). Raj's comment incited an irate and frustrated response from some readers in the room. Monali, a young physician who expressed a lot of interest in this particular element of the narrative, questioned Raj in disbelief at the implication that Missy would be complicit in her own sexual abuse: "Are you serious?" And the hostess, Kamal, followed up by asking, "But how could she know what [sexual abuse] was?" (NetSAP book club meeting, *The Red Carpet*).

I conjecture that these readers felt that Raj's comment implicitly blamed the victim for "enjoying" the ayah's sexual abuse or, at the very least, suggested that Missy accepted the abuse. Raj, in response, referred to passages in the story in which Missy explains that she began trying to emulate "the sensations of Mary's hands" when she was alone (70). Monali reconsidered her reaction to Raj's comment and agreed that the association of sexual abuse with Missy's masturbation was confounding:

> It was hard to discern. So is she a sexually abused child who now is masturbating? [. . .] You could've just taken masturbation alone in a strict sense [. . .] as a theme. [group laughter] Like, is this girl, is she marriage-suitable or whatever? But to throw in the sexual abuse part, I don't know. I didn't really care for it. I think the whole power play with the ayah and the child alone, that was interesting though" (NetSAP book club meeting, *The Red Carpet*).

The hostess's brother, Vikram, who had been an active and lively member of the discussion, was likewise skeptical about the isolated depiction of sexual abuse in the story. He felt that the author didn't provide context for it: "I didn't like that story at all, and it was because all of a sudden you drop that in, and it's like you're just you're adding pieces. I don't think it's a, a sexual abuse [story] really—it's there, but it doesn't run throughout the story" (NetSAP book club meeting, *The Red Carpet*). In an effort to defuse the awkwardness of the conversation, Sri, the group leader intervened, addressing Raj: "I know that you're trying to say there is another layer—there's unresolved questions because it's written one way, and how the ayah is portrayed is another way, and probably the actuality is very clear-cut—how we all see it. But how [Sankaran] wrote the sensations, that makes you believe that maybe she was okay with it" (NetSAP book club meeting, *The Red Carpet*).

I linger over how this conversation unfolded because it exemplifies how the process of group reading brings to light a distinction between the interpretations that group members explicitly report and their more embedded and tacit tastes, dispositions, and responses.[11] In other words, there may be inconsistency between what readers are comfortable saying to one another and what they are really feeling in the social and communal setting of the book club. The overall discomfort in the meeting had become palpable in the wake of this conversation, a perfectly reasonable response given that sexual abuse and masturbation are generally taboo topics in any social setting.

And yet the book club's responses to this story also entail the possibility that when narratives depart from normative South Asian experience, they are harder for South Asian or South Asian American readers to apprehend. The story itself offers reflection on these culturally inflected taboos. Missy gets in trouble for making up sexually explicit stories because "this crossed over into the realm of Dangerous Thoughts that had no place in Girls from Good Families. This was Chi-Chi" (68). Later, when recounting how she went from a triumphant athlete whom her classmates cheered on to being shamed and punished, she makes up a rhyme: "Two Four Six Eight. Indian girls don't masturbate" (71). One person in the book club meeting, Lalita, spoke up to defend Sankaran's depiction of sexual abuse as well as her depiction of sexual pleasure; her comments on the value of the depiction not only reflected the general discomfort that such a story might create in a group discussion but also showed that in communal settings, the group's tastes might lean toward normative narrations of South Asian identity.

Lalita's perspective was largely informed by her profession as a certified social worker and therapist working mainly with victims of domestic abuse in the DC area. I would later interview her at the safe house for victims of domestic abuse where she was employed. She spoke up tentatively in the meeting, explaining quietly that it was one of her favorite stories in the collection because of its potential to raise awareness of taboo subjects such as sexual abuse:

> I really liked that part because I work with a lot of [women who are] sexually abused, and they're survivors. I think the way they described the girl's experience was very typical. I liked that it was in there because it is so common for children to experience, and it is something that nobody wants to talk about or likes to talk about. Because it's just [. . .] not in a lot of novels. In a way, it was so normalized for her. That was just a common experience, and the way, for like a whole year I think they said, she didn't think of it as abnormal. (NetSAP book club meeting, *The Red Carpet*)

While other participants in the discussion excluded the possibility that a child might have trouble separating her abuse and feelings of pleasure, Lalita's experience in domestic abuse social work allowed her to see the value of the narrative's description of abuse and its confusing association with childhood sexual pleasure. From her perspective, the story provided a realistic representation of the interrelated workings of class, ethnic mores, and social taboos and constituted an unusual contribution to the body of transnational South Asian writing.

When I interviewed her, I asked her to revisit her comments on sexual abuse during this book club meeting. She explained to me she was nervous to speak up in the group that night and to share an opinion that diverged from the consensus:

> I don't know if I articulated myself very well. I didn't know anyone in the group. So I was kind of nervous. But I think it can help people, like in mainstream culture to build more awareness. In the book the writer talked about sexual abuse. And that's not something that people talk about that often because it's very stigmatized. [. . .] Destigmatizing and educating people is such a huge part and creating awareness is such a huge part of what we do and what I do. I enjoy reading about it because I feel like someone else is doing the same job that I'm doing. [. . .] So having literature that addresses something like that is so important I think. The South Asian women we see come here and they have no clue. And they are the ones that are more—so much more likely to—any Asian woman that comes here is so much more likely to go back.

Her unease at speaking up to offer a dissenting opinion suggests that the NetSAP book club is a complex and not always inclusive site of imagined community. The responses of the members of the club to *The Red Carpet* exemplify how transnational South Asian literature renders South Asians visible within its various reception contexts and, perhaps more unexpectedly, how this literary culture renders South Asians visible to each other. That is, Lalita's hesitance about sharing her opinion in the group reminds us of how difficult it can be to speak up even in (if not particularly in) situations that are supposed to be sites of community that we belong to already. In such contexts, a desire for narratives that render the South Asian community homogenous, legible, and familiar to South Asians themselves, to each other, and to non-South Asians, within particular parameters of educational, class, and professional privilege, produce a form of cultural gatekeeping. This gatekeeping, in turn, means that narratives associated with South Asian identity that are unfamiliar and do not conform to pervasive ideologies of authenticity that construct South Asian culture in the United States as chaste, family-oriented, model-minority citizens cause discomfort.

The NetSAP book club's uneasy staging of ethnic community reflects broader structures of inclusion and exclusion within the South Asian American community. In their reflections on the book club and in the construction of the book club as a public institution, its members speak to the importance of constructing heterogeneous forms of South Asian identity to enable their belonging. And yet subject to the vagaries of neoliberal multiculturalism, South Asians in the United States feel and exert pressures on one another to conform to particular cultural norms and to value familiar narratives that shore up ideologies of authenticity. Their practices of reading demonstrate the persistence of structures of exclusion in the United States and illuminate the ways that South Asian American subjects respond to such exclusions through ambivalent constructions of ethnic identity and contradictory ideals of community. In the chapter that follows, I continue tracking how readers understand the formation of South Asian community identity in the NetSAP book club through screens of class and privilege.

2

THERE'S A WHOLE OTHER CLASS

Model Minorities, Privileged Subjects, and the Question of Caste

Professional status and its associated privileges take on a strange duality in the NetSAP book club: professional status, as much as ethnic affiliation, is a determinative feature in the constitution of the book club's membership, but privilege remains for the most part a tacit and buried element of participants' practices of reading. During a lengthy interview with Afrah at her apartment in DC one afternoon, the role of South Asian American class status and privilege in the NetSAP book club became apparent when she contrasted the rewards of reading with coethnics to the experience of a South Asian friend who was disappointed with her experience attending a (non–South Asian) book club meeting:

> I think [the NetSAP book club] is a place where you don't have to be defensive. Because the story with her is that she went to her book club. And they were reading *White Tiger* and someone there was like, "Oh, my God. I can't believe how classist Indians are and they treat their servants so terribly!" And my friend was back up against the wall and just like, "It's not worse than anywhere else!" And then being there she had to defend it. Whereas in our book club everyone is South Asian. They can just say what they want to say and they're not having to defend the entire race or whatever.

Aarvind Adiga's critically acclaimed novel *White Tiger*, which won the Man Booker prize in 2008, is set in modern-day India and tells the story of Balram Halwai, a poor man who unethically works his way up the social and economic ladder. After murdering his boss, the son of a feudal landlord, he steals money to start a taxi business in Bangalore specializing in transporting high-tech workers to and from their jobs. Balram's story joins India's rapid economic growth to a narrative of social corruption and harsh economic divides. As Akash Kapur summarizes in a *New York Times* book review, the novel's global reception was divided because of how it depicts Indian socioeconomic issues: it was celebrated abroad for exposing the ongoing inequality of Indian society and complicating the image of India as a bastion of technological progress and Bollywood-style opulence. And yet, in India, critics felt it denied the nation's economic and social progress in an effort to pander to Western audiences.

Afrah's metacommentary on her friend's experience defending South Asian culture among non-South Asians at this book club meeting serves to emphasize her ease with coethnic readers in the NetSAP book club—as she says, "Everyone is South Asian." While she explicitly cites the shared ethnicity of the group as the main factor in her dedication to the book club, there is an equally significant assumption of shared class background buried in her statement. She emphasizes that in NetSAP there is no obligation to "defend the entire race" partly in order to suggest that South Asian culture in the United States is not monolithic. At the same time, Afrah's assertion that everyone in the group "can just say whatever they want to say" reveals that their comfort in the group is built at least partially on their shared cosmopolitan privilege, which in this case and others was indicated by their familiarity with and complacency about the socioeconomic hierarchies of modern, affluent Indian society.

The tacit and yet structuring function of privilege in the NetSAP book club, what Sunaina Maira identifies as the "under-discussed and overdetermined" role of class in the construction of South Asian American identity ("Ideologies" 146), can be understood as a direct effect of neoliberal multiculturalism. In a broad sense, neoliberal ideology among socioeconomically elite ethnic subjects encourages identification with commodified forms of ethnic authenticity (such as traditional dress and exotic cultural practices) as a means to earn belonging and cultural citizenship in the United States while obfuscating the economic exigencies and structures that bring ethnic communities into being (Melamed 141; Thoma 19). In this chapter, I explore how practices of reading in the NetSAP book club reflect the workings of neoliberal multiculturalism among South Asian Americans, manifesting particularly in readers' ambivalence about the model minority paradigm.

The model minority paradigm refers to a complicated discourse, originally used to disparage other racial minorities, in which Asian Americans are commended for their self-sufficient, hard-working, and family-oriented approach to assimilation (Song 167).[1] For Asian American subjects, and one might say South Asian American subjects in particular, one cannot overstate the significance of the model minority paradigm in shaping belonging in the United States.[2] Even though the term originally stratified racial difference among diverse minorities, its long-term effects have come to organize difference and belonging via intersections of racial and classed meanings within Asian America.

As erin Khue Ninh explains, the dominant consensus among Asian Americanist scholars and activists is that the model minority paradigm is a *myth* based in stereotypical associations of Asians with accommodation, obedience, and sacrifice (9). Refutations of the model minority paradigm, Ninh explains, have thus tended to rely "on indicators of Asian American failure or deviance" and "statistics of poverty or criminality" (9). Such defenses fall short, however, because, as Ninh and other scholars have demonstrated, they do not account for the ways that model minority discourse has been assimilated within Asian American communities (Ninh 9; see also Koshy, "Morphing" 154). These scholars argue that it is inaccurate to call the model minority paradigm a myth when it is such a "crucial element of [Asian American] racial formation and agency" (Ninh 9).

NetSAP book club participants' relationship to the model minority discourse emerges in their practices of reading as a tension between their conscious resistance to positive stereotyping and a more complex affiliation with the core values associated with the model minority ethos. The first section of this chapter details readers' dissatisfaction with the over-representation of affluent South Asian characters in transnational South Asian literature and their objections to the racist structure of the model minority paradigm. The remainder of the chapter studies how the communal practice of reading in evidence during the discussions of Kamala Markandaya's *Nectar in a Sieve* (1954) and *The Marriage Bureau for Rich People* (2009) by Farahad Zama raised issues of socioeconomic inequality, class, and caste and served to complicate these objections.[3] Discussants nostalgically praised the traditionalism depicted in these narratives, contrasting it with their own cosmopolitanism. Even though readers explicitly disavowed affiliation with model minority status in interviews and meetings, their concern for narrative elements of "sacrifice, obedience, hierarchy, and gratitude" (11)—key values, as Ninh explains, of the model minority paradigm—demonstrates that ambivalence regarding this discourse is nevertheless a powerful feature of contemporary middle- and upper-middle-class South Asian American subject formation.

Questioning Privilege and the Model Minority Paradigm

From 2000 to 2010 the South Asian community in the United States grew by 81 percent. Indians still comprise the largest segment of the South Asian population in the United States, making up 80 percent of the total, followed by Pakistanis, Bangladeshis, Nepalis, Sri Lankans, Bhutanese, and Maldivians.[4] According to the 2010 census, "Asian Indians" comprise the third-largest Asian group in the United States after Chinese Americans and Filipino Americans.[5] The median income for Indian American households is $90,711 and is reported to be the highest median household income of all ethnic groups in the United States—far exceeding the overall median household income in the United States of $52,250.[6] Indian Americans participate in the U.S. workforce at a rate of 72.3 percent, and 57.7 of that 72.3. percent are employed in managerial and professional specialties. At the same time, there is significant class variability within the South Asian American community, as well as uneven access to resources, education, and economic and cultural capital among its subgroups; for example, for Bangladeshi Americans the median income is below the national level at $48,471 (U.S. Census, *Asian Population*).

Many professional and highly educated South Asians were the beneficiaries of the 1965 Immigration and Nationality Act. Sociologists have noted that due to their professional background these South Asian Americans "earn large incomes, live in large suburban homes located primarily in white neighborhoods, drive luxury cars, and send their children to expensive private liberal arts colleges and Ivy League schools" (Bhatia 187).[7] The NetSAP book club is made up primarily of second-generation South Asian Americans who tend to be the beneficiaries of this post-1965 boom. They are a privileged subset of the "children of 1965"—what Min Hyoung Song identifies as the generation of Asian Americans who started to reach adulthood in the early 1990s, many of whom constitute an educationally and economically advantaged Asian American mainstream. There are also several readers in the book club who are more recent transplants to the United States and who, already experienced, tend to have come for professional or educational advancement.

First- and second-generation NetSAP book club participants' professional and cultural capital mitigates the social disadvantages of racialization to which working-class South Asian Americans are subject.[8] That is, affluent South Asian Americans such as those who populate the NetSAP book club constitute the visible, model minority face of the ethnic community; their experiences of assimilation have been eased by the education and professional status acquired in their South Asian countries of origin.[9] In contrast, family reunification policies and the influx of undocumented South Asians have created a large and yet relatively unseen working-class population of South Asian immigrants laboring in the service and manufacturing industries (Mani, *Aspiring* 20; Song 32).[10] With that said, South Asian Americans of varying class levels still struggle with how to place themselves within U.S. systems of racial categorization (Mani, *Aspiring* 19). Affluent ethnic subjects still encounter racism in the United States, even if they react to it from a relative position of privilege.[11]

In interviews, NetSAP book club members noted that particularly in the literary realm (as opposed to film or television) there has been a lamentable overrepresentation of narratives that focus on the affluence of South Asians in the United States.[12] My aim here is not to weigh in on the credibility of this claim but rather to examine what NetSAP book club members' views on this alleged overrepresentation can tell us about their ambivalent and contradictory relationship to their own privilege and the model minority paradigm. Their disidentification with images of affluence in transnational South Asian literary culture demonstrates a desire for intraethnic solidarity across class and a savvy awareness of how cosmopolitan privilege affects which South Asian narratives become globally popular and accessible. Furthermore, when we spoke one-on-one, they downplayed their own assimilation and the deracialization afforded by model minority modes of belonging, arguing forcefully that the paradigm was unreliable and tenuous.

Maya, for example, felt that popular transnational South Asian literature tends to mirror her own class positioning: "I feel like there's a lot missing with South Asians who are poor or who are not like me. I had a college education and graduate school and in many ways was overeducated and privileged. I don't see a lot of literature on—I haven't sought it out, to be fair, literature on that growing, large population [of poorer South Asian Americans]." Maya has no illusions about her own privilege or educational status and distinguishes herself, quite consciously, from South Asians who are "not like" her, meaning poor, unassimilated, and less educated. Maya's observations align with those of literary critics who have noted that the poor and working classes are often left out of popular narratives of South Asian immigration, thereby making these experiences seem less representative not only among mainstream audiences but among cosmopolitan South Asians as well (Ghosh 28; see also Shukla, *India Abroad* 15).

NetSAP book club members savvily attributed the elitism of transnational South Asian writing to the privileged, cosmopolitan subjectivity of many popular South Asian writers. Afrah, for example, observed that "South Asian literature used to really focus on upper class South Asians because those were the people that were writing. And often they'd moved from India and they moved to England or America, and their families were richer [than other South Asians]. And that was interesting and I liked it at the time, but it's nice to go beyond that." Anil, a young South Asian man who at the time of our interview was attending medical school, said, "There's a whole other class. The people that are the writers are the ones that are in the upper class. And the lower class, they can almost be invisible because [the upper class] does not see them."

Scholars such as Inderpal Grewal and Bishnupriya Ghosh attribute the fact that economic advantage and social privilege permeate the production of transnational South Asian literary culture largely to the English-medium education that the middle and upper classes in India receive. British policies during the long history of colonial occupation created an English-educated middle class, the members of whom were originally intended to function as intermediaries between the Indian population and colonial state. In the postcolonial context, this group emerged as an elite subset of the population, a privileged class whose immigration to the West was eased by their fluency with the English language and English literary culture (Ghosh 3; Grewal 41). The ensuing cultural capital associated with fluency in English not only enabled South Asian emigration to English-speaking nations by opening up professional opportunities and cultural assimilation but also assured familiarity with Western literary culture and generic forms. By contextualizing which South Asian narratives become globally accessible, NetSAP book club participants draw attention to how elite cosmopolitanism comes to define global South Asian identity.

Given the educational levels of NetSAP book club members and their predilection for educating themselves about South Asian American identity formation, it is perhaps unsurprising that they offered incisive critiques of the model minority paradigm while acknowledging that they may be held up as exemplars of it. Anil, for instance, objected to the idea that South Asian American subjects who were economically successful were touted as the authentic ethnic representatives of the group through its literary culture. Anil granted that model minority discourse, grounded in a positive stereotype, granted South Asians "the benefit of the doubt," as people often assume, "Oh you're Indian, you must be smart, right?" However, he was very aware of the ways that this stereotype could pit South Asians not only against other minorities but against one another:

> The model minority thing is hurting everyone, all minorities, because it makes it worse for the Blacks and Hispanics. Everyone is like, "Oh, why don't you look at the Asians?" They're so successful and they make up less than one percent of the population. They make up 10 percent of the physician population. That hurts everyone. Then there's this whole segment of South Asians that aren't very wealthy and they're not in the public eye at all. I see them all the time, right? Because my parents were actually not very wealthy at all. They actually came through family reunification and not directly because of education, and I think that people like me, [whose] parents were not very wealthy, but [whose] children went on to become physicians or whatever, that's kind of rare. Because I see a lot of my parents' friends who live in these typical poor ethnic ghettos and the kids all end up doing what the parents are doing which is running gas stations or convenience stores and they sort of stay at that kind of life.

Anil's comments demonstrate an awareness not only of the more divisive elements of the model minority myth but also of how it obscures working-class South Asian American experiences in favor of narratives of professional success. He references the family reunification policies during the mid-1980s that followed the 1965 Immigration Act and that, along with diversity visas, substantially contributed to class-based disparities and regional diversity among South Asian immigrants in the United States. His own experiences as a medical student from a working-class background have prompted him to reflect on the shortcomings of model minority discourse as a way to understand the complexities of South Asian American experience.

Similarly, Aarthi, a South Indian reader, objected to South Asian American complicity with the model minority paradigm because, as she explained, to do so cedes control to dominant groups to define South Asian American identity and because it ascribes a false exceptionalism to South Asian immigrants:

> I resist the idea of trying to be something that fits into people's stereotype. I'm not saying that we should commit crimes just to prove a point or something. But the model minority is essentially a way in which—I didn't really want to say "white people"—it's a way in which the dominant culture can recognize someone as a good group versus a less-than-ideal group. And who doesn't want that as a community, you know what I mean? Everyone wants their kids to work hard and go to school and get an education and get a good job. So, Indian Americans, in particular—or South Asian Americans, in particular—are obsessed with education but then that's also true for a lot of other minority groups, too.

Aarthi objects to positing certain groups as models for others and notes that the mainstream power to grant model minority status includes the power to deny it. She connects South Asian American experience to a longer history of immigrant aspirations and a desire for education and opportunity in the United States. Notably, Aarthi justifies South Asian American complicity with the model minority paradigm while noting that it's a problematic identification.

Raj insisted that the model minority was a paradigm that South Asians perpetuated themselves rather than one that was imposed wholesale by dominant groups. He also emphasized that South Asian privilege in the United States was not a given, particularly after the events of 9/11:

> The reason I hate the term "model minority" is because I think that white people don't really think of us as the model minority. I think we think of ourselves as the model minority. The best case scenario is if we're going to be here anyway, they want 100 percent assimilation. No accents. You speak English. You dress like them. You go to church. You don't bring foreign flags at sporting events, or anything else. You just do everything just like that. And if you do all those things you will be successful. But really I think that this is an idea that Asian Americans have designated [for] themselves. But I guess we're not the ones that invented it, you know. I feel like too many Asians identify with whites rather than with, say, Hispanics, you know? And I think that that model minority thing is part of that. It just takes 20 crazy Hindus to destroy one U.S. building, and we are not the model minority anything anymore. We're dirt. We're all getting frisked at the airports. That's all it takes.

Raj gestures to the post-9/11 racialization of South Asian Americans in the United States. Rather than referencing the stigmatization of Muslim South Asian Americans, he imagines a scenario of Hindu religious fundamentalism in the United States. I conjecture that Raj purposefully wanted to emphasize that religious fundamentalism is not the unique purview of Islam and, in doing so, to reinforce connections among South Asians in America along lines by which they are usually divided. He connects South Asian American modes of assimilation to their deemed successes in America but notes that the process of assimilating can be one that is coerced rather than voluntary. His comments oscillate between the assertion that model minority status can only be achieved through complacent assimilation to norms of whiteness and the notion that it is a self-imposed designation, even if it didn't originate from within the Asian American community. He concludes by observing the tenuousness of model minority status for subsets of South Asians who do not conform to the image. Perhaps the most striking feature of his commentary is his disappointment that South Asian Americans don't attempt to establish links to other nonwhite minority groups but rather seek to consolidate their economic capital by colluding with white privilege.

These comments encapsulate the overall awareness among NetSAP book club participants of the inadequacies of the model minority paradigm. In fact, their explicit resistance to the paradigm can be understood as a marker of their educational and professional status: it demonstrates their knowledge, as privileged ethnic subjects, of the positive and negative stereotypes that have come to circumscribe South Asian identity in the United States. Moreover, it reveals that they have the cultural and economic capital to distance themselves explicitly from such limitations in their self-presentation.

In the remainder of this chapter, I explore how in spite of the stated objections of NetSAP book club participants to the exclusive, classist, and racist elements of the model minority paradigm, it is a discourse that has had structuring effects in shaping South Asian American reading practices and community. In the discussion of Markandaya's *Nectar in a Sieve,* the participants fetishized the narrative of South Asian authenticity that is configured in it through premodern, rural representations of South Asian poverty and village life. In the discussion of *The Marriage Bureau for Rich People,* attendees neglected the economic effects of caste in shaping privilege among South Asians in the United States by treating caste as a strictly *cultural* artifact of South Asian diasporic identity. Because poverty, social mobility, and class are central themes in these novels, class played a significant role in these particular discussions, but otherwise, it was seldom a sustained topic, therein demonstrating the structuring and yet silent effects of class in shaping this book club.

In comparing the NetSAP book club's responses to these two novels, I do not mean to elide their stark historical and generic differences. Even though they are set in different time periods, are of different genres, and have been written by authors from very different religious, regional, and educational backgrounds, they share some striking similarities in their concerns with economic and social hierarchy. NetSAP book club participants' practices of reading with respect to these two book club meetings demonstrate the possibilities and perhaps more sharply the limits of literary encounters with sameness and difference. David Palumbo-Liu instructively notes that in the modern era of globalization, literature can inspire empathy for others by representing transhistorical and transnational forms of sameness and difference. He notes, however, that there are limits to using literature as an empathic tool, one that can familiarize, domesticate, and mitigate otherness: "How much otherness is required [to inspire empathy], as opposed to how much is excessive, disruptive, disturbing?" (*Deliverance* 2). In these two book club meetings, participants encountered "other" forms of South Asian identity, and this experience was tempered through an imagined ethnic kinship with literary characters. But as their conversations make clear, it is a constructed, tenuous kinship stymied by powerful situational, historical, economic, and locational differences.

NetSAP book club members' yearnings for what they deemed an authentic version of South Asian identity figured in these two meetings through two of the main tropes of model minority discourse: tradition and hierarchy. Their appreciation of these tropes conflicted with their rejection of the model minority paradigm as a path to belonging for South Asian Americans in the United States. In general, their discomfort with and ambivalence about privilege is a vital component of their cosmopolitan subjectivity and understanding of South Asian American community formation. As educated, elite South Asian subjects they are suspicious of how stereotypes of upward mobility shape South Asian American culture. And yet they also tend to overlook how model minority discourses and economic privilege shape the ways in which South Asians in the United States construct ideals of ethnic authenticity.

Discussing Privilege, Poverty, and Caste in NetSAP Book Club Meetings

Book club meetings tended to be held in the tonier neighborhoods of the Washington, DC, metro area, a region known for its expensive housing, and the meeting on Markandaya's *Nectar in a Sieve* was no exception; it took place in a young female reader's well-appointed downtown DC penthouse apartment, which provided a striking contrast between the setting of the book club and that of the novel we were discussing.[13] Markandaya's social realist novel about the difficult life experiences of a rural peasant woman in South India is a version of South Asian experience that is temporally, situationally, and contextually removed from this group of South Asian diasporics. And yet through their practice of reading, the discussants worked, for better or for worse, to establish links between their experiences of South Asia and the one described in the novel.

The novel focuses on the story of an Indian peasant woman named Rukmani and the trials that she faces once she is married and raising a family. It is a domestic narrative that confronts several social and political issues, such as the effects of colonialism, industrialization of rural communities, poverty, and starvation. Although it is represented as a realist narrative, at the time of its publication, critics questioned whether the novel's depictions of village life, poverty, and destitution could be authentic given that they were written by an expatriate author of middle-class background.[14] Each reissue and most book reviews of *Nectar in a Sieve* have been accompanied by a short biography that authenticates Markandaya as native informant and provides a peculiar validation of her unlikely rise to success, as has likewise been the case with notable contemporary South Asian female writers such as Arundhati Roy and Jhumpa Lahiri (Almeida 43; Pais n.p.). As the story goes, born in India, Markandaya eventually settled in England, where she spent most of her adult life. Yet with the publication of the critically acclaimed and popular *Nectar in a Sieve*, she became an international literary presence. The novel garnered praise and success in the United States, Canada, and England, was reviewed in several major publications, and established Markandaya as one of the most internationally celebrated writers of Indian origin at the time. Arguably, however, the novel was most celebrated and esteemed in the United States, where it was a dual selection for the Book of the Month Club in 1955, earning Markandaya a $100,000 prize. It was also a notable book selection by the American Library Association in the same year.

Echoing the popular criticism that circulated around the time of the novel's publication, recent academic criticism on the text tends to focus on three issues that tie clearly into debates as to whether Markandaya's work is authentic in its representations of peasant life: first, critics question whether the novel's social concerns are sincere enough to qualify it as a work of social realism, second, they debate Markandaya's choice to use standard English for the speech of a rural Indian peasant woman, and third, they lament Markandaya's inclusion of ethnographic details, which they regard as an attempt to pander to an English-speaking literary market.[15]

The NetSAP book club's general response to the novel, in contrast, was one of admiration for its authenticity: some minor reservations about the novel's writing style and ethnographic features notwithstanding, they felt the novel's greatest strength was its realistic representations of village life and the way it humanized poverty.[16] They deemed it as "very authentic, simple but not in a simplistic way," as "more real" than other South Asian diasporic fiction, and a "classic" that is "still very resonant today" (NetSAP book cub, discussion of *Nectar in a Sieve*). Their assessment of the novel's authenticity reflects its categorization as a work of social realism, a genre popular in mid-twentieth-century India in both film and literature in which the plight of the impoverished masses is humanized through stories of individual struggle, hardship, and hope.

Repeatedly during the book club meeting, discussants referred to Markandaya's work as "refreshing," idealizing the novel's depictions of poverty and labor struggle as a sort of antimaterialist, anticapitalist manifesto:

> **VIKRAM:** I liked how it gave social depth to this peasant class that is always often kind of stereotyped in very simplistic terms. In their marriage and in her relationship, they were quite sophisticated despite their circumstances.
>
> **AISHA:** Well, they had a good relationship, too. It's like they encouraged each other. They supported each other.
>
> **VIKRAM:** When they went to the city and everyone was like, "No beggars allowed." They never—they weren't egotistical in any way. You would've thought after being called a beggar six times that—yes, we have no material wealth, but we're not here for material reasons. It was just kind of refreshing.
>
> **KAMAL:** I think it still bothers me that [someone said] that they had nothing. I think they had something that none of us here will ever

> have is that happiness with what they—and acceptance for what they have. It's almost like breaking that cycle of need and want and desire and possessions. (NetSAP book club meeting, *Nectar in a Sieve*)

Arun in turn commended the novel for the way it provided an unfamiliar representation of South Asian culture:

> **ARUN:** [It appealed] to me for the same reason that some documentaries appeal to me—because it's an abstraction out of your reality into someone else's and—she's not trying to make the story relatable to the reader. She wants to affect something. She wants to affect the reader, but she doesn't hit you over the head with it. I think a lot of the South Asian writers today think so much of themselves that they're not trying to communicate through their words. They're trying to impress. (NetSAP book club meeting, *Nectar in a Sieve*)

Arun, along with his fellow readers in this meeting, insisted that the novel offers a productive defamiliarization of the dominant, cosmopolitan construction of South Asian culture in modern transnational writing.

Locating their comments in a specifically South Asian American context, other participants built on Arun's assertion by contrasting Markandaya's social realist concerns with their frustration at the proliferation of South Asian American novels about bicultural identity crises:

> **NIHA:** It was refreshing to me that I didn't sort of have to spend hours and days with some existential crisis about identity. That's my life anyway, so it was very refreshing and transporting to read something that was not nostalgic. I probably wouldn't have picked this up on my own. If this hadn't been suggested by the book club; [. . .] it wouldn't have occurred to me to be next on my reading list.
>
> **ANJALI:** It was a very different perspective, [. . .] and we're not used to reading books about poverty, about people going through so much struggle and like you were saying, months or years or whatever to travel and knowing that you're never going to see their kids again, things like that, it's so hard to imagine that. [. . .] I was back and forth between being intrigued by "Oh, my God, there's people [. . .] who have this kind of life in different parts of

the world." And we're so used to having all the struggles that we're going through but never having to really worry about money so much; [. . .] it was kind of a refreshing, different perspective.

AISHA: Yes, I agree. [. . .] It was just simple life and how you get through it. It makes our problems look so trivial. But the book is not trying to belittle other people's lives. That's the difference between then and now. Now we're so overdramatic about everything. Even in the writing that we read. (NetSAP book club meeting, *Nectar in a Sieve*)

Indeed, at this moment in the meeting, participants were comparing *Nectar in a Sieve* with Jhumpa Lahiri's *The Namesake*. As I explain in chapter 4, during this book club meeting, readers used Lahiri's body of work to stand in for what they perceived to be the profusion of narratives on affluent Hindu characters resettled in the United States. Aisha lamented that "the writing that we read" in the NetSAP book club generally reflected the complacent cosmopolitan preferences of South Asian American readers. All four readers agreed that the otherness of Markandaya's novel instructively exposes the privilege of modern South Asian American subjects, whose primary concerns as they are reflected in transnational South Asian literature tend to be bicultural identity crises rather than the day-to-day survival and struggle of the characters in *Nectar*.

Notably, however, the elements of the narrative that they seize upon as the most defamiliarizing, strange, and challenging to their privileged status as members of the professional class were framed quite explicitly in terms of values endemic to model minority discourse, such as social hierarchy, sacrifice, and selflessness. Readers are interpellated by the model minority discourses from which they seek to consciously distance themselves, revealing a key contradiction in constructions of South Asian American community and identity. As one reader, Kamal, explained to the book group:

> I did kind of appreciate it as an ethnographic study actually. As I was reading it, I was just thinking, she's describing the life of poverty and these very specific segments of society, whether it took place in a village in India or any other place on the globe where there's definite classes and definite limits to where someone can move forward. She gets out the feeling of living for survival. I kept picturing people that I've worked with in villages in poverty in different parts of the world, and it's exactly this. I think she describes it so well, this feeling. [. . .] You go from day to

> day, not only just surviving, but there is some substance to your life, and there's drama, and there's people that cheat, and do these things to fulfill their personal needs, but it's still sort of static. I really took it as a social study, not so much as a beautiful piece of literature. (NetSAP book club meeting, *Nectar in a Sieve*).

Kamal draws a direct connection between the novel and his professional experience as an aid worker, authenticating his own assessment of the novel's strengths as an ethnographically accurate depiction of rural poverty. He commends Markandaya's humanization of the poor in rural villages and sees truth in her descriptions of the social order, the "definite classes, and definite limits" that determine this world and its set of values.

Responding in part to Kamal's observations that the novel captures Rukmani's struggle for survival, Niha and Aisha explained that they were inspired by the characters' perseverance:

> AISHA: Well, people are in a worse situation than us. When I go to India, the poorer class of people are just happy with what they have and they realize that other people are worse—in a worse condition. So that's something. It's a very tragic book because it just tells about her life and all the bad things that happened, but at the same time it's kind of nice to know that there's no complaining about it and there's no villain. It's—they just deal with it as they go, so it is tragic, but when I finished the book, I was like it's not that negative at the end because it makes you realize that somebody's life is much worse.
>
> NIHA: You just have to deal. You deal with what you're dealt. And it was incredible to me that something as simple as traveling took months and months. They had to think, okay, if we stay for a year we're going to have enough for this journey. That's just so overwhelming and hopeless; [. . .] it's not that I was depressed at the end of it. I found it a beautiful book. I didn't really feel she was trying to talk about, "this noble struggle." (NetSAP book club meeting, *Nectar in a Sieve*)

On the surface, one could say that Kamal's, Aisha's, and Niha's responses problematically deal in the trope of the "happy peasant" whose premodern life is desirable for its simplicity, freedom from capitalist desire, and gratitude for survival. Niha is such a savvy reader that she even names and disavows this romanticization of poverty, lending further credibility to her own interpretive admiration for the struggles that Markandaya describes. All of these readers unabashedly respect the protagonist's endurance, obedience, and sacrifice and described these features as instructive and pedagogical, having the ability to make them "realize that somebody's life is much worse." They ironically juxtapose these ideals with their own privileged position within the U.S. social order, even while it is precisely these filial values and principles that have been used to prop up dominant narratives of South Asian American success (Ninh 9).

The book club's initial reaction to Farahad Zama's contemporary novel *The Marriage Bureau for Rich People* was, in contrast, rather dismissive, owing to its status as a romance.[17] As one participant put it, the novel is "entertaining on a very, very, very superficial level" (NetSAP book club meeting, *The Marriage Bureau*). The first in a series of novels devoted to the narrating the ups and downs of Mr. Hyder Ali's thriving marriage bureau, the novel is set in the town of Vizag in Andhra Pradesh on India's east coast. Mr. Ali, with help from his wife, decides in his retirement to open a marriage bureau that caters to wealthy clientele. The novel tells of Mr. Ali's slow start in the business and eventual success at matchmaking, along the way offering commentary on the effect of religious and caste restrictions that still shape romantic union in modern-day India. For example, one of the main narrative threads focuses on Mr. Ali's talented, bright assistant Aruna. When her family's financial troubles force her to give up her graduate study and go to work, Aruna, a Brahmin Hindu woman, teams up with the Muslim Mr. Ali and helps him to make even the most difficult matches work. In the course of her work with Mr. Ali, she ends up meeting and falling in love with Ram, a wealthy, handsome young Brahmin doctor whose parents are seeking an equally affluent daughter-in-law. In a fairy-tale ending, Aruna and the doctor manage to convince their respective families that they make a good match despite the class difference and end up marrying. In a subplot, Mr. and Mrs. Ali's son, Rehman, much to their disappointment, has devoted himself to social activism, protesting the incursion of special economic zone development in a community of locally owned farms.

Even though the conversation about this novel began with a few attendees suggesting that it wasn't much more than "brain candy" and that it was about as unrealistic, fanciful, and "escapist as a Bollywood movie," it quickly shifted when one reader argued that *Marriage Bureau* had a lot to say about class and intercaste marriage. Tara, a new member, suggested that the novel, while seemingly frivolous in its concerns with romance, offered a social message:

> **TARA:** But that's a message. That's a social message. Either way it's a social message.
>
> **AFRAH:** What is the social message?
>
> **TARA:** That a poor woman wouldn't marry a rich guy or is not able to marry. That's [the] caste or the class system at work. [. . .] But the barrier should be broken. That's a message. (NetSAP book club meeting, *The Marriage Bureau*)

Here, Tara explicitly refers to the romance between the protagonist Aruna and Ram. She notes that this romance offers a progressive view of rigid social stratification in India, an observation that sparked an extended discussion of the lingering cultural effects of caste in Indian society particularly in relation to marriageability. Most participants in this meeting pointed out that caste was an entrenched and even perhaps useful element of the Indian social order. But as the conversation developed they also demonstrated their own distance and unease with the rigid hierarchies of caste as well as their reluctance to discuss how caste and class privilege intersect to shape the cultural and economic capital of South Asians in the diaspora.

A survey of matrimonial pages in newspapers throughout India and in the popular Indian American newspaper *India Abroad* indicates that when it comes to social and cultural life, caste identity, alongside other factors such as age, skin color, and educational background, still carries significant weight. While politically and professionally it is illegal to discriminate against an individual on the basis of caste in India, it is a social structure that retains significance in South Asian and diasporic cultures as an everyday fact of life (Tickell 24). *Marriage Bureau* reflects the enduring legacy of caste in Mr. Ali's matchmaking business: it is one of the primary criteria that he and Aruna use in determining romantic matches. That is, Mr. Ali and Aruna keep track of their clients' preferences for particular complexions, religions, and regional backgrounds but tend to arrange marriages along caste lines. Responding to the spark of interest in the issue of caste and class, the book club leader and moderator Raj posed a question to the group:

> **RAJ:** So one of the things Mr. Ali says is, "When people come in and say, 'Caste no bar,' it makes it harder to find a match. And when

people are specific, it makes it easier. So I guess I have two questions about this. [. . .] Number one: do you think, is there truth to that? And number two, do you find something about that morally objectionable? Do you think the author is trying to say something stereotypical? Let's just start with the true part. What do you think?

LAKSHMI: I could see it being true because you don't want to seem like you're desperate, and maybe by saying anybody will do, "Oh, it doesn't matter if she's fat, ugly, whatever. Just anybody will be fine," is very desperate. We all have to work within society, and I think he's reflecting Indian society. I mean, people—especially in a smaller kind of town and community—they do follow caste networks. You kind of hang out with certain people because you've been marrying each other for generations and you all are sort of the same caste. And [if] you go against that, maybe it seems a little rebellious, a little bit desperate. For me, that was believable. (NetSAP book club meeting, *The Marriage Bureau*)

Raj refers to a section in the novel when Mr. Ali explains that in his experience, "it was actually more difficult to find a partner for somebody who said 'caste or religion no bar.' It was ironic, but true, thought Mr. Ali, that the more specific the requirement—a Turpu Kapu from Krishna District who owned at least twenty acres of land, for example—the easier it was to find a match" (35). Raj asks readers to weigh in on the veracity and ethics of this representation of Indian caste mores. The consensus of the group—which was signaled by members' concurrence with Lakshmi's remarks—was that the novel presented an accurate portrayal of the imperative within modern Indian society, particularly in smaller towns, to marry within caste networks. No one at the meeting felt that ideologies of caste endogamy were particularly objectionable in the novel or in real life. When relegated to the seemingly innocuous realm of social and romantic union, caste seemed to most attendees of the book club meeting to be a perfectly reasonable way to define social commonality, particularly in small-town society.

Indeed, some readers even offered justification for the persistence of caste stratification in India, seeing it as a way to adjudicate and reinforce social difference in a context where poverty was inescapable and pervasive:

SHASHI: Every time I'd travel [to India] as a kid, it was like my family was intentionally [saying], "Don't look outside" [. . .] and tried

> to shelter me. In India, speaking strictly from having been to Mumbai and Delhi, poverty exists in such a way you can't ignore it. And that's part of daily life. People just put up their barriers. Whereas in the United States, the way neighborhoods are constructed, the way Washington, DC, is constructed, with a quadrant system that's very much racially segregated, it's set up in a way that we can ignore [poverty] if we're coming from positions of class privilege. But in India, you have to create other boundaries. (NetSAP book club meeting, *The Marriage Bureau*)

Shashi offers a complex justification of the caste system, conjecturing that because poverty in India is so inescapable and overt, caste offers a structure through which to manage social inequality. She notes that in contrast to the United States, where racial and economic segregation mitigates the privileged subject's exposure to poverty, in India, the rich cannot escape the poor. Both this justification of caste as well as the one that represents it as a harmless social tool in India draw attention to NetSAP book club participants' privilege, their inculcation to model minority discourse, and their acquiescence to systems of social hierarchy, however rigid they might be.

In part, NetSAP book club participants' justification of caste might have at least partially been influenced by the novel's own logic, namely, the idea that caste is an ethnocultural tradition that might bridge class divides. When Aruna's uncle intervenes on her behalf to speak with her parents about Aruna and Ram's desire to marry, caste is the means by which he smooths over their main transgression—having fallen in love with each other outside of the conventions of arranged marriage:

> Shastry-uncle said, "At first, I too did not believe that a well brought-up girl like Aruna would find her own husband, but the more I have found out about Ramanujam and his family, the more convinced I am that our daughter has done no wrong. Ramanujam is a Brahmin. Aruna has not run away with him" (267).

Aruna's and Ram's shared caste status in the upper echelons of the caste hierarchy ultimately trumps her undesirable lower-middle-class status and enables both sets of parents to agree to their marriage. The novel's seemingly progressive vision of class thus relies on the entrenched system of caste stratification.

It was my sense throughout this conversation, and perhaps more accurately as I reflected on it afterward, that the misunderstandings that arose in this meeting regarding caste and class were manifestations of participants' guilt about their own privilege. This tension emerged most sharply in an uncomfortable interaction between Maya and Meena, both regular book club attendees. Maya, a Punjabi woman of Indian origin—who both in our interview and in various book club meetings emphasized her identification with India rather than the United States—was from outward observation highly assimilated (she spoke English with an American accent, wore Western clothes, seemed familiar with American popular culture, and had been educated at an American university). Meena had been attending book club meetings for many years and did not fit into the general postcollegiate demographic of the group—I estimate that she was in her fifties at the time. Meena was of Indian origin and had spent a good part of her adult life there. Maya was sharing her thoughts on caste with the group, explaining that when she was growing up in New Delhi, caste did not inform her sense of self—indeed she explained that it wasn't until she was a teenager that she even thought to ask her parents what caste they belonged to:

> **MAYA:** I grew up in New Delhi and I don't think that I've had a single conversation about caste in my life with anyone in my family. I grew up learning about it. I knew that this was a problem. But I've never heard anyone in my family ever mention caste ever. I think I asked my parents [about it] one time because I was learning about it in school. I was like, "What caste are we?" And I didn't know. I was like fourteen or fifteen.
>
> **MEENA:** What caste are you?
>
> **MAYA:** It doesn't matter. (NetSAP book club meeting, *The Marriage Bureau*)

The tone in which Maya had responded to Meena was one of irritation. It became clear from the reaction in the group, the silence and nervous laughter that followed, that this had been a relatively tense and unpleasant exchange. In the comments that followed, various participants chimed in to disavow the importance of caste in their families and social circles. What happened in the moment between Meena's direct question about Maya's caste and her palpable, discomfort at being asked this question?

Meena often visibly irritated other members of the group by making overtly disagreeable or incendiary statements. While I do not believe that her interpersonal communication style was related to her lack of cultural assimilation or age, these factors may have played a part in how she fit into the group and in how her comments were received. Meena, after all, had revealed to me in an interview that she thought of herself as a bit of an outsider to the group because of her age, but she felt strongly that she had to continue attending the meetings in order to serve as an unofficial steward of NetSAP's literary culture, especially after the group's original founder passed the reins onto the next generation of book club leaders.

I believe, however, that there was more at work in this awkward exchange than a violation of social mores. Maya prefaced her remarks about the novel by saying that she had read it on her flight back to visit relatives in New Delhi. The kind of economic privilege that such mobility exemplifies was common among book club participants and was frequently naturalized in book club discussions—readers would often talk about flying back to various South Asian countries for vacations and to see relatives. And yet the overall privilege of members of the group and their shared social background, while a salient commonality, was never addressed explicitly as such.

I conjecture that when Meena directly asked Maya what caste she was from, Maya and other readers in the group bristled because they felt that to discuss caste privilege was akin, in some ways, to discussing class privilege—a taboo and gauche topic in the United States. In other words, for relatively assimilated, privileged Indian Americans, caste is seen as a retrograde vestige of India that they want to disavow. While they might see class as a discourse of mobility, caste, a system that one is born into and cannot change through achievement, is associated with rigid, regressive, and inescapable socioeconomic hierarchies that stand in direct contradiction to narratives of American meritocracy.

At the same time, as noted, participants also relegated caste to the realm of ethnic and cultural tradition, treating it as a fairly innocuous system that governs marital union and allows for the maintenance of social order. However, in emptying caste of its economic effects in this way, they failed to acknowledge the link between high-caste privilege and affluence, particularly in the diaspora. As Sinthujan Varatharajah explains, the Indian caste system eases the migration of upper-caste Hindus from backgrounds of relative educational and economic privilege, who very often emigrate to countries like England, the United States, and Canada in search of further opportunity. In contrast, lower-caste and Dalit individuals who face unemployment in India have historically emigrated more often to Africa and the Caribbean, often through bonded labor systems. Varatharaja asserts that caste has always been a buried and yet powerful marker of difference among South Asians in the diaspora:

> In diaspora we have removed caste from the public into the private while the public is invisibly still constructed around caste allegiances, differences and prejudices. Today, the majority of marriages in diaspora are still negotiated along caste lines, the majority of friends circles are situated along caste sameness and the majority of South Asian political, social, cultural and economic spaces and centres of power are in the hands of those who have traditionally spoken, explained, observed, analysed and written caste away.[18]

While South Asians in the United States are attuned to how educational attainment, family wealth, and other forms of privilege might facilitate their belonging in the United States, there is much less acknowledgment of how these factors also have been influenced by caste privilege.

Readers' ambivalence about caste—their relativist excusal of caste as an ethnic tradition crucial to the maintenance of Indian society and their failure to acknowledge its effects in shaping their own privilege—exemplifies the impact of social ideologies of neoliberal multiculturalism on South Asian American subject formation, which rely on the obfuscation of the economic and social structures that prop up American fictions of meritocracy and determine wealth. Varatharajah observes that it is the exclusive prerogative of the caste- and class-privileged to suppress these social and economic structures and to make caste and its attendant hierarchies appear trivial as a structuring inequality in the diaspora; caste does not appeal to South Asians as a rubric through which to understand the workings of privilege for South Asians in the United States because of how it occludes the idea that the American dream is attainable for all who work hard enough.

Through practices of reading in the NetSAP book club, participants ambivalently confront and suppress the undesirable, unequal foundations of South Asian cosmopolitan identity in the United States as mediated through shared discourses of ethnicity, privilege, model minority paradigms, and caste hierarchy. In the following chapters, I shift from a close examination of the communal process of interpretation in the NetSAP book club culture to an examination of lay practices of reading South Asian American and diasporic texts within the broader institutional contexts of mainstream reviewership and literary academia.

3

A NARROW VIEW OF THE WORLD

Gendered Literary Culture and South Asian American Belonging

In January 2006, Manish Vij, at the time a regular contributor to the popular South Asian American cultural interest blog *Sepia Mutiny*, posted an incisive visual send-up of the commodification of transnational South Asian novels in Western markets. The illustration (titled "Anatomy of a Genre") satirizes the book cover art of Amulya Mulladi's *The Mango Season*, which features two brown, cupped palms cradling an orange and red mango and resting in the lap of woman wearing a South Asian traditional dress. The image is bordered on the top and bottom by a gold sari motif. Vij labels this image and elements of the back cover, identifying several of the more common clichés that figure in popular representations of South Asian culture in the West: Eastern sensuality, ethnic dress, Indian cuisine, arranged marriage, interracial romance, and second-generation cultural confusion—a set of cultural symbols so identifiable that they can be easily labeled (see figure 1). One blog reader even amended the infographic by suggesting that with the addition of a few more clichés such as "crazy aunty," "wedding scene," "white boyfriend/girlfriend," or "reconciliation with 'East' and 'West' (pathos filled)," "Anatomy of a Genre" could offer a veritable guide to writing the exoticized Indian diasporic novel. Eliciting more than fifty enthusiastic comments, "Anatomy of a Genre" reveals a community's self-consciousness and indignation about the powerful marketing initiatives and strategies of commodification employed in the service of selling South Asian culture in Western literary markets.

The frustrations that inspired "Anatomy of a Genre" and elicited such fervent commentary seem to contradict another instance of everyday

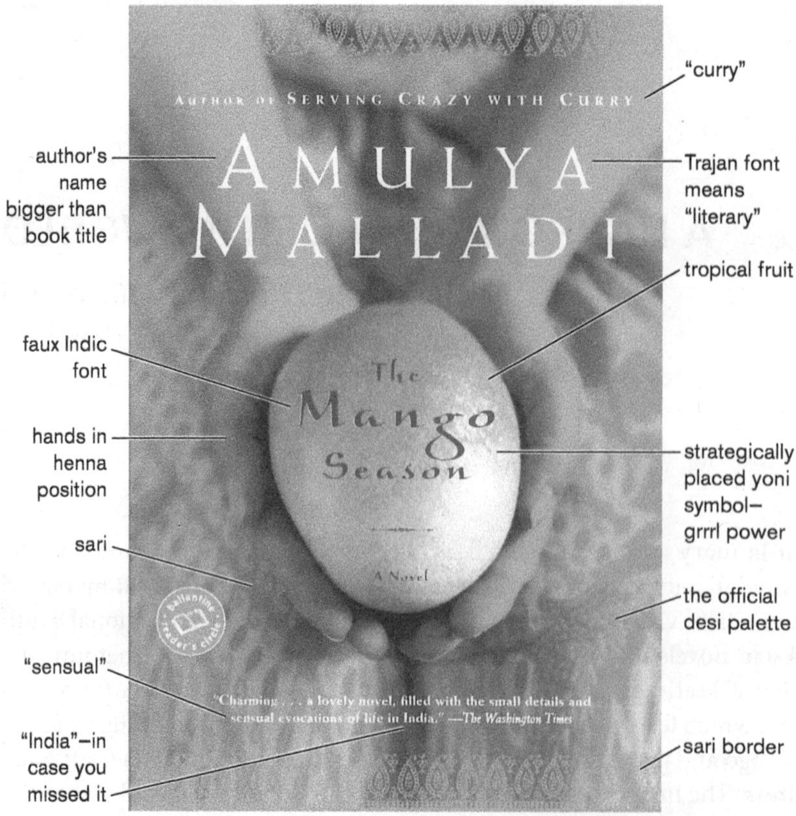

Figure 1. Anatomy of a genre. Redrawn from a schematic by Manish Vij; originally published on sepiamutiny.com.

readership that I encountered in the NetSAP reading group. Describing how popular transnational South Asian literature affects her life, Priya, a young Indian American woman, said that her encounters with this body of literature elicited a powerful sense of familiarity from her. In fact, Priya explained that after her marriage ended, she took solace in reading transnational South Asian literature, particularly by women, because it helped her make sense of the cultural and romantic struggles she faced as a young Indian American woman:

> I think whether you get an arranged marriage or whether you marry somebody that you fall in love with, you still face a lot of the same struggles, especially with family. [. . .] And a lot of the stories that I read explored

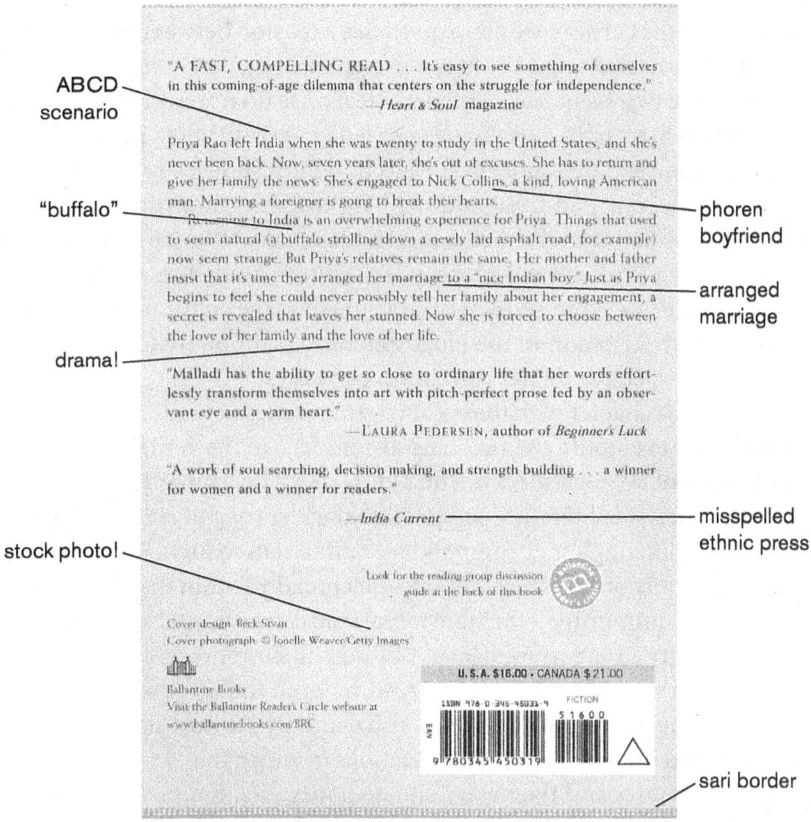

Figure 1 (*continued*). The back cover.

that whole conflict. I think for somebody with my own personal experience—[marriage] didn't go very well for me—I like reading about it. It makes me feel like it is research, you know? You learn something.

At a basic level, these two sets of responses are concerned with the possibilities of belonging that popular, commodified transnational South Asian literature produce for South Asian Americans. Vij's and Priya's commentaries demonstrate that, even among readers of similar class and ethnic background, there are differences in readerly expectations, desires, and subject positions.

The difference between the blog readers' and Priya's responses to popular transnational South Asian literature reveals that in either scenario, the skeptical or the earnest, we can experience a tension between who we feel we are and how that sense of self is represented in literary culture.[1] In other words, these two scenarios of readerly response do not necessarily differ regarding what tropes and themes pervade popular transnational South Asian literature; rather, they part ways in their responses to and uses for them. On the one hand, Vij and the blog readers humorously indicted this genre of literature for being a formulaic, neo-Orientalist rendering of South Asian culture and identity for Western audiences.[2] And on the other hand, Priya expressed a deep attachment to the cultural symbols that inspired such irritation in the blogosphere, explaining that they provide her with perspective on her own life experiences.

I begin this chapter with these contrasting scenes of readership because of how they exemplify the two central concerns in the remainder of this book. First of all, regardless of context, readers' investments in transnational South Asian literature suggest that the literary culture shapes paradigms of belonging for cosmopolitan South Asian readers in the United States. Both responses evince a desire—felt broadly within the South Asian American community—for nonstereotypical representations of South Asian identity in literature because of how these representations shape South Asian American belonging. And yet even though these responses overlap in their basic concerns, they also demonstrate how such responses are mediated by the contexts and situations in which they are called forth.

In this chapter and the next, I situate nonacademic practices of reading in the NetSAP book club within the broader institutions and reading formations—or "discursive and intertextual determinations"—that constitute transnational South Asian literary culture (Collins 45). Various reading formations intersect in the NetSAP book club—the members exemplify what Jim Collins terms a "variant literacy" among modern-day nonacademic readers whose literary pleasures are defined and "shaped by elements drawn from reading protocols of both academic and popular interpretive communities (44)." In the contemporary United States, educated lay readers such as the members of the NetSAP book club are not only interpellated by the consecrated critical discourse around them, including academic works and mainstream popular reviews, but are also frequently exposed to the tastemaking effects of social media, online book clubs, discussion boards, Amazon reviews, and blogs like *Sepia Mutiny* (see Collins 78). The following chapters argue that while seemingly discrete, practices of reading among academic critics, literary reviewers, and nonacademic readers operate on a continuum of literary desires that are shaped by overlapping and also at times competing political, personal, and communal agendas.

The juxtaposition of these two scenes of readership offers a springboard into the crucial role of gender in shaping transnational South Asian literary culture—a category of analysis that is central to this chapter and the next. Both instances of readership present distinct responses to popular transnational South Asian literature written by women.[3] *Sepia Mutiny* commentators situate *The Mango Season* and novels like it among a broader field of popular transnational South Asian literature that traffics primarily in the commodification of ethnic difference, and in their analysis of this genre, the influence of gender is an incidental, almost invisible influence. The blog readers' wry, witty commentary on "Anatomy of a Genre" suggest that they take a jaded view of tropes of arranged marriage, interracial dating, and exoticized South Asian femininity in popular transnational South Asian literature—tropes that are gendered even if they don't consciously or explicitly deem them so. In contrast, Priya notes that she is drawn to the comfort offered in writing by South Asian women on South Asian women's experiences.

Whether readers are or are not conscious of how the workings of gender impact their literary preferences, the contemporary marketing of South Asian diasporic women's writing and the construction of authorial personas within this writing has been plagued by gender bias. I begin the chapter by examining how the gendering of transnational South Asian literary culture is overtly at work in the literary marketplace, particularly in book covers. In this arena, male authors' work tends to be visually coded as serious, literary, intellectual, and historical, while that of female authors is sexualized, exoticized, and stereotyped. In the second section of the chapter, I analyze a salient gendered literary historical moment in South Asian diasporic writing, the polemical juxtaposition of Arundhati Roy with the canonical figure of Salman Rushdie by literary critics, the media, and lay readers in the wake of the publication of Roy's critically acclaimed novel *The God of Small Things* (1997). Both authors have been celebrated for representing Indian culture on the world stage but have also simultaneously been deemed inauthentic because of their associations with a particular cosmopolitan moment in modern Indian history. However, I argue that among cosmopolitan readers across a variety of settings in the late 1990s, Rushdie's associations with elitism did nothing to diminish his perceived mastery as an author, while Roy's associations with provincialism served ultimately to undermine her literary authority.

In the final section of the chapter, I invoke and build on the gendered juxtaposition of Rushdie and Roy to expose the foundations of a lingering gender bias in the construction of contemporary transnational South Asian literary culture. As scholars of Asian American literary studies have noted, regimes of multiculturalism interact with hierarchies of value, in which divides between high and low culture are themselves racialized (Chuh 16; Kang 4–5). I examine how racialized hierarchies of high and low culture within transnational South Asian literary culture are further compounded by associations with male and female writers, respectively. In transnational South Asian literary culture, especially as it has developed in academic institutions in the United States, women authors carry the social burden of transmitting culture. This imperative minoritizes South Asian women's writing in the United States, connecting it with particular ideologies of authenticity through tropes of exotic sexuality, traditional Indian culture, provincialism, and ethnic American representation. For cosmopolitan South Asian readers such as those in the NetSAP book club, the minoritization of South Asian women's writing in the United States through gendered tropes of authenticity not only diminishes women's literary contributions but also devalues ethnic American paradigms of belonging. I contend that this feminized discourse of minoritization, prevalent in transnational South Asian literary culture, shapes and reflects South Asian Americans' ambivalent and unresolved attitude toward Asian American paradigms of cultural citizenship.

Judging a Book by Its Cover: Authenticity and the Politics of the Paratexts

The intersectional politics of race and gender have been a definitive concern in Asian American literary history. As Viet Thanh Nguyen writes, "Asian American writers, male and female, often articulate their concerns about race and class *through* gender and sexuality" (6). Indeed, one of the most famous controversies in Asian American cultural politics is the debate between Maxine Hong Kingston and Frank Chin over the representation of Asian American masculinity in Chinese American literature (Thoma 14). The veritable cottage industry of analyses on the conflict between Kingston and Chin signal the centrality of politics of gender and racial authenticity in defining Asian American literary studies (Kang 54). Similarly, the sexualization and sensationalism around the character of *Jasmine* in a novel by the same name, and the oversignification that accompanies Jhumpa Lahiri and her work in the field of South Asian American studies, which I discuss in the following chapter, all offer sites of literary contestation that are entrenched in issues of gender and sexuality. The reception of these texts demonstrates how powerfully gender mediates constructions of race and class among South Asians in the United States. These examples reveal that the racialization of Asian American subjects is underwritten by Asian American norms, ideals, and distortions of masculinity and femininity.

For South Asians, particularly those in the United States, legacies of British colonialism and Indian nationalism haunt the formation of idealized male and female South Asian diasporic subjectivities. These histories have had a particular impact on South Asian American women, who are routinely authenticated in various types of cultural production through tropes of sexualization and exoticization originating in discourses of British colonial conquest and also in Indian nationalist traditions. As historian Partha Chatterjee explains, as they pursued their "civilizing" mission in India (119), British colonialists assumed a proprietary sympathy with oppressed Indian womanhood (121). Indian nationalist anticolonial discourse in the early- to mid-nineteenth century responded to the British colonial objectification and sexualization of Indian femininity by representing Indian women as the authentic bearers of national identity, asserting that British "had failed to colonize the inner, essential, identity of the East, which lay in its distinctive, and superior, spiritual culture" (Chatterjee 121).[4] Within this framework of Indian nationalist ideology, women were fashioned as keepers of a spiritual realm that inculcated traditional Brahminic values. Feminist scholars who study transnational South Asian American cultural production have noted that the longing for authenticity and tradition initiated by anticolonial nationalist movements and perpetuated by displacement imbue the South Asian diasporic experience. As a result, in diasporic contexts South Asian women are both exoticized and objectified while also being charged with the task of maintaining an authentic South Asian identity and enabling the assimilation of the family (Gopinath 9; Das Gupta and Das Gupta 327).

These contradictory depictions of South Asian femininity are perhaps most obvious and exaggerated in the marketing of South Asian literature through book cover art, which is why the cover of Mulladi's T*he Mango Season* was such an obvious target for Vij's satire.[5] Speaking of the marketing elements of book publication, Lori Ween argues that book covers, book reviews, and author interviews—elements that Gérard Genette calls the paratexts of literature—have particular importance in selling ethnic American literature (Genette 2–4; Ween 91). Ween notes that through these seemingly innocuous paratexts, publishers seek to convey "authenticity" and "difference (or exoticism)" and circulate "limiting and limited ideas about ethnic groups" (91). Similarly, Shazia Rahman notes that despite the "multiplicity of feminisms and narratives" available in texts by South Asian female writers that posit "mobile, diasporic, and feminist subjectivities" (90), the literary production of South Asian women is pigeonholed by "eye-catching and exoticised book covers" that construct them and their work as authentic cultural objects (88).[6]

This dissonance between the texts and paratexts of transnational South Asian women's writing has been powerfully illustrated in a recent online survey, "Red Sari: An Analysis of South Asian and Diaspora Book Covers," conducted by Mary Anne Mohanraj, that presents solid evidence that male and female writers of South Asian descent are marketed unevenly through their book cover art. Mohanraj asserts that the imagery used in these covers implies that women write simple, accessible stories, while male writers produce serious narratives. Mohanraj begins the survey by chronicling her own experience selecting the cover art for her collection of short stories *Bodies in Motion* (2005) published by Harper Collins. She explains that originally her publisher selected a cover that featured the open, fanned-out pages of a book, spread across a green backdrop (see figure 2). After receiving negative marketing feedback from book buyers, her publisher decided to change the cover.

The next iteration of the book cover attempted, it seemed to Mohanraj, to market the book based on the scant sexual themes of the collection, which—like the food motif—are only present in a handful of the stories. Although her publisher did not tell her what criteria they used to chose the replacement cover, she heard that there had been marketing feedback that suggested using the cover art to foreground the stories that focused on "food and sex" over those that that focused on family relationships. The next cover presented an image of a woman's body, her head not visible, wearing a translucent red sari. Mohanraj felt that the new cover was overly sexualized and misrepresented the variety of themes in the collection. After speaking with her publisher about her reservations, they came to an agreement to revise the cover design by photoshopping the image to make the sari opaque and move the focus away from the woman's breasts (see figure 3).

Figure 2. First cover for *Bodies in Motion.* Courtesy of Mary Anne Mohanraj, *Red Sari: An Analysis of South Asian and Diaspora Book Covers.*

Surveying book covers by several other South Asian female and male authors, Mohanraj concludes that her experiences reflect a broader trend in transnational South Asian literature wherein book covers for female authors tend to feature women's truncated bodies (usually with a focus on the body rather than face or head) sexual poses, red saris, the color red in general, and images of food, plants, or flowers. In contrast, the book covers of male authors' work tend to feature "ancient paintings, people in motion, buildings or cities, large landscape features, such as bridges

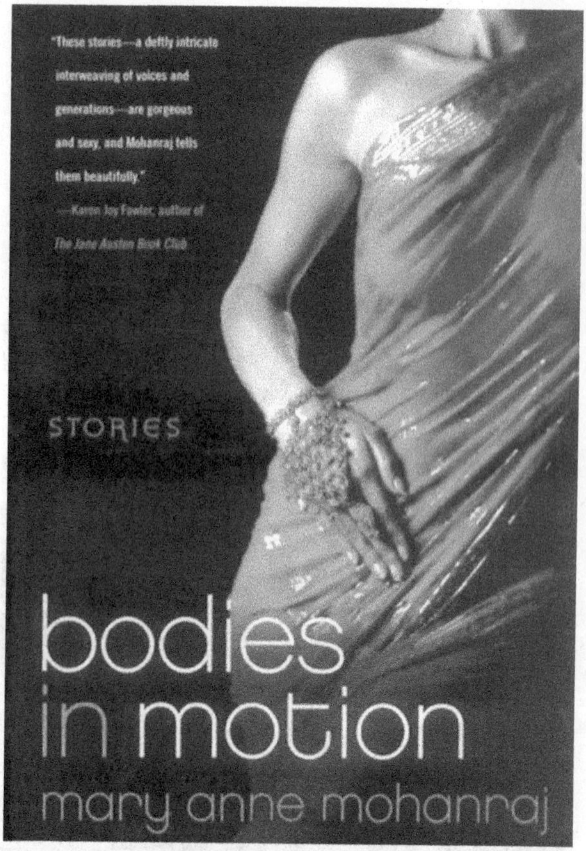

Figure 3. Final cover for *Bodies in Motion.* Courtesy of Mary Anne Mohanraj, *Red Sari: An Analysis of South Asian and Diaspora Book Covers.*

or mountains, abstract images, the author's name and title, and the color blue." She argues that the covers "South Asian male authors receive by default are designed to signal a serious 'literary work.' Whereas women authors' covers are designed to signal something else entirely, that the books are sexy, accessible, popular, easy reading."

Mohanraj's observations on the gendering of book covers expose the peculiar burdens of authenticity and representation with which South Asian female writers are saddled. In her analysis, the red sari, the central motif of her argument, is an image that both sexualizes the South Asian female, signifying her as an object of desire, and that carries the promise that the South Asian female (both as author and cover art object) will reproduce a traditional, authentic version of South Asian culture for literary consumption. Indeed, all of the imagery that Mohanraj points to (including flowers and food) construct South Asian women's literature as feminized, consumable, and traditional. Such feminization extends colonial associations between sexually objectified Indian womanhood and the preservation of an authentic, traditional, Indian culture into the postcolonial diasporic present.

Mohanraj's analysis reveals that the associations between South Asian women's literature and sexuality, food, and ethnic difference are an effect of marketing rather than an intentional, pandering element of their work included to appeal to Western readers. Through her online project, she works to identify and undermine this persistent trend and in doing so responds to the marketing initiatives that seek to characterize her work in terms of the gendered clichés of commodifiable South Asian culture.

Mohanraj's project further demonstrates that ideologies of authenticity manifested in book cover images assume and reproduce different sets of expectations for male and female writers. South Asian male writers are not entirely free from burdens of representation, but the images used on their book covers to convey the impression of exotic authenticity, such as ancient buildings or natural landscapes, do not devalue their work in the same way that sexualized and exotic associations with red saris and mangoes devalue the work of female writers. In other words, through the book cover art chosen and promoted by their publishers, male writers and their work are associated with history, difficulty, and intellect, while female South Asian writers are affiliated with identity, accessibility, and emotion through the cover images chosen for their books. As I discuss in the next sections, the gendered binaries that are so obviously at play in book cover imagery are more tacitly present in the complicated construction of the authorial personae of Arundhati Roy and Salman Rushdie and in the institutionalization of South Asian American literature.

"The Talented but Flawed Child of Rushdie": Arundhati Roy and the Gendered Construction of Authorial Persona

Nineteen ninety-seven is a crucial year in the history of South Asian diasporic writing.[7] India was already on the world stage, preparing celebrations for the fiftieth anniversary of its independence when two notable publishing events coincided drawing further attention to Indian politics and history across the globe. The first was the media frenzy around Arundhati Roy's Booker Prize–winning debut novel, *The God of Small Things*. And, the second was Salman Rushdie's controversial introductory remarks as editor of an anthology *Mirrorwork: 50 Years of Indian Writing in English* in which he infamously declared diasporic South Asian literature in English superior to the work being written in native South Asian languages.[8] These events along with Amitav Ghosh's 2001 repudiation of the Commonwealth Prize for Literature are retrospective flashpoints in the ascendance of the Indian diasporic novel as a vehicle for social commentary (Ghosh 6).

I contend that the impact of this cosmopolitan moment still reverberates, marking transnational South Asian writing as a site of critique of Indian nationalist politics, globalization, and of representation in South Asian diasporic culture.[9] This critique takes shape between the oppositional paradigms of nationalism and cosmopolitanism that determine the authenticity of particular transnational South Asian writers. Critically acclaimed transnational South Asian writing that emerged at this time was often branded, depending on the politics and location of the author in particular, as either nationalist or cosmopolitan—sometimes both simultaneously—in the international media and by literary scholars.[10]

There has already been significant attention paid to how this renaissance of Indian diasporic literature in the late twentieth century and early twenty-first century was an expression of the tensions and collusions between resurgent Indian nationalism and the cosmopolitan globalization of South Asian culture. Here, I build on these examinations, investigating how these paradigms shape the authorial personae of Rushdie and Roy in particularly gendered terms. While both Rushdie and Roy were seen during this time as capitalizing on the global popularity of cosmopolitan South Asian literature, Rushdie's preeminence in the field has been naturalized and nationalized in academic and lay sites of readership through his positioning as the father of modern Indian diasporic literature. During this time, Rushdie was charged with inauthenticity, a charge brought on the grounds of his elite, highbrow, cosmopolitanism. His presumed inauthenticity was thus attended by a narrative that attributed to him a patriarchal expertise among various readerships. It was a narrative that appointed him as the literary father who enabled his South Asian literary kin's success and provided his offspring the opportunity to bring international attention to South Asian politics. Furthermore, even as Rushdie's association with elite cosmopolitan culture might have served to deauthenticate his representative Indian status, it also granted him and his work the veneer of difficulty, historicity, worldliness.

In contrast, at the time that her first and only novel was published, Roy was represented in contradictory ways in the media. On the one hand, she became an overnight cosmopolitan literary superstar; every story of Roy's rise to literary fame was accompanied by her compelling rags-to-riches biography.[11] As Padmini Mongia notes, "for six months or more in 1997, it was difficult to get away from the attention surrounding Arundhati Roy and her novel" (103). And yet on the other hand, she was often cast in the media as Rushdie's subordinate progeny. In some media and scholarly analyses Roy's success was attributed to her supposed self-fashioning as a national object of beauty or else she was derided for her lack of skill in representing various facets of Indian culture. Roy's alleged inauthenticity as a cosmopolitan writer tethered her novel to a discourse of provincialism, thus diminishing her value as an acclaimed writer among cosmopolitan readerships.

Before deepening my analysis of Rushdie's and Roy's reception during this time, I want to acknowledge the limitations of such a comparison while emphasizing its importance. First, I do not intend to ignore the vast differences between the localities and subject positions of these two authors: Rushdie, a prolific fiction writer, a Muslim-Kashmiri man of privileged background residing in London and New York, would of course be received differently from Roy, a self-made, South Indian female activist residing in New Delhi who has published far more essays and political manifestos than literary fiction. Since the late 1990s and early 2000s, critical treatment of and lay responses to these two writers has been widely varied. Additionally, I want to acknowledge that the reception of these two authors was never monolithic: Rushdie, while very well respected among various readerships is not a universally celebrated author, as the famous 1989 *Satanic Verses* fatwa controversy attests—nor is Roy's success and her work entirely dismissed as an effect of her pretty face.[12] However, in what follows, I purposefully juxtapose these two figures at a watershed moment in the formation of contemporary transnational South Asian culture to expose a crucial instance in which gendered associations with male and female writers become starkly apparent in the media and in academic criticism as well as among lay readers. That is, even though Rushdie's earlier work arguably engages feminist cultural politics, at this moment in South Asian diasporic literary history he was portrayed in various sites as a patriarch and the progenitor of transnational South Asian literature through an elaborate and complex comparison to Roy.

Upon, and even prior to Roy's literary debut, writers, academics, and tastemakers repeatedly compared her to Rushdie, frequently using metaphors of paternity meant to compliment her literary prowess but that instead subordinated her talent to his. Pankaj Mishra, a well-respected Indian novelist who was also an editor at HarperCollins and an early champion of her work there, was the first to endorse the novel as "the biggest thing since *Midnight's Children*" (qtd. in Wachinger 82). Elleke Boehmer notes that Roy was hailed as the "long-awaited female Rushdie" (64). The hyperbolic narrative of Rushdie's influence on Roy and other writers of her tradition was undoubtedly pervasive at the time: Makarand Paranjape wrote that "heaps of novels" have been shaped by "Rushdie's liberating touch" (220); Anita Desai claimed that Rushdie showed Indian novelists writing in English "a way to be 'post-colonial'" (qtd. in Jani 14); Tobias Wachinger suggested that "without Rushdie, there would probably be no Shashi Tharoor, no Vikram Chandra, no Arundhati Roy, or at least not the highly celebrated, globally read authors as we know them" (73); and finally, Timothy Brennan somewhat jokingly asserted that "*Midnight's Children* exploded this literature of constipation and threw open the doors to an entire generation of younger novelists for whom empire, race, immigration, and religious fundamentalism had been the basic food" ("Cultural Politics" 112). Rushdie's ascendance was granted dramatic visual representation in a special issue of the *New Yorker* in 1997 that included a group photo titled "India's leading novelists" to commemorate the fiftieth anniversary of India's independence. In the photo, Rushdie occupies a central position, presiding magnanimously over a group of South Asian authors. Roy is positioned below Rushdie, who has his hand placed jovially on her shoulder. Critics have not only read this positioning as evidence of Rushdie's centrality in the field of transnational South Asian literature, but have also suggested that Rushdie singles Roy out as a sort of literary protégé.[13]

Roy and her debut novel were subordinated in the media to Rushdie and his work through the masculinist language of paternity and authority.[14] In "India's Post-Rushdie Generation; Young Writers Leave Magic Realism and Look at Reality," Mervyn Rothstein of the *New York Times* describes how the new generation of South Asian writers, among whom he asserts Roy is prominent, "are often called Midnight's Grandchildren in homage to another seminal Indian novel, Salman Rushdie's *Midnight's Children*" (n.p.). This notion that Roy is one of "Midnight's Grandchildren" not only suggests a generational connection between their novels but also implies that Roy's success originates with Rushdie. Evoking a similar language of descent even more superlatively, James Wood writes in a 1997 review of *The God of Small Things* that "Arundhati Roy's good and flawed *The God of Small Things*, which is a perfect child of Rushdie's, offer[s] a picture of what Indian writing looks like today." In Wood's comparison, Rushdie is the enabling, masterful father, and Roy his talented but flawed child.

Conversations with NetSAP book club members in the mid-2000s indicate that the effects of this Rushdian moment, his construction as a paternal and foundational figure in South Asian diasporic literature, persisted among lay readers. As Raj, the book club moderator, insisted, Rushdie enabled Roy's success: "There was clearly a relationship between *The God of Small Things* and Salman Rushdie. That Arundhati Roy says she never read a Salman Rushdie novel. [. . .] okay. But I bet her publisher did. And they know that the audience did, and I think that Rushdie enables certain kinds of stories to be published" (NetSAP book club meeting, *The Royal Ghosts*). Raj's assertion that Rushdie's success facilitated Roy's publication echoes similar sentiments in literary academia and popular reviews, indicating a synchronicity in these cultures of reading.

NetSAP book club participants would often appeal to Rushdie as the gold standard of transnational South Asian literature to which all other writers were compared. Sunil in an interview emphatically insisted that "if you don't like Rushdie, then you don't like to read", and during a book club meeting on Kiran Desai's *The Inheritance of Loss*, a set of readers compared it to Midnight's Children, describing the latter as "epic," "classic," and ultimately as "better than the Bible" (NetSAP book club meeting, *The Inheritance of Loss*). As Padma, a NetSAP book club member, exclaimed in an interview, "I would say that *Midnight's Children* is just the best South Asian literature that I think has ever been written." Uma accounted for Rushdie's dominance by universalizing his appeal and influence as a writer: "Salman Rushdie kind of fell into a great writer category as opposed to great South Asian writer." Additionally, readers calibrated Rushdie's overall cachet in the literary world through his work's aesthetic experimentation: Ajay described his work as "kaleidoscopic" and "phantasmagorical"; Afrah said it "well-written and cheeky"; Sunil thought it would earn acclaim well into the future: "Rushdie is probably going to win the Nobel Prize in literature, Naipaul did, Tagore did." Many of these comments speak to the idea that Rushdie was able to surpass South Asian themes even as he incorporated them. For these readers, this ability allowed him to masterfully respond to the imperative that transnational South Asian literature be authentic.

NetSAP book club members were drawn to Rushdie's canonized status because of how it reinforced their cultural capital, shored up their educational privilege, and deepened their intellectual engagement with history. They felt edified by his difficult subject matter and challenging prose style, noting that they were proud to have made it through his dense prose: "It's super-rewarding," Sunil remarked. "He never forgets anything and all the threads get tied at the end. [. . .] It rewards careful reading." "*Midnight's Children* took me forever to read," Padma stated. "It was very long drawn and very difficult to get through." "I literally had to concentrate so much and I had to read little by little, week by week to get through it," Pooja said. Arya said she respected Rushdie's work for resisting the "mass market": you can't "pick [his work] up and flip through [it] on the beach. [. . .] I find him [to be] a real writer, and one of the more challenging writers for me personally that I try to read." Sunil explained that Rushdie's novel gave him a uniquely creative perspective on historical events: "I could read history as it is presented on *Wikipedia*. Similarly, there is something lost that you get by reading Rushdie's *Shame*, which is based on [that history]. You can't read Rushdie and think this is exactly what's factual, what happened; [it's] based on the truth but not necessarily conforming to it." Rakesh likewise explained that Rushdie gives the reader a sense of how "India works. [. . .] You not only get an idea of who the characters are but why they're doing what they're doing [. . .] that very few people can capture in travelogues or history books." Related to readers' admiration for Rushdie's representations of history was the sense that he captures an authentic vision of South Asian culture. As Meena, who described herself as a first-generation Indian American, said, "People may not understand Rushdie, but when you read his books there is something very true." Maya, a young woman and regular participant, noted Rushdie's use of "Hindustani language rather than strict Oxford English," which she deemed authentic.

The universality, difficulty, historical consciousness, and representative status that the media, literary academics, and lay readers ascribe to Rushdie's oeuvre are ideals typically associated with male writers within the broader politics of literary culture.[15] Time and again, feminist literary scholars have noted through analyses of multiple literary genres and periods that while work by male authors is valorized for its naturalized associations with history, intellect, and the public realm, women's writing is devalued through its associations with easiness, popularity, sentiment, and the personal.[16] But what emerges as particularly noteworthy in Roy's and Rushdie's contexts of reception is how these gendered oppositions are brokered differently for each of them through discourses of ethnic authenticity. During the late 1990s and early years of the twenty-first century, Rushdie was constructed among his various readerships as perhaps the most adept cosmopolitan writer of modern Indian history (Jani 15).[17] That is, even if there were elements of his authorial persona that were flawed in their associations with the vagaries and elitism of cosmopolitan discourse, Rushdie's role as the progenitor of a modern literary renaissance among South Asian diasporic authors, his competence as a writer, and his ability to illuminate modern Indian politics to a global audience never came under serious question at this time.

Even though Roy and Rushdie had moved onto other projects, publications, and affiliations, taking them beyond this cosmopolitan moment of the late 1990s, my conversations with NetSAP book club members demonstrate the enduring effects of how they were constructed during this boom in the global popularity of South Asian literature. Roy turned exclusively to writing nonfiction and shifted her focus to activism in South Asian politics. A year after the raging success of *The God of Small Things*, she published an essay condemning the Hindu right-wing Bharitya Janata Party (BJP) government for its nuclear posturing, a political move that had been largely supported by middle-class Indians who identified with Hindu nationalism. In her essay "The End of Imagination," Roy condemns supporters of the BJP's policies, claiming that instead of addressing India's rampant poverty, BJP party leaders and their supporters were reveling in empty displays of military power (see Deb). The essay marked a shift in Roy's career as a writer, taking her from the status of national icon to firebrand activist. She subsequently published essays protesting the series of megadams to be built on the Narmada River, the massacre of Muslims in Gujarat in 2002, plans for bauxite mining in Orissa, the military operations in India against tribal populations and Naxalites, and India's occupation of Kashmir (Deb). As of spring 2014, she was at work writing the introduction to the new edition of "The Annihilation of Caste" written in 1939 by B. R. Ambedkar—a controversial project given that Ambedkar's essay includes a denunciation of the caste system and rebukes Gandhi for wanting to abolish untouchability but supporting the perpetuation of the caste system (Deb).

On all fronts, Roy has done much to counter the image of the beautiful, fortunate, globally appealing, feted author—an image that has informed her glamorous activist personae. Following a one-day prison sentence in Tihar Jail after being held in contempt by India's Supreme Court for using incendiary language in a petition, she cut her hair short; she employs no servants; and she donates current royalties from *The God of Small Things*, her nonfiction writing, and other prizes to charitable organizations in India. It is only recently that she has turned her attentions back to writing fiction—the subject of which she is carefully guarding from the press (Deb).

Regardless of Roy's reinvention as a nonfiction writer and her profound political commitments, the effects of the "Roy phenomenon" (Tickell 104) linger on, particularly the sexist attention to the physical appearance of South Asian women writers that ultimately diminishes and obscures their artistry. Roy's looks rather than her political activism and literary contributions continue to be the focus in the media. As recently as November 2014, a profile of Roy in the *Guardian* by Anthony Andrew began with a physical description: "Small, delicately boned, a beguiling mixture of piercing dark eyes and bright easy smile, she is a warm presence. [. . .] The grey tint to her curls lends depth to a still strikingly youthful face. Looking at her, it's not hard to detect the author of the richly empathetic *The God of Small Things*." This characterization of Roy as delicate, attractive, and diminutive and the association Andrew makes between Roy's physicality and her work is just another entry in a long line of well-documented comments of this sort. It echoes, for example, a 1997 review by Jan McGirk for the London-based *Sunday Times*, in which she seemingly compliments Roy for her beauty, but in doing so conflates the content of Roy's work with Roy herself as an author and South Asian woman: "With her mass of untamed curls and smoldering dark eyes Arundhati Roy could be the model for one of her romantic heroines." Such physical descriptions render her a part of a colonial legacy that regards South Asian women's bodies as promising authentic, direct access to South Asian culture (Boehmer 65).[18] This desire for access is not only objectifying but also encodes a problematic expectation that South Asian female writers will offer uncontrived, genuine accounts of South Asian experience—an expectation that makes them vulnerable to dismissal when their work fails to indulge these desires.

NetSAP book club members accounted for this attention to Roy's appearance by suggesting that it was a way to market South Asian women's writing to a broad, non–South Asian audience. Uma, a regular and vociferous participant in the book club, made this point concisely during an interview: "Arundhati Roy is gorgeous. I'm not saying she's not talented, but she is hot. And that probably helped market her because it's—so much of [success] is about marketing." Uma, attuned to the ways in which South Asian women are objectified in the Western media, meant to implicitly critique the fetishization of Eastern beauty. Inadvertently, however, she also attributes her success not to her work but to her sexual appeal.

The subject of Roy's exotic beauty and accusations that she was complicit in using her looks to promote her novel also emerged in literary academia. In *The Postcolonial Exotic* Graham Huggan argues that popular writers of the South Asian diaspora, such as Rushdie, Vikram Seth, and Roy mobilize a kind of "*strategic* exoticism designed to trap the unwary reader into complicity with the Orientalisms of which the novel[s] so hauntingly relate" (77). Huggan questions the tendency in popular review and academic criticism to conflate ethnic writers with their texts; however, he frames this conflation as one through which South Asian diasporic writers ironically pose a challenge to neo-Orientalist hankerings for exotic representations of the East (72–76). Overall, he argues that Rushdie, Seth, and Roy deliberately exploit Western desires for exotic literary representations of India, noting that all three authors are "highly skilled at self-promotion, and at the media-friendly manufacturing of exotic ('Oriental') romance" (77).

However, he repeatedly associates Roy's strategic exoticism and self-fashioning as a result of her "incorrigibly photogenic" good looks, and he claims, with no real substantiation, that she "has clearly worked hard on her image, her marketably exotic looks" (77). As Julie Mullaney explains, Huggan singles Roy out among these other writers through a focus on her physical appearance. He renders Roy in gendered terms, casting her as the primary author of her own sexualized and desirable image, and in doing so, he not only downplays the fact that this image is both created and sustained by her Western readership but potentially adds to the discourse of her objectification (59).

Presumably, Huggan's desire to critique the neo-Orientalist imperatives at work in the publication, marketing, and reception of ethnic texts leads him to overlook gender as a determining and unique factor in shaping Roy's critical reception. Huggan notes that for many literary critics in the academy and general media, the marketing and reception of *The God of Small Things* provided an "object lesson in commodity fetishism" (76), yet, he fails to see in his own interpretation how expectations of unmediated access to South Asian culture function differently for male and female

South Asian authors, in this case serving to make Roy into the literal embodiment of a neo-Orientalist desire for authentic access to Indian culture in the global literary market.

Even when Roy was celebrated as an authentic Indian writer who took part in a cosmopolitan moment, her cosmopolitan appeal hung precariously on questions of her expertise, not only her knowledge of Indian regional politics but also her skill as a writer.[19] In the global media she was celebrated for being the first Indian residing in India to win the Booker. An *India Today* cover published on 27 October 1997 captioned a large photograph of Roy with the text "Princess of Prose: By winning the Booker Prize, Arundhati Roy gives Indian writing in English global acceptance." Reviewers commended its authentic representation of the caste system, cultural rituals (such as Kathikali dance), and political life (Marxist activism) in Kerala in the late 1960s (Boehmer 64). But as a result of her cosmopolitan appeal and global popularity, she was also challenged in her role as a representative of Indian culture abroad. Following the novel's release, Roy was taken to court in Kerala for an obscenity suit filed by traditionalists who were concerned that the novel's depiction of an intercaste relationship between a Christian woman and untouchable man corrupted public morals.[20] Ghosh explains that this suit can be seen as a challenge by local and regional communities, who refused to be spoken for and represented by an elite, cosmopolitan, bourgeoisie intelligentsia disconnected from the everyday realities of Indian life and politics (38).

Kerala locals were not the only ones who did not share the international admiration of the novel. According to Lisa Jardine, Carmen Callil, the outspoken chair of the 1996 council of Booker judges, said on television that the novel was "execrable" and should not have even made the shortlist. Similarly, Jardine reports that after attending the Booker Prize ceremony, the announcement of Roy's win was followed by "much bad-tempered whispering behind hands amidst the mostly male editors of the broadsheet newspapers' literary pages." Jardine notes that this mean-spirited reception took on gendered undertones; not since "the last novel by a woman (Pat Barker's *The Ghost Road*) won in 1995" had she "heard such an immediately ungenerous response to the announcement."

Several reviewers complained at the time of the novel's publication that Roy's writing is ungrammatical and clumsy; Amanda Craig, for example, noted that "her novel like most such debuts, is a mixture of outstanding promise and wonky style. Roy badly needs a good editor to sieve the gold from the chaff." Others pointed out that her prose style is excessive, emotional, and coy.[21] NetSAP book club member Sunil echoed this critique with an ostensible compliment: "I thought that girls would like it a lot more than guys would like it. It was very intensely emotional. [. . .] It requires the reader to invest in it in order to get into it. It was well-written but it was just too much." This backhanded compliment in which Roy's unfulfilled potential as a writer is ascribed largely to her allegedly overwrought writing style and emotional excess is the kind of denigrating remark that reviewers, critics, and readers commonly make about women's writing.[22]

However, at another site of reception, Roy's linguistic choices were blamed for making the authenticity of the novel inaccessible to non–South Asian readers who desired a real "racial/ethnic encounter"; according to Gita Rajan and Shailja Sharma, readers "complained of having to stumble over difficult Indian words, which distracted them from getting the meaning. In other words, even when readers understood that it would be a racial/ethnic encounter, they wanted the text to be transparent, and were unprepared to work through the rough terrain of a cultural translation." Rajan and Sharma came to this conclusion after speaking with librarians from major metropolises, who informed them that readers felt more comfortable with the novel in its audio form because the "authentic sounding" narrative voice helped readers to navigate the novel's representations of cultural difference (153).[23] As this example demonstrates, for certain audiences the encounter with the other that *The God of Small Things* ostensibly offers has to be presented to its audiences through an embodied layer of authentic narration. As I explore in the final section of this chapter, the criticism of Roy's stylistic choices that serves to deauthenticate and decontextualize her and her novel reflects broader patterns of reception of female South Asian diasporic writers particularly in the context of the United States.

Gender and Transnational South Asian Literary Culture

In a sensationalistic interview at the Royal Geographic Society on 31 May 2011, V. S. Naipaul was asked whether he considered any women writers his literary equal. He responded by deriding Jane Austen's writing, insulting the award-winning work of his former editor, Diana Athill, and claiming that he could easily discern the difference between writing produced by male and female writers because, as he explained, women's writing is mired in "sentimentality, the narrow view of the world." Journalists at the event reported that he concluded his response to this question by stating that "inevitably for a woman, she is not a complete master of a house, so that comes over in her writing too" (Fallon). He concluded the interview by stating "I don't mean this in any unkind way." Unsurprisingly, Naipaul's rant drew responses from authors, critics, and bloggers, ranging from humorous dismissal to admiration to outrage.[24]

There are, of course, several reasons to dismiss this entire episode as merely curmudgeonly and attention seeking, or, as Pulitzer Prize–winning writer Jennifer Egan puts it, "the ravings of an old man" (Sehgal). Indeed, Naipaul is no stranger to this sort of controversy; this is only the most recent chapter in a long history of blatant and well-documented sexism (see Nixon and Gorra). And yet regardless of his behavior (or perhaps because of it), Naipaul is for some beyond reproach; in fact, others admire his arrogance: "Happily, the recognition—like the criticism—has done nothing to mellow him, or to shake his conviction that he's top of the pile, and that no woman is going to push him off it," claims William Langley.

At the most basic level, Naipaul's comment is just another unsurprising instance of sexism in literary culture. And yet because Naipaul is an acclaimed author in the field of transnational South Asian literature, framed as a "father figure" in this literary tradition and summarily "canonized by a Western literary establishment" (Gopinath 69), his blatant sexism is more difficult to just brush off, as he has the cachet to influence how others perceive South Asian authorial personas. Even though in this instance Naipaul was not speaking specifically about transnational South Asian women writers, his assertion that women writers are not the "master[s] of a house" and therefore have "a narrow view of the world" that is reflected in their writing implies women writers are impotent and lack perspective. Because Naipul is commonly thought of as one of the founding fathers of transnational South Asian literature, his longtime denigration of female authors as narrow has affected broader trends in how South Asian female writers are or are not recognized by the literary establishment. Naipaul's emphasis on female writers' "narrow view of the world" suggests a gendered limitation on their capacity to think globally and historically—an implication that speaks to the focus of my conclusion to this chapter on the formation of gender hierarchies in the reception of transnational South Asian literary culture.

In book club meetings and interviews with NetSAP book club participants, gender was not often an explicit subject of conversation. Rather, as I discuss in greater detail in the final chapter, the topic emerged more often in participants' praise for or complaints about the way male and female characters were characterized. Their assessments were not simple: that is, they did not necessarily condemn literature that was stereotypical in its representations of South Asian masculinity or femininity or commend it for breaking with these stereotypes. Even in the cases when a female character was depicted as weak, sexualized, oppressed, alienated, nagging, dependent, or defined by marriage and maternity, they sought to complicate the characterization through their interpretive strategies. As the case of Priya, the reader whom I quote at the start of this chapter, reveals and as my examination of the female characters in *The Namesake* in the following chapter further suggests, NetSAP book club members' desires and motivations in reading this body of literature often shaped the ways they interpreted depictions of male and female characters.

While NetSAP book club participants were sensitive to how gender stereotypes in transnational South Asian literature could potentially impact real world perceptions of South Asian cultural norms and mores, particularly in the diaspora, they were less concerned with how these stereotypes shape the construction of the field itself. In the rare instances that gender emerged as an explicit topic of conversation in interviews, interviewees would often generalize about South Asian literary gender politics in ways that echoed scholarly associations of male writers with politics and history and female writers with the personal and emotional. Gayatri, for example, told me that "there's maybe a certain emotion to female writing that I don't sense in men particularly. [. . .] This may not be politically correct, but there's a certain arrogance I sense in the male writing that maybe I don't sense in the female writing. It has a more friendly authority versus an arrogant authority." Uma similarly asserted that "men write more about the macro and women the micro." Maya, who in several meetings and in our interview emphasized that she approaches literature from a feminist perspective, offered an assessment of the difference between male and female South Asian writers that was strikingly similar to literary critical analyses. In meetings she always raised issues of gender and pointed out stereotypical or sexist depictions of female characters. I had asked her to name a few of her favorite South Asian writers and the list turned out to be mainly established, canonized male writers. When I noted this to her, she explained that she was more attracted to the subject matter of male writers: "I think male writers tend to gravitate towards a more plot-centric narrative, while female writers write a lot more about emotion and characters." None of these book club members were aiming to denigrate South Asian women's writing; indeed, a number of them were commending its focus on emotion and character development. However, their associating women's writing with emotion and identity suggests that they are building and responding to pervasive generalizations in various literary contexts that essentialize differences between men and women's writing.

In recent criticism there have been similar instances where transnational female writers have been celebrated for their accessibility and for their embrace of emotion and (ethnic) identity. Several of these scholarly examples associate the formation of the South Asian American literary tradition with female writers of South Asian descent. Sandhya Rajendra Shukla notes that "the first Indian authors to have U.S. literary celebrity have been female" (161) and that the foundational Indian American writer Bharati Mukherjee self-consciously identifies her work with "paradigms of ethnicity" in contrast to U.S.-based male South Asian writers such as Abraham Verghese, whom she suggests frames his stories of Americanization within the context of Indian diaspora (170).[25] Similarly, Vinay Lal argues that because the novel requires an intimate "grounding in the social order [. . .] male Indian American novelists have not generally been able to set their stories to American life" (109). In contrast, he asserts that "Asian Indian women writers, among them Bharati Mukherjee, Meena Alexander, [and] Jhumpa Lahiri, [. . .] speak more directly to the condition of being an Indian in the United States" (111). And most recently, Anupama Jain offers an insightful critique of how the process of assimilation for South Asians is most often narrativized via "fictions of Americanization published about South Asian immigrant women" (146).

These inadvertent and minoritizing associations are also evident in Gita Rajan and Shailja Sharma's efforts to differentiate between what they see as "new" and "old" forms of cosmopolitanism. "writers such as Roy and Lahiri," they assert, "are actors on the public culture stage, and their appeal lies in combining a new kind of narrative texture with a mass appeal factor. [. . .] One does not need specific knowledge of history, geography, or civilizations to understand Lahiri's narrative world" (156). Their work, Rajan and Sharma maintain, represents a newer globally conscious and globally marketable strain of writing, a new kind of cosmopolitanism that is more widely recognizable because it moves beyond "oppositional, emancipatory, or center-periphery narrative threads" (158). In contrast, they claim that understanding writers such as Rushdie, Naipaul, and Amitav Ghosh requires knowledge of the history of empire and colonialism (157). In their effort to challenge masculinist forms of cosmopolitanism and promote the recognition of South Asian female writers, Rajan and

Sharma reinforce the gender dynamics of the Western canon, casting the identity-oriented, authentically ethnic and accessible voice as female and the historical, postcolonial, and difficult voice as male.

In one way, these critics are merely identifying and analyzing trends that they see at work in the formation of transnational South Asian literatures. In fact, each critical treatment offers a theory as to what underlies this gendered pattern: Shukla explains that, regardless of the diasporic reach of her stories Mukherjee self-identifies as an ethnic American; Lal attributes the difference in thematic concerns between male and female authors to historical patterns of immigration, and for Jain these South Asian narratives reflect how "processes of assimilation are always gendered" (137). All of these critics offer viable explanations that account for why the South Asian American literary tradition has been pioneered by female writers. And yet their observations contribute to the gendered associations that minoritize the contributions of South Asian female writers within the broader field of transnational South Asian literary culture.[26]

This minoritization, as it is scripted through regimes of neoliberal multiculturalism, relegates South Asian women's writing to paradigms of ethnicity. Rajini Srikanth and Lavina Dhingra point out that these associations with ethnic paradigms are themselves devalued within the institutionalization of minority literatures because ethnic literatures are associated with the commodification of ethnic identity for Western consumption whereas postcolonial literature is associated with intellectually rigorous content and is seen as being harder to commodify.[27] Even though it is clear that these critical tendencies are founded in a broader project to recognize the literary contributions of transnational South Asian writers, they end up binding these writers and their narratives to discourses of unmediated authenticity and tradition through their allegedly nation-based concerns.

In closing this chapter, I want to consider how these constructions of gender in transnational South Asian literary culture may be impacting and reflecting U.S. South Asians' ambivalent relationship with paradigms of Asian American identity. Several scholars have remarked on this relationship, noting that in the United States, people of South Asian origin often prefer to define themselves through national affiliation (as Indian, Pakistani), regional origin (as Gujarati, Punjabi), or religious background (as Hindu, Muslim).[28] Bakirathi Mani argues that this tenuous connection to Asian American and American representational politics is the result of South Asian exclusion (followed by inadequate additive inclusion) in the field of Asian American studies. She also explains that South Asian postcolonial histories have until recently exceeded the purview of Asian American paradigms of belonging (6–7). Similarly, Anupama Jain argues that South Asian diasporic affiliations with nations outside of South Asia and the United States complicate South Asian American assimilation (24). In *A Part, Yet Apart,* a groundbreaking anthology on South Asians in America, Rajiv Shankar explains that unlike South Asians who did not directly experience U.S. military power during the Cold War, East and Southeast Asian nations and people were subject to U.S. cultural influence through multiple military conflicts and wars. He argues that this legacy of military intervention meant that Japanese, Korean, Vietnamese, and the Filipino immigrants were already familiar with U.S. culture by the time they emigrated, while "South Asia and America have been far more distant associates" (xi).

I speculate that there is yet another way to comprehend the stronghold of South Asian ambivalence toward paradigms of Asian American identity formation, a way that is embedded in the gendering of transnational South Asian literary culture. The reception of transnational South Asian literature among a variety of audiences reveals that ethnic American paradigms of belonging are devalued in the powerful cultural arena of literature through feminized discourses of minoritization, access, commodification, and assimilation. In contrast, South Asian affiliation with postcolonial histories and diasporic modes of belonging integrate masculinist narratives of complexity, agency, autonomy that contribute to South Asian cultural capital in the United States. For elite South Asian Americans, I conjecture that this tacit gendering of the literary culture shapes and reflects their ambivalence toward Asian American models of citizenship. That is, I believe that the gendered constructions of transnational South Asian literature reflect and construct how South Asians in the United States relate to different modes of belonging. Perhaps the global paradigm of South Asian displacement, captured in terms like "diasporic," "cosmopolitan," and "postcolonial," offers a more appealing, worldly, and powerful version of South Asian identity in the United States than the paradigm of ethnic American identity. In the final chapter of this book, I examine the gendered, representational pressures that engulfed the reception of a quintessential, widely read South Asian American novel, *The Namesake* by Jhumpa Lahiri.

4

THINKING AND FEELING WITH HER

Representation and Affect in Jhumpa Lahiri's The Namesake

In July 2004, Roohi Choudhry, a regular contributor to Bookslut.com—a well-respected literary review website that prides itself on prioritizing "excellence" rather than prestige or popularity—published an unusual review of Jhumpa Lahiri's first novel, *The Namesake,* in the website's features column.[1] Following on the superlative success of Lahiri's award-winning, critically acclaimed debut collection of short stories, *The Interpreter of Maladies* (1999), for which she won the 2000 Pulitzer Prize and the Pen/Hemingway Award, *The Namesake* has become a watershed text of South Asian American experience, highly significant and widely discussed among a variety of readers. Choudhry opens the review by describing her own ambivalence about the novel. She admits that she found the novel so engaging at times that she twice missed her stop on her evening commute because she was so engrossed in reading, and yet at the same time, she describes frustration with *The Namesake*'s "borderline-ADD narrative and the wandering, almost non-existent plotline." Ultimately, Choudhry concludes that her own hesitation arises from the unfair representational expectations—particularly among South Asians in the United States—with which the novel was burdened from the moment of its debut:

> Few novels (and even fewer by South Asian American writers) have the ability to polarize readers into competing, sulky, defensive camps as *The Namesake* has done. [. . .] Lahiri is perhaps the only South Asian American writer familiar enough to the mainstream to earn a feature in *Oprah* magazine. A lot of people wanted her to get all their personal stories right in one go.

Explicitly breaking with the generic conventions of review essays, the "usual highhanded Kakutani review and subsequent murmurs of assent," Choudhry seeks to democratize her review of this novel and to resolve her ambivalence by "solicit[ing] the opinion of other South Asian women." What she finds is that some "greeted *The Namesake* with skepticism," while others "cried at every page."

The four readers she interviews via email, express far less ambivalence about the novel than Choudhry does—overall, they relate a deep appreciation for the narrative's description of middle-class, second-generation South Asian American experience and Lahiri's ability to make issues of bicultural confusion significant to non–South Asian readers. Suparna Banerjee-Emanuel, an English teacher who lives in New Jersey, describes her experience of reading the novel:

> I cried and laughed through much of the book—the naming drama, the awkwardly handled love affairs, the painful love/embarrassment that Gogol's parents bring him, the Ivy League pressure, the foods and the presentations, the crazy, desperate nature of Bengali gatherings. I loved it and it made me sad, made me miss my childhood and made me miss my own parents. But I also felt connection—my life was not in isolation.

I begin with Choudhry's commentary, a testament to the potential and increasing influence of nontraditional, internet-based forms of reviewership, because my concern in this final chapter is the range of interpretive possibilities *The Namesake* admits. Choudhry's review illustrates the different meanings that this novel has for different audiences. But furthermore, it grants particular weight to lay readerly response in determining the novel's worth and how true it is to the experience of South Asian Americans who might identify with the central themes of the narrative.

For reviewers, academics, and lay readers, *The Namesake* is arguably one of the most oversignified texts in representing and shaping South Asian American cultural identity. As evident in Choudhry's unconventional review, for affluent South Asians in the United States, the plurality of meanings engendered by *The Namesake* encapsulates South Asian Americans' abiding ambivalence about their racial and communal identity. Some readers relate strongly to the novel's aesthetics and description of South Asian American experience, while others are suspicious of Lahiri's capacity to "get all their personal stories right in one go." The contradictions that inhere in *The Namesake*'s interpretive field reveal the central contradictions of neoliberal multiculturalist subject formation: affluent

South Asian Americans aspire to particular ideals of cultural citizenship by embracing ethnic heterogeneity, gender equality, and class solidarity and are also shaped by the complacency their own privilege gives rise to. Furthermore, the myriad interpretations that *The Namesake* affords deepen the idea that the gendering of discourses of authenticity in transnational South Asian literary culture embeds regimes of value differently for male and female writers.

As I explore in this chapter, in Lahiri's case these gendered discourses of authenticity are the filter through which she and her novel are interpreted by both scholarly and lay audiences. There is a substantial set of scholarly analyses of *The Namesake*, particularly in the field of South Asian American literary studies, that converge in their disappointment with the novel's representational failures: its attractive depictions of consumerism, its fetishization of South Asian culture for white audiences, and its uncomplicated account of patriarchy and Hindu-Brahmin culture. Conversely, middle- and upper-middle class South Asian American lay readers, the class NetSAP book club participants typically are members of, are less interested in the materialist narrative threads of the novel and strongly identify with its account of second-generation bicultural confusion around issues of dating and family relationships. By the time I began participating in the NetSAP book club and developing my ethnography in 2005, the group had already met to discuss *The Namesake* (see appendix 3). However, two years after its publication in 2003 it was still a touchstone text for readers: out of thirty interviews I conducted with NetSAP book club participants, twenty-four offered unprompted, extensive commentary on the novel and eighteen conveyed the impression that they strongly identified with it.

While ostensibly diverging in their responses to the novel, both scholarly and lay analyses of the text are affectively invested in the question of whether *The Namesake* offers an authentic, realistic, and representative narrative of contemporary South Asian American culture. The role of affect in representation has been much debated in literary criticism and is particularly fraught in Asian American literary scholarship. And yet it is clear from the discursive field that has emerged around this novel that political, critical, *and* emotional desires inform both scholarly and lay practices of reading. That is, even when literary scholars critique the novel and Lahiri's work more broadly for acceding to the ethnographic demands of white audiences, the response of lay readers reminds us that realist accounts of ethnic difference are received differently among various audiences. Within its contexts of readership, the novel offers up a range of interpretive possibilities that readers are attracted to depending on the political and personal desires that animate their practices of reading. Texts like *The Namesake* that have become very meaningful within particular ethnic American reading communities make manifest the myriad ways that readers, both academic and lay, use a text to make sense of their own and others' complex subjectivities, cultural identities, and social affiliations.

The Namesake: Text and Context in Published Reviews

Reviews of *The Namesake* in major media outlets immediately after it was published were very positive overall.[2] The critical consensus commended Lahiri's spare yet descriptive prose, her ability to bridge first- and second-generation experiences of displacement, and her capacity to evoke sympathy for flawed characters. Moreover, these reviews cited her attention to detail in describing Bengali culture, her complex treatment of romantic relationships, and her successful transition from the genre of the short story to the extended form of the novel.[3] The novel tells the story of Gogol Ganguli, whose Bengali parents immigrated to the United States in the 1960s. It follows Gogol through his adolescence into his young adulthood, focusing mainly on his romantic life—specifically two long-term relationships with Anglo-American women and his failed marriage to a second-generation Bengali woman. The plot is also driven by an intergenerational conflict between Gogol and his parents that is metaphorized in Gogol's dissatisfaction about having been named after the Russian author Nikolai Gogol. As Gogol grows up he begins to resent this name and to go by Nikhil instead. He does not make peace with his name or his culture until years later when he learns that his father's immigration to the United States was initiated by his desire to leave India after a near-fatal train wreck. Lying among the train's wreckage, Gogol's father, Ashoke, used pages from Gogol's "The Overcoat" to signal for help.

The intertextual story behind Gogol's naming encapsulates the complexities of South Asian migration and speaks to the ambivalence of immigrant identity (see Mani, *Aspiring* 59 and Jain 194). Bakirathi Mani explains that despite the novel's narrow focus on a particular demographic of South Asian immigrants, *The Namesake* has been a popular novel in the United States because of how it provides a coming-of-age tale that fits into the tradition of ethnic American stories of assimilation (*Aspiring* 57). The novel's appeal as a mainstream representation of South Asian identity in the United States was consolidated among South Asian and non–South Asian audiences alike in 2007 with the release of Mira Nair's film adaptation of the novel featuring popular South Asian American actor Kal Penn in the lead role of Gogol.[4] More than a decade after its publication, the novel stands as one of the most popular and well-known accounts of South Asian America by one of the most acclaimed South Asian American writers.

This success has not come without cost for Lahiri, and she has discussed her hesitation to take on the mantle of the authentic second-generation South Asian American cultural spokesperson. Lahiri, like her fiction, has accrued an abundance of representative meanings among her various audiences, a representative status that only deepened after she won the 2014 National Humanities Medal.[5] In the mainstream media Lahiri's authorial persona has been subject to representational scrutiny on two fronts. First there is a repeated emphasis on her beauty. In one recent example, Lara Adair observes in a review of Lahiri's second collection of short stories, *Unaccustomed Earth* (2008), in the *San Francisco Chronicle* that "expensively and chicly dressed, Pulitzer Prize-winning writer Jhumpa (pronounced Joompa) Lahiri is at 36 as beautiful as any movie star."[6] Repeated references to Lahiri's style and beauty imply that her success has been enabled by these superficial qualities—her exotic beauty makes her a more appealing representative figure. Such references also suggest that her elite, fashionable persona reflects the elite South Asian diasporic milieu with which she is most familiar.[7] Second, just as readers of her short stories and novels question whether or not she offers an authentic rendering of South Asian American culture, they debate whether she herself can function as an authentic representative of that culture. This conflation of Lahiri and her work can have positive effects on readers: as NetSAP book club participant Aarthi phrased it, "When I read Jhumpa Lahiri, I am thinking and feeling with her." Aarthi's statement encapsulates the attachment that readers felt to Lahiri's narrative world as it is embodied in her second-generation, bicultural construction in the media. At the same time, Lahiri's authorial persona, just like Roy's, is gendered and limiting: her talent is both authenticated and diminished through the strong association reviewers and lay readers make between her and ethnographic, realistic, autobiographical accounts of South Asian culture.

In 2006, responding to the problems of her representative status, Lahiri wrote a personal essay for *Newsweek*, in which she speaks powerfully about ethnic ambivalence: "I have always believed that I lack the authority my parents bring to being Indian. But as long as they live they protect me from feeling like an imposter." Here Lahiri reveals her own thwarted desire to inhabit a truly "authentic" Indian identity and the difficulty of realizing that desire as someone who lives between South Asian and American cultures. Similarly, when she was asked in a 2003 *New York Times Magazine* interview with John Glassie about what she makes of the surge of interest in all things Indian, she responds, "I've always been very ambivalent about all things Indian. [. . .] When I see someone like Madonna sporting the Indian look, it's very ironic to me. I grew up with people saying, 'What's that on your mom's forehead? And not in a good way." In Boris Kachka's interview with Lahiri in *New York Magazine*, Lahiri rejects the idea that she is limited as an ethnic American writer. Kachka notes that "*Unaccustomed Earth* is, once again, about upwardly mobile South Asians from New England, and so is the novel she's working on." He then asks Lahiri why she focuses solely on South Asian experience, and she responds, "Is that all you've got in there? I get asked the question all the time. [. . .] It baffles me. Does John Updike get asked this question? Does Alice Munro? It's the ethnic thing, that's what it is. And my answer is always, yes, I will continue to write about this world, because it inspires me to write, and there's nothing more important than that." Even though Lahiri continually questions ideologies of South Asian ethnic authenticity, she is constructed as its embodiment.

A significant number of academic readers of *The Namesake*, many of whom are of South Asian descent themselves, express concern over the fact that Lahiri's work is popular with non–South Asian readers on the grounds that all she offers is a bland multiculturalism. In a recent anthology devoted entirely to Lahiri's oeuvre, editors Lavina Dhingra and Floyd Cheung note that while there is a vein of criticism on Lahiri that tends to focus on the formal qualities of her fiction and its transnational themes, there is a larger body of criticism that emphasizes how her work represents South Asians and South Asian culture in the United States. They explain that "some critics look to her identity as an Indian American and expect her to engage with the politics of ethno-racial and cultural identity in her writing—ideally in a way that they see as progressive" (xv).

Rajini Srikanth, for instance, argues that in *Unaccustomed Earth* Lahiri's artistry lulls the reader, particularly the white and non–South Asian

American reader, into a complacent acceptance of "her beautiful universe" ("What Lies Beneath" 69). Srikanth critiques the short story collection and by implication Lahiri's work more broadly for dehistoricizing South Asian immigration to the United States and propagating a superficial "multicultural ethos" in which difference is blunted and rebranded as exotic and desirable. She notes that Lahiri mainly depicts middle- and upper-middle class South Asian professionals who "listen to Chopin's Nocturnes and buy their groceries at gourmet food stores" and that she limits her representations to a small, elite sliver of the Indian American population, namely the Bengali Hindu community, thereby excluding the operations of race, power, and privilege among South Asian Americans in her narratives.[8]

Similarly, Anita Mannur, writing on how Lahiri's work changed after the initial success of *The Interpreter of Maladies*, notes that race in her stories has become less important as her work has become increasingly commodified and exemplary of a "palatable multiculturalism" that "reaffirms the view that Indian Americans enter the wider terrain of American culture easily" (162). Lavina Dhingra Shankar was among the first critics to advance this kind of argument about Lahiri's fiction.[9] As she says, Lahiri's success derives from her exotic but "not too spicy" rendering of South Asian culture and from an "identification (and either regret or self-exoneration) among (Caucasian or other non–South Asian) readers who might have indulged in a [. . .] rejection of the barbaric Other" ("Not Too Spicy" 40). And finally, Ambreen Hai agrees that Lahiri's work is valuable for creating narratives that evoke empathy and build community, but she laments that Lahiri's fiction is not overtly political. Hai is wary of critical tendencies that exhort the author to "do what a critic wants," (206), but she nevertheless maintains that it is unfortunate that Lahiri's work does not "carry a radical or transformative political edge" (205).

After I first read the novel, prior to conducting my ethnography of readership, I had the same concerns that Srikanth, Mannur, Dhingra, and Hai express about Lahiri's attractive, affluent, and consumerist narrative worlds. Before starting graduate school, my affective response to the novel had been one of strong identification with the narrative of bicultural displacement. However, after I entered literary academia and learned more about the field of Asian American studies, my reading of the novel, although still influenced by affect, shifted to a concern with issues of representation and authenticity. Whenever *The Namesake* came up in conversation with NetSAP book club participants, I stated my reservations, which were that it presented what I felt at the time were limiting, stereotypical representations of Indian women and objectifications of the three main female characters as materialistic consumers, victims of brown male oppression, and repositories of ethnic tradition.

I was particularly concerned with depictions of class and gender in the novel. As I explained (usually only partially) in these conversations, I felt that the narrative pivoted on Gogol's relationship with his father and his uneasy return to his own cultural heritage as the prodigal ethnic son, evoking what Gayatri Gopinath argues are the "patriarchal and heteronormative tropes of the term 'diaspora'" (5). Additionally, I was convinced that the novel's female characters acted as foils to the male protagonist's development, contributing to simplistic notions of what constitutes authentic South Asian female subjectivity in the West.[10] Finally, I saw privilege and affluence as structuring themes of the novel, evident in descriptions of consumption, brand-name materialism, Gogol's Ivy League educational advantages, and his desire to leverage his cultural capital to move up the social class hierarchy. Relatedly, I believed that the economic motives that have historically driven immigration and assimilation among first- and second-generation South Asian immigrants of the professional class to the United States are obfuscated by Gogol and his father's quests for self-realization and individuality. In sum, I was unable to reconcile my initial identificatory and emotional connection with the novel with my representational investment as a literary scholar. I felt, like other critics, disappointed that the novel wasn't more inclusive, that it depicted South Asian aspirations for upward class mobility, celebrated an unexamined Indo-chic ethos, and encouraged collusion with the model minority myth.[11]

The Many Meanings of *The Namesake*

Of course, not all scholarly assessments of Lahiri's work have found it dissatisfying: there is a small but influential body of scholarship that commends Lahiri's work for challenging traditional notions of authentic South Asian American narratives through its transnational engagements and its revision of traditional tropes of Asian American narratives, thus reading her texts in ways that go beyond the concerns of authentic ethnic or national representation (see Koshy, "Minority Cosmopolitanism" 594 and Mani, *Aspiring* 69). These critics praise Lahiri's work for revising common representations of "traditional" Indian culture in transnational South Asian literature and humanizing the cliché elements of the ABCD narrative.[12] I note this strain of scholarship not only to acknowledge the heterogeneity of scholarly interpretations of *The Namesake* but also to draw attention to the representational stakes of Lahiri's work. In other words, the fact that her work receives both criticism and acclaim suggests how fraught the cultural politics of Asian American literary studies are.

Asian American literature has, to some degree, been popularized through representational debates: Many of the major controversies in Asian American literary studies—such as the alleged denigration of Chinese masculinity in Maxine Hong Kingston's *The Woman Warrior* (1989), the negative depiction of Filipinos in Lois Ann Yamanaka's novel, *Blu's Hanging* (1998), and the gender, racial, national, and religious stereotypes in Bharati Mukherjee's *Jasmine* (1989)—have concerned representation. Such controversies encode well-founded anxieties about the role of representation and affect in reading Asian American literatures. They demonstrate the political and social stakes of readerly identification with literary representations of Asian American subjectivity and the effect that such representation can have on individual and group esteem. At the same time, these debates also demonstrate the problems that arise when readers identify closely with Asian American literature. Asian American scholars have long been concerned that reading for ethnographic or sociological truth fetters minority authors with an unfair representational burden that can have the effect of limiting their creativity and diminishing the complexity of their literary mediations of subjectivity. Ultimately, as Min Hyoung Song writes, whether or not one believes that focusing on representation, affect, esteem, and the self-worth of a particular group produces naïve and retrograde readings, these issues structure the debate over Asian American literary representation for a number of Asian American subjects (6).

Even though Lahiri disavows the various representational claims that are associated with her and her work among various readerships, what makes Lahiri's *The Namesake*'s so central in South Asian American literary studies is the way its mixed reception captures the quandaries of South Asian American belonging. The novel's reception in both academic and nonacademic contexts reflects South Asian American preoccupation with formulating a nonreductive and complex idea of authentic ethnic identity. Readers' ambivalence about the text captures their fraught relationship to ideologies of authenticity that thwart as well as enable their assimilation in a neoliberal era in which commodified forms of difference are valued. As Thoma writes, popular Asian American literature provides guidance for Asian American subjects by "disclosing the limitations of neoliberal models of belonging" as well as showing Asian American readers how to negotiate such constraints (179). NetSAP book club participants' response to *The Namesake* makes such practices of reading manifest, evoking Kenneth Burke's characterization of literature as "equipment for living" (qtd. in Long 131). Elizabeth Long explains that when seen in this mode, literature becomes "less a platonic ideal than [. . .] something that is pressed into service for a task beyond itself, a tool employed in the construction of human lives" (131). Book club readers focused on the novel's representations of the second-generation experience, including the effects of ethnic difference and similarity in romantic relationships, the comfort of shared experience, and a longing to connect to their parents' histories of immigration. The personal dimensions of their interpretations politicized the seemingly benign, second-generation coming-of-age narrative, exposing their anxieties about authenticity as mediated through class, racialization, and gender roles.

Of course, given the demographic of the members of the NetSAP book club—college educated, middle to upper-middle class, mainly of Indian extraction and Hindu background—it is unsurprising that these readers felt such a connection to the novel. In interviews, I found that readers identified with the novel in three main ways. First, they strongly identified with the male protagonist Gogol, regardless of their own gender, largely because he embodies the narrative of bicultural displacement on which the novel centers. As Sunil, a Bengali American put it, "*The Namesake,* I remember just reading it and it blowing my mind. [. . .] I mean so much of my life I realized was not unique after all. [. . .] I related to it on so many levels. I thought [Gogol] was really me. I came from Michigan, and I really thought I was white." For Lalita, the novel provided a relatable narration of her own desire for assimilation and belonging: "I was drawn to Gogol's experience of living in America [. . .] and wanting to assimilate to more of a mainstream American culture." Or as Priya said, "Even though it was a guy's perspective, a lot of [the] things [it describes are] like how I would have lived my life, [. . .] dating someone non-Indian, moving away from the Indian stuff, balancing the relationship with his parents."

Second, they identified with what they described as the novel's unique representation of the fraught experience of assimilation for *second-generation* South Asians in the United States. Sri, the NetSAP book club's founder and first moderator, exemplified this attitude: "[Lahiri's] voice is America. Her stories are very true" (NetSAP book club meeting, *The Red Carpet*). Sri emphasized that Lahiri writes South Asians into U.S. cultural citizenship through the narrative rendering of Gogol's difficulties reconciling South Asian and American values. Rinki, a reader of Sikh-American origin, explained that she had read all three of Lahiri's books and felt a strong connection to them because each had "something an Indian American can relate to," particularly in terms of the "second-generation themes." Meera and Raj found the novel particularly compelling for its descriptions of intergenerational and intercultural negotiation. Meera described Lahiri's success at describing the multiple roles that second-generation South Asian Americans were expected to inhabit: "The way that she articulates going through this identity crisis, [. . .] coming to terms with the world the you live in and the household you grew up in, and going back to South Asia a lot. [. . .] You are constantly playing multiple roles at once." Similarly, Raj described this multiplicity in terms of a tension between the generations: "I really liked *The Namesake.* [. . .] If you're second-generation Indian [. . .] you know there's a tension between the world you're growing up in and what you need to know and the values you need to have to survive versus your parents and where they came from, what values they had." Aarthi eloquently summed up the narrative's description of bicultural negotiation: "I think [Lahiri] does a good job of capturing the ambivalence that people feel when they're, you know, American-raised but Indian-born."

Third, readers identified with the novel because they felt Lahiri's exemplary writing, popularity, and acclaim helped to make the South Asian American experience more mainstream by offering the best of what South Asian American writing has to offer: "Jhumpa Lahiri, she just captures what you're thinking," Moira remarked. "If I wanted a non–South Asian friend to read any South Asian author, and something that I would be proud of them reading, then it would be [*Interpreter of Maladies* and *The Namesake*]." Reflecting on Lahiri's popularity in the United States, Rakesh, a NetSAP book club participant born and raised in Rajasthan, explained that Lahiri offered a "model of a second-generation writer" and that she captured a shared experience: "You have people [in the book club] going through the same experiences, the same [bicultural] turmoil, and that's what I think attracts people to her books." These remarks about Lahiri's transcendence of ethnicity connect to how other NetSAP book club participants' saw Rushdie as an author whose mastery and skill made his writing "universally" acclaimed. NetSAP book club members felt they were able to consolidate their cultural capital through the association with a literary culture in which beloved writers like Lahiri and Rushdie transcend ethnic difference to become part of an Anglo-centric canon in which South Asian diasporic writing is not entirely minoritized.

In addition to sharing the ways they identified with the novel, NetSAP book club members demonstrated a savvy critical engagement with the novel's main themes as they are dramatized through the three main female characters. In the section that follows, I situate academic (a category in which I include my own analyses) and lay readers' interpretations of the novel in dialogue with one another. Each major relationship in the novel encodes key themes of South Asian ethnic authenticity: first, Gogol's interracial romance with Maxine exposes how class privilege shapes ethnic affiliation and the process of assimilation; second, his intraracial marriage to Moushumi depicts the ambivalent performance of traditional South Asian identity through the recurring trope of arranged marriage; and finally, Gogol's relationship with his mother, Ashima, challenges and reinforces the persistent stereotypes that drive the narration of South Asian female characters. The complexity of each of these relationships—particularly, as they are interpreted in scholarly and lay cultures of reading—shows ambivalence to be a structure of feeling for affluent South Asians in the United States. In each of these relationships, practices of reading reinforce dominant images of South Asian class privilege, a desire for whiteness, and the fetishization of authentic, traditional culture. And yet at the same time, lay readers' analyses of these relationships raise questions of race and class, reminding readers of their familial histories of immigration to the United States and disrupting the patriarchal leanings of the novel.

"Being and Feeling That You Are Gogol"

As the main interracial romance in the novel, Gogol and Maxine's relationship raises questions about how assimilative desires, whiteness, and national belonging are mediated through class privilege for South Asian Americans.[13] As a character, Maxine Ratliff represents, as Sheng-mei Ma describes in another context, "the disadvantaged group's fallacy of assimilation. White bodies [. . .] become not only an exotic physical entity [. . .] but also a political symbol with which lies the promise of power" (67).[14] Maxine is an affluent white American, a New Yorker by birth, and privileged in every sense. She functions as a representative of Western high culture and international sophistication. From the moment Gogol meets her parents at the house she grew up in and still lives in, an insurmountable difference in their class and ethnicity becomes evident: "He is stunned by the house, a Greek Revival, admiring it for several minutes like a tourist before opening the gate" (130). Maxine's affluence and lifestyle are alien to Gogol; he is merely a visitor without hope of permanent residence in her world.

Lahiri's portrait of Maxine can be seen as ambivalent and somewhat critical. She is a character drawn largely through catalogues of her consumption and materialism. Detailed lists of what Maxine instructs Gogol to eat, drink, and buy abound, implicitly commenting on their class difference. Maxine becomes a cultural usher, teaching Gogol how to effect the highbrow tastes that will enable him to realize the cultural capital of his Ivy League education and gain proximity to the advantages of whiteness. In the description of Gogol and Maxine's relationship consumption and class status are pervasive and presented as relatively benign forces. Gogol ruminates, for example, over the affluence and easy privilege of the Ratliffs, comparing his experience vacationing with them at their lake house with the childhood family trips that he and his family took to visit other Bengali families:

> The Ratliffs own the moon that floats over the lake, and the sun and the clouds. [. . .] Yet he cannot picture his family occupying a house like this, playing board games on rainy afternoons. [. . .] They would have felt lonely in this setting, remarking that they were the only Indians. [. . .] He feels no nostalgia for the vacations he's spent with his family, and he realizes now that they weren't vacations at all. [. . .] They had stayed in motels, slept whole families to a single room, swum in pools that could be seen from the road. (155)

Gogol's distaste for those family vacations of the past with other Bengalis and his desire to partake in the leisure that characterizes Maxine's family vacations symbolize his ethnic assimilation, deracialization, and upward mobility.

In one way of looking at their relationship, the full impact of Gogol's racial difference from Maxine, which is rooted in his ethnicity and the limitations it imposes on his social and class status, is blunted by the narrative's turn to stereotypical tropes of bicultural incompatibility. For example, the failure of Gogol and Maxine's relationship can be attributed to her inability to understand Gogol's returning to his family and culture after his father dies: "[Maxine] had not understood being excluded from the family's plans to travel to Calcutta," and she expresses jealousy toward his mother and sister (188). In other words, cultural difference overshadows the incomplete racial and class critique that the novel initiates. Maxine's presence in the narrative and the attendant issues of class, assimilation, and national belonging that her relationship with Gogol foregrounds are eclipsed by ethnic alterity—once an object of sexual desire for Gogol in his quest for a more advantageous class position in America, Maxine now becomes an object against which he defines himself.

And yet despite the novel's obfuscation of class difference and its reliance on clichés of interracial romance, NetSAP book club members focused on *The Namesake*'s representations of affluence and were wary of its attractive materialism. Referring to the description of Gogol's family vacations, Raj explained: "My mom read it. And my dad's deceased now, but they moved here in the late 1960s, and my dad moved here to go to grad school, and they had no money, and the first friends they make here are other Indians." In Raj's reading, the novel doesn't obscure the effects of class and economics but instead seamlessly incorporates class aspiration as part of the narrative of migration. In a similar vein, during the book club meeting about Markandaya's *Nectar in a Sieve* (1954), Aisha, a Pakistani American participant in the club, contrasted her experience of reading *The Namesake* with her experience of reading Markandaya's novel: "I found [*Nectar in a Sieve*] very refreshing. I kept thinking of the book *The Namesake.* I have no idea why. I was thinking, 'Gogol's problem was that he didn't like his name and look at [Rukmani's] problems.' It was so refreshing because the books that we're reading nowadays are so materialistic." Her comment sparked a degree of consensus among book club attendees, but readers were careful to take into account the historical differences between the two novels. Eventually, the hostess of the meeting, Niha, suggested that the difference between the two novels was that readers identified less with Rukmani than they did with Gogol: "*The Namesake* is about being and feeling that you are Gogol" (NetSAP book club meeting, *Nectar in a Sieve*)."

Because *The Namesake* provides such a relatable representation of second-generation South Asian American experience, it requires the reader (particularly readers invested in South Asian American identity formation) to reckon with the authenticity of that depiction. As the book club members who participated in the discussion of *Nectar in a Sieve* pointed out, such reckoning is not as straightforward as it may seem. Rather, as these readers observed, *The Namesake* overtly confronts some of the material realities that South Asian Americans face, such as the difficulties of immigration and second-generation experiences, but obscures others, such as the differences in class and economic privilege within this ethnic community.

In addition to analyzing the role of affluence in Gogol and Maxine's relationship, NetSAP book club participants attended to the tension between a desire for assimilation and a desire for ethnic authenticity that this relationship exposes. Whether or not they had personal experience with interracial romantic relationships, readers explained that such relationships in the novel spoke to a desire to successfully negotiate their own complicated cultural affiliations. As Nishi explained, reading South Asian diasporic literature reinforced her sense that she would be more comfortable dating within the Pakistani American community:

> [The more I read] South Asian literature, the more I really wouldn't want to marry someone who didn't share some of those experiences, like going to Pakistan, like the richness of the culture, or the cultural values. I guess my values are [shaped by] South Asian literature. Not to say I don't want to be adventurous, or want to meet other types of people, but I love the history that I have, and I want to see it in other people that I know.

Nishi's sense that South Asian literature shaped her moral values was also reflected in her remark that the novel's portrayal of the longing to "connect with your parents' history" was "touching in a way" but also alienating when "your reality at school or in college is changing" and when having "white friends shapes what you're like and who you are and what you're attracted to." In Nishi's reading, the complexities of interracial dating can be daunting and thus encourage ethnic insularity. However, her assessment of interracial relationships also encodes the broader difficulties of negotiating a bicultural identity and a strong desire to respect her family's wishes while also fitting in with mainstream Anglo-American culture.

In another instance, Meera, a recent Indian American transplant to the DC area, explained that Gogol's longing for Maxine could also be read as a longing for racial acceptance:

> The American girl [that Gogol] was dating in New York was the epitome of what he wanted. [She] was everything that he wasn't: total upper class, very cultured, very worldly, in a European sense. [. . .] I saw like him just going after what he didn't have and what he wasn't, because that is what he thought he wanted to be and [. . .] could become by being with her.

Nishi's and Meera's readings retool the economic homogeneity and bicultural clichés of the narrative, insisting on the value of the novel's depiction of South Asian desires for assimilation and the privileges of whiteness.

Their readings don't completely challenge what Srikanth terms "Lahiri's brand of desirable difference" ("What Lies Beneath" 51) or, in other words, the attractive multiculturalist materialism of the novel; rather they provide evidence of the range of interpretive possibilities that this novel inspires among readers. Writing about Lahiri's short story "Sexy" in *The Interpreter of Maladies*, Susan Koshy explains that Lahiri's work challenges the idea that interracial romance can bridge racial and national difference ("Minority" 595). NetSAP book club participants' interpretations of Gogol and Maxine's relationship align with and build on this observation; for them, interracial romance in *The Namesake* symbolizes pressures to conform to the norms of Anglo-American taste, and they see the failure of interracial romance in the novel as reflecting South Asian Americans' thwarted desires for mainstream social standing and political inclusion.[15]

At the same time, one could say that NetSAP book club participants' interpretations of Gogol and Maxine's relationship reflects what scholars such as Bandana Purkayastha characterize as an assimilative strategy wherein the group asserts an upwardly mobile ethnic identity in the symbolic realm and at sites of political coalition in order to avoid being "incorporated into the U.S. racial system" (10).[16] However one interprets Gogol and Maxine's relationship, it is clear NetSAP book club participants' recognition of the novel's complex rendering of interracial romance overlaps with scholarly observations illustrating that representations of sexual desire, tethered as they are to longings for racial and national belonging, impact South Asian American racialization in the United States.[17]

While the themes of ethnic authenticity, romantic desire, and second-generation assimilation introduced in Gogol and Maxine's romance are carried over to Gogol and Moushumi's relationship, in this case the romantic narrative addresses problems of ethnic similarity rather than ethnic difference. Gogol and Moushumi's relationship is founded on a shared desire to remedy their cultural displacement by being together. They initially agree to meet at Ashima's request, thus invoking the trope of the arranged marriage. Moushumi, a Bengali American woman, has recently ended an engagement with a white American man due in large part to their cultural differences. Gogol and Moushumi function as cultural correctives for one another, not only healing each one's heartbreak but also counteracting the feelings of ethnic alienation that their forays into interracial romance produced. In fact, the initial basis for their attraction is described through their shared background and heritage: "They talk endlessly about how they know and do not know each other. In a way there is little to explain. [. . .] He can imagine her life, even after she and her family moved away to New Jersey. [. . .] There had been the same frequent trips to Calcutta, being plucked out of their American lives for months at a time" (211–12). They are united by their common culture, shared experiences, and the second-generation problem of their ethnicity leading to misperception and misunderstanding in the United States. For example, a waiter at an Italian restaurant where they eat lunch asks if they are brother and sister. Gogol is "at once insulted and oddly aroused. In a way he realizes, it's true—they share the same coloring, the straight eyebrows, the long slender bodies, the high cheekbones and dark hair" (203). They both seem somewhat pleased by the mistake because it reminds them once more of their common ground. This moment offers a potential critique of insular South Asian communities in the United States by foreshadowing the false sense of security based in a shared background that unites Gogol and Moushumi.

When they get married, the wedding is portrayed as an expectation that they meet but of which they are not entirely a part: "He is aware that together he and Moushumi are fulfilling a collective, deep-seated desire—because they're both Bengali, everyone can let his hair down a bit" (224). Their courtship, marriage, and newlywed life satisfy a sense of cultural obligation to their parents, extended family, and the wider Bengali community. This trope of a quasi-arranged marriage encodes a desire for belonging and assimilation as well as an anxiety about choice and displacement. Sunaina Marr Maira explains that the trope of arranged marriage "provides the counterpoint to the image of a hypersexualized land of Kama Sutra. Public discussions of dating and marriage among second-generation Indian Americans, and their underlying erotic fantasies, are thus fraught with the politics of not only gender and sexuality but also nation, generation and race" (*Desis* 153).[18]

A number of critics have interpreted the dissolution of Gogol and Moushumi's union as a progressive choice, a refusal of identity politics, and the triumph of Western individuality over Eastern fatalism. For example, Robin E. Field interprets the divorce as an assertion of individuality and newfound American subjectivity, replete with the freedom to make messy decisions about romantic preferences and sexual infidelity: "In *The Namesake,* marriage is a complicated manipulation between the traditional expectations of immigrant parents and the desires of the second generation. [. . .] Lahiri [. . .] underscores how cultural similarities do not necessarily lead to personal compatibility, as this marriage crumbles by the end of the novel" (173). Field claims that Lahiri's "most significant contribution to contemporary American literature" is how she captures the "delicate balance between cultural prerogatives and personal agency" (168). Song notes that Moushumi's decision to have an affair can be seen as a "willful denial of social arrangements" and "rejection of identity" (173). The failure of Gogol and Moushumi's intraracial romance thus potentially signifies the triumph of individuality and the transcendence of ethnic obligation.

NetSAP book club participants offer another way to read Gogol and Moushumi's romance—as a commentary on identity. They suggest that in the novel romantic choice does not signal an embrace of either Western modernity or Eastern tradition but rather of a more fluid understanding of bicultural identity.[19] They interpreted Gogol and Moushumi's doomed marriage as a powerful representation of the romantic obligations and struggles that face second-generation South Asian Americans. As Padma, a reader who generally objected to portrayals of passive female characters in transnational South Asian literature, explained, "We're still in that generation where we are dealing with the whole arranged marriage thing and [the] difficulty of finding people who understand the whole East-West mix, and I think maybe that was part of *The Namesake* that maybe people really connected with." Priya saw the novel as presenting the dilemma of family and tradition versus individuality and development through tropes of romance: "The struggle between marrying somebody your parents want you to, versus someone you love, that struggle, [that's what] *The Namesake* did, and I lived that for a while. I feel I can totally relate to those things." Priya strongly identified with many South Asian novels' depictions of failed or doomed romances because, as she explained, they helped her make sense of her own recent divorce and its cultural implications.

The fact that the collapse of Gogol and Moushumi's romance is triggered by Moushumi's decision to leave Gogol for another man is important to both Padma's and Priya's readings of the novel. Some critics see Moushumi's decision to leave the marriage as a sign of her independence from cultural obligations (Kaur 40) or her unwillingness to conform to the expectations of the Bengali community as an assertion of her global identity, forged by personal choice rather than national or ethnic affiliation (Field 176; Song 173). However, because Moushumi's narrative arc is also defined by a choice between brown or white men (the former representing oppression and the latter rescue from that oppression) the novel also reinscribes reductive and gendered Orientalist paradigms. Lahiri offers an insight into Moushumi's motivations:

> And yet the familiarity that had once drawn her to him has begun to keep her at bay. Though she knows it's not his fault, she can't help but associate him, at times, with a sense of resignation, with the very life she had resisted,

> had struggled so mightily to leave behind. He was not who she saw herself ending up with, he had never been that person. (250)

Moushumi met Gogol when she was on the rebound from Graham, the white American man whom she had broken up with weeks before they were to be married after she overheard him complaining to friends about the provinciality of Calcutta, where they had visited her relatives. In essence, Gogol rescued her and "obliterated her former disgrace" (249). Graham's presence is a shadow in the narrative that causes Gogol to feel insecure in his relationship to Moushumi. Graham's race was a factor in his appeal to Moushumi because marrying him would have ensured her a degree of cultural rebellion. Predictably, when Moushumi wants to escape from her marriage to Gogol, she has an affair with another white man, Dimitri. Whiteness—specifically, whiteness universalized through the gender of the male subject—ostensibly becomes an unmarked and uncomplicated signifier of freedom of choice and escape from tradition. Thus, interpretations that see Moushumi's choice as liberating potentially reaffirm racial and gender hierarchies; such interpretations are complicated by what Gayatri Spivak identifies as the familiar narrative structure whereby the white man rescues the brown woman from the stultifying and rigid expectations of the brown man (297).

For Priya and Padma, the complexities of Gogol and Moushumi's romance produced a range of anxieties relating to the hegemony of whiteness and how it inflected their own bicultural identity. They described being anxious about denying their heritage if they were to date a non-South Asian and the struggle to honor their individuality and family obligations. Their readings offer further insight into why the failure of Gogol and Moushumi's marriage does not necessarily represent an escape from Eastern oppression and a movement toward Western choice. Pooja, another NetSAP book club, explained that her reading of the novel prompted her to reconsider thinking of dating according to cultural binaries:

> [*The Namesake*] really was a huge eye opener to me, realizing that you can date an Indian or South Asian [but that] we're all pretty much growing up with American values these days. So it really doesn't mean anything at the end of the day, because if you're marrying someone who grew up here, you're pretty much marrying someone who's not probably growing up with those values.

Pooja's remark also demonstrates a tendency among South Asian Americans to essentialize identity along national and racial lines by creating a divide between South Asian and American culture. Yet at the same time, by reading *The Namesake,* she became aware that her South Asian value system is destabilized by what she perceives as a competing American value system in which divorce is acceptable.

Overall, readers in various contexts acknowledge that race and ethnic affiliation impact romantic involvement, but they also emphasize that *The Namesake*'s romantic narratives challenge rigid notions of a divide between Indian and American cultures and encourage consideration of what categories of racial affiliation might signify. In particular, lay readers' interpretations of romance in the novel indicate that Moushumi's rejection of an Indian man in favor of a white suitor does not ensure her liberation, just as Gogol's marriage to an Indian woman after leaving his white girlfriend does not guarantee that he will succeed in conforming to ethnic expectations. In this way, NetSAP book club participants understand Gogol and Moushumi's marriage as a negotiation of the untenable divisions between East/West, tradition/modernity, and oppression/liberation in favor of more fluid, dynamic constructions of ethnic affiliation.

The most blatant clichés of South Asian ethnic authenticity, identity, and femininity in the novel are arguably those used to depict Ashima, Gogol's mother. And yet despite this heavy-handed characterization, readers in the NetSAP book club interpreted her story as the central one in the novel, providing one of the most compelling and powerful displays of how the practice of reading can legislate a variety of ambivalent interpretive meanings around discourses of authenticity.[20]

Descriptions of ethnic cuisine, cooking, and eating dominate Ashima's appearances in *The Namesake.* A common trope in South Asian diasporic literature links descriptions of food to particularly classed and gendered identities under the rubric of national affiliation (Mannur 3). Ethnic Indian cuisine comes to symbolize Indian culture through a language of consumption, creating a set of culinary metaphors that mirrors the consumption of ethnic texts in the literary marketplace. Anita Mannur makes this connection explicit: "Cursory examinations of many ethnic-themed novels will demonstrate how a visual rendering of food on novel covers is frequently also the means by which publishing houses market Asian Americanness to a readership hungry to consume delectable renditions of alterity" (14). Ashima's association with Indian cuisine marks her as the keeper of cultural tradition and national purity in the domestic space of the American household. In fact, the novel opens with Ashima alone in the kitchen of the apartment she shares with her husband, Ashoke, in

Cambridge, approximating *chaat*, an Indian snack, with "Rice Krispies and peanuts" to satisfy her pregnancy cravings (49). Food provides a connection to the homeland of India and a way to both temper and underscore her displacement in the West.

Yet while food metaphors encode Ashima's cultural adjustment, they also reinforce stereotypes of South Asian female subjectivity that figure the South Asian woman as the authentic bearer of Indian national purity and unchanging ethnic tradition. As the traditional wife, Ashima reproduces India in the home through her culinary skills, and food also provides a way to deepen the intimacy in her marriage and to learn more about her husband: "She has come to know him. [. . .] By now she has learned that her husband likes his food on the salty side, that his favorite thing about lamb curry is the potatoes, and that he likes to finish his dinner with a small final helping of rice and dal" (10). The food metaphor contributes to a limited characterization of South Asian female subjectivity, and Ashima is read according to several clichés: the obedient daughter, the diligent wife, and the forbearing and sacrificing mother (Prashad 105).

The drama of pregnancy and the language of (re)birth pervade characterizations of Ashima and Ashoke's immigration experience in particularly gendered ways. Ashoke's reinvention in America is a redemptive experience; his narrative arc is defined by rebirth in America after his near-death experience in India: "He was born twice in India, and then a third time in America. Three lives by thirty" (21). But Ashima's assimilation is by contrast characterized by her experience as an isolated mother engaged in the task of insular cultural reproduction: "For being a foreigner, Ashima is beginning to realize, is a sort of lifelong pregnancy—a perpetual wait, a constant burden, a continuous feeling out of sorts. [. . .] Like pregnancy, being a foreigner, Ashima believes, is something that elicits the same curiosity from strangers, the same combination of pity and respect" (49–50). By equating pregnancy with the alienation of immigration, the narrator provides a gendered spectacle of what it means to be a foreigner. The "pity and respect" that foreignness elicits is likened to a perpetual pregnancy, suggesting that the transition from immigration to assimilation at once partakes of public recognition and is also an insular, private, an internal process that carries with it the promise of resolution. In fact, it is literally motherhood that enables her adjustment to American self-sufficiency and independence: "She begins to pride herself on doing it alone, in devising a routine. Like Ashoke, busy with his teaching and research and dissertations seven days a week, she, too, now has something to occupy her fully, to demand her utmost devotion, her last ounce of strength" (34–35).

As mother and wife, Ashima represents familiar, stereotypical modes of authentic, traditional South Asian femininity. The metaphor of pregnancy that characterizes her adaptation to living in the United States reinforces the trope of the long-suffering Asian mother.[21] However, by the end of the novel, Ashima eschews the more staid elements of Indian cultural tradition. She has no trouble adjusting to Gogol and Moushumi's divorce and is in fact proud of them for not settling for an unhappy married life: "They are not willing to accept, to adjust, to settle for something less than their ideal of happiness. That pressure has given way, in the case of the subsequent generation, to American common sense" (276). Ashima participates in the "progress" of the second generation by acclimating to the values of American individuality and is figured as an increasingly multicultural subject, albeit one that participates in a complacent and gendered East/West binary of developmental progress from tradition to modernity.

NetSAP book club participants' interpretations of Ashima's character development did not attempt to resist, resolve, or defy the more determinative narrative elements that define her—namely, her associations with consumption, domesticity, and motherhood. Rather, by reading Ashima's story of immigration as central, they modified and refocused the patrilineal, masculinist themes of the novel. They deeply related to Ashima, explaining either that they learned about how difficult their mothers' immigration was by reading the novel or that they were touched by their own mothers' empathy for Ashima's character. As Auditi, a Bengali American reader who Choudhry interviewed for her Bookslut.com article, observed:

> For the first several chapters I just kept crying as I saw my own mother reflected in Ashima (Gogol's mother). I think that the way that Gogol views her is characteristic of how a second generation Bengali-American might look at his or her mother. It was only as an adult that I came to understand and appreciate what my mother had gone through, and Gogol goes through that same process. At the end of the novel Gogol is 32, my age, and I felt I had learned something with him.

Pooja described a similar experience of reading the novel: "I know my cousin was telling me her mom really identified with the first half of the book more. And so did my mom, because they could understand the whole thing, getting married, coming here, adjusting to the life and bringing up your children here." For Auditi and Pooja, the novel allows both first- and second-generation readers to compare their experiences. During an interview with book club participant Raj, I asked if he felt that there were troubling gender stereotypes in the novel. He replied that his mother's identification with Ashima recalibrates the stereotypes: "You could say Gogol's parents are stereotypical, but my mom said it's just like her life, so I don't know what to tell you." Raj valued the novel for giving voice to his mother's immigration experience and offering a context for his personal history.

By allowing NetSAP book club members to recognize their parents' unwritten immigration experiences, the novel offers an example of how lay readerly desire can recast gendered clichés. These readers enacted a "politics of articulation" wherein "they show how the meanings of texts change as they hook up with different interests and interpretive communities" (Felski 10). In bypassing the dominant patriarchal narrative of Ashoke and Gogol's reconciliation and instead focusing on Ashima's isolation, struggle, and eventual adaptation to life in the United States, they strategically reinterpreted Ashima's story to locate the displaced South Asian female subject within a representational system that may otherwise occlude or dismiss her experience. In many ways, their reading of her character suggests Ashima *is* the truly compelling transnational and cosmopolitan figure in the novel, capable of moving back and forth between Indian and American contexts.

The many meanings of *The Namesake* that scholars, book reviewers, and lay readers have formulated demonstrates that the novel simply cannot be understood in a singular way, and, indeed, the breadth of its social influence among South Asian Americans is apparent in the multiple interpretive possibilities it has engendered. Read in one way, the novel captures, in both its reception and content, a set of quandaries facing South Asian Americans in their desire for authentic descriptions of intergenerational tension, class aspirations, experiences of migration, and gender equality. And in another, *The Namesake* and the academic and nonacademic field of interpretation that it has generated itself dramatizes the ambivalence characteristic of South Asian cultural production as it mediates forms of South Asian belonging in the United States. NetSAP book club participants read the novel in ways that distance it from what Rajini Srikanth describes as the more "overdetermined" "Orientalist perceptions" of South

Asian sexuality—"repressed women, domineering men, female feticide, loveless marriages, crude and unsophisticated sexual desire" (*The World Next Door* 98)—even as these elements might be present in the text.

In this way, the novel's interpretive field instantiates the dualities that structure the depiction of South Asian experience and the ambivalence over what constitutes an authentic account. *The Namesake*'s multiplicity of meanings stages the salient quandaries that inform second-generation South Asian American community formation, demonstrating a deep ambivalence about the relationship between racialization and upward mobility, the pressures to adhere to South Asian cultural tradition and assimilate to American culture, and finally, the increasing distance between second-generation South Asian Americans and their parents' histories of migration. Ultimately, the plurality of readings and interpretations that circulate around this novel reveal both the aspirations and limitations of belonging among South Asians in the United States caught between the complacencies of their own privilege and the desire to imagine a more cohesive, unified, and inclusive sense of South Asian identity in the United States.

AFTERWORD

BEYOND AMBIVALENCE?

Throughout this book, I study the role of ambivalence, authenticity, and representation in contemporary South Asian American reading practices. In the current neoliberal multiculturalist context, ideologies of authenticity have had a strong influence on how South Asians in the United States negotiate their sense of belonging. Through practices of reading and other everyday cultural activities, South Asian Americans advance their own claims to authentic ethnic identity; they use these practices as a form of gatekeeping, as a means of regulating the parameters of South Asian American identity, and also as a way of expanding community and constructing new forms of it. As several scholars—myself included—have maintained, ambivalence has been the primary affective response to this complex process of identity and community formation.[1]

And yet ambivalence is not an easy resting place. Even though it has become a defining feature of the cultural politics of middle-class South Asians in the United States, it is inherently an unstable, limited structure of feeling, and one that may soon prove to be inadequate as a way to describe the complexities of South Asian American belonging in the second decade of the twenty-first century. In the ten years that have passed since I first conceptualized this project, the number of South Asians in the United States has grown significantly, and they are now widely represented in film, television, politics, and the arts. This past decade has seen the emergence of several South Asian American figures in U.S. popular culture: Kal Penn of the popular *Harold and Kumar* franchise, Mindy Kaling of *The Office* and *The Mindy Project*, Padma Lakshmi, the host of *Top Chef*, and comedians Aziz Ansari, Aasif Mandvi, and Hari Kondabolu. These are just a few of the South Asian public personalities who have gained a mainstream, non–South Asian following. South Asian Americans are also playing a more active and visible role in politics. Penn worked on Barack Obama's campaign arts policy committee in 2007–8, and then took on a position as associate director in the Office of Public Engagement under the Obama administration, where he served as a liaison to Asian American and Pacific Islander communities (see Del Rosario). Nikki Haley has been governor of South Carolina since 2011 and Bobby Jindal served as governor of Louisiana from 2008 to 2016. In 2008 Jindal was under consideration as a running mate for Republican presidential candidate John McCain.

As images of South Asian Americans multiply across a variety of representational venues, I find myself wondering if this array of platforms will allow South Asians in the United States to move beyond ambivalence, and if so, what that would that look and feel like. Will all the variety in cultural representations of South Asian American identity loosen the stranglehold of ideologies of authenticity, providing South Asian Americans with new ways to imagine their cultural citizenship and belonging? And given the boom in South Asian American representation in popular, political, and institutional American culture, I can't help but wonder what role literature might play in the future formations of South Asian American identity and community.

Indeed, I see this book as part of a broader scholarly conversation that is already charting how South Asians in the United States use everyday cultural practices, such as eating ethnic cuisine, viewing films, watching television, attending art exhibits, and consuming fashion to think beyond ambivalence about representational forms (see Mannur, Desai, *Beyond*, Dave, Mani, and Reddy). These practices, like the practice of reading in NetSAP book club, allow South Asians in the United States to define a sense of identity and establish sites of community *for themselves*, rather than continually be defined by others or the white gaze. Of course, this process of self-definition has the potential to reintroduce limited notions of authenticity. But it also has the potential to complicate such notions and to insist on more progressive, inclusive parameters for South Asian American identity and community formation, as the readers in my study demonstrate. In other words, even as this body of scholarship attests to the persistence of ideologies of authenticity in shaping intraethnic forms of identity and community, it also suggests a tipping point of South Asian American frustration with the limitations of authenticity and its attendant representational paradigms.

I am equally curious as to what the future holds with respect to the second main concern of this book, the exploration of how modern practices of reading shape identity and community belonging. In an increasingly technological, digitized, media-saturated environment, what will the role of reading be in shaping constructions of South Asian American identity and community formation? It is clear that the South Asian diaspora continues to consist of a highly literate reading public, as evidenced in the fairly recent formation and subsequent globalization of the Jaipur Literature Festival and in the continuing prestige of transnational South Asian literary culture.[2] Transnational South Asian literary culture offers South Asians across the globe a unique experience of connection and imagined community that other material and cultural production does not—or at least not in the same way. I believe that the practice of reading will continue to be culturally valuable among South Asian Americans precisely because reading literature is both a quotidian cultural practice that contributes to community formation and enrichment as well as gatekeeping cultural activity. It is a cultural practice that provides a unique outlet and expression for South Asian Americans' relationship to privilege, cultural capital, and the model minority myth.

While I believe that practices of reading will *endure*, I can't say how they will *change* in light of the growing popularity of other representational platforms. But in this troubling moment of Indian American enthusiasm over the election of Hindu nationalist Narendra Modi as prime minister of India, I hope that in general, South Asian American cultural practices will continue to be robust and restless, to undermine narratives of model minority success, and to destabilize the allure of ethnic authenticity. Modi—who was denied a visa to travel to the United States in 2005 over allegations that during his tenure as chief minister of Gujarat, he was complicit in riots that left over one thousand Muslims dead—has gone from persona non grata in the United States to a strong political ally, his rags to riches story speaking to ambitious, affluent Indian Americans (see Mandhana). His election has ushered in a moment of resurgent Indian nationalism among Indians in the United States, particularly of the professional classes, that reinforces hierarchies of privilege and promotes ideologies of authenticity.[3] Because reading offers a particularly powerful cultural practice through which the future of South Asian America can be shaped, I believe it has the potential to provide a much-needed antidote to the nostalgic nationalism and ethnic insularity that Modi's election has incited.

This is not to downplay the fact that reading is a practice of South Asian American identity formation that could easily be subsumed into the neoliberal rhetoric of self-improvement, investment in education, and professionalism that Modi promotes and that is so popular among his Indian American fans. Practices of reading have the capacity to bolster these elements of twenty-first century South Asian American identity, and yet I am confident that they will also continue to provide the historical context that is necessary to challenge narrow thinking, to demonstrate the diversity of the South Asian American experience along lines of gender, sexuality, and religion, and most of all to promote open-minded discussion about the future of South Asian America among those invested in it.

As I hope I have made clear throughout this book, I am in general optimistic about the future of reading. I have no nostalgia for the past, nor, in contrast to some public intellectuals and institutions, do I lament some supposed decline of reading in the modern world.[4] In fact, it seems to me that while practices of reading are changing and dynamic (as they have always been), they continue to manifest socially and privately (as they long have), and they are, in these varied, new and old forms, expanding rather than contracting. As illustrated by recent popular literary phenomenon, such as the Oprah Winfrey book club's culture wars, the denunciation of the mainly female readers of *Fifty Shades of Grey* or the *Twilight* series as antifeminist, gullible, cultural dupes, and the ongoing and unapologetic canonization of white authors in yet another "best of" list, practices of reading, communally, individually, and institutionally remain crucially relevant to the vagaries of commodity culture and its gendered and racialized judgments, values, and meanings.[5]

The work that remains to be done as we think about reading and readership is to explore how readers use literature in complex, meaningful, and messy ways to understand themselves, each other, the world they live in, and worlds they cannot (but might do well to) imagine. This book asks its own readers to take this simple, expansive view of reading as a shared point of departure. I advocate, in my closing thoughts, for a capacious view of reading, not as an anointed, elite tradition but as a living and breathing cultural practice. A practice that prompts those of us who love to read, in one form or another, to examine the nature of that love and to ask how the seemingly beneficial (or at the very least benign) practice of reading entails conscious and unconscious omission, division, and self-interest just as often as it fosters inclusion, connection, and empathy. In this ambivalence, I can comfortably reside.

APPENDIX 1

LIST OF INTERVIEWEES

Alias	Date of Meeting	Gender and Self-Identified Ethnic Description
Manju	10/22/2005	Female, Indian American
Moira	10/27/2005	Female, South Asian American
Madhu	11/14/2005	Female, Indian
Sujata	7/7/2006	Female, Pakistani American
Sunil	6/16/2006	Male, Bengali or South Asian American
Nishi	6/11/2006	Female, Pakistani American
Raj	7/12/2006, 12/12/2009	Male, Bengali or South Asian American
Priya	7/14/2006	Female, South Asian American
Meera	7/15/2006	Female, South Asian American
Padma	9/10/2006	Female, South Asian American
Pooja	9/10/2006	Female, Indian American
Priti	9/11/2006	Female, Indian
Ash	9/12/2006	Female, Indian
Ajay	9/12/2006	Male, Indian
Raima	10/11/2006	Female, Pakistani American
Anil	10/12/2006	Male, South Asian American
Lalita	10/13/2006	Female, South Asian American
Monali	11/7/2006	Female, Indian American
Sri	10/8/2009	Female, Indian American
Rinki	11/27/2009	Female, Sikh American

Alias	Date of Meeting	Gender and Self-Identified Ethnic Description
Aarthi	12/5/2009	Female, South Indian, or South Asian American
Afrah	3/6/2010	Female, Punjabi and South Indian and Indian Canadian, educated and raised in Hong Kong
Maya	2/18/2010	Female, Punjabi and Indian
Sneha	3/27/2010	Female, Sri Lankan
Uma	3/27/2010	Female, Bengali and South Asian American
Rakesh	3/27/2010	Male, Jaipuri, Rajasthani and Indian
Gayatri	3/28/2010	Female, Punjabi and Indian American or South Asian American
Meena	5/1/2010	Female, Indian
Pawan	5/2/2010	Male, Punjabi and Indian
Arya	5/2/2010	Female, Punjabi and Indian or South Asian American

APPENDIX 2

BOOK CLUB MEETINGS ATTENDED (2006–2007, 2009–2010)

Book	Author	Date	Number of Participants
The Feast of Roses	Indu Sundaresan	5/11/2006	7
The Red Letters	Ved Mehta	6/8/2006	6
Two Lives	Vikram Seth	7/13/2006	5
The Red Carpet	Lavanya Sankaran	9/14/2006	25
The Royal Ghosts	Samrat Upadhyay	10/12/2006	3
The Inheritance of Loss	Kiran Desai	11/9/2006	10
Nectar in a Sieve	Kamala Markandaya	2/8/2007	10
In Other Rooms, Other Wonders	Daniyal Mueenuddin	10/8/2009	11
Three Cups of Tea	Greg Mortenson and David Oliver Relin	11/12/2009	14
Delhi Noir	Hirsh Sawhney, Ed.	12/10/2009	23
Cutting for Stone	Abraham Verghese	1/14/2010	5
The Marriage Bureau for Rich People	Farahad Zama	2/18/2010	11
The Hamilton Case	Michelle de Kretser	3/12/2010	5

APPENDIX 3

COMPLETE LIST OF BOOKS READ BY THE NETSAP DC BOOK CLUB, 1998–2014

Month	Title	Author	Fiction / Nonfiction	Country of Setting	Gender of Author
2014					
January	*The Lowland* (2013)	Jhumpa Lahiri	Fiction	India / United States	Female
February	*The Billionaire's Apprentice* (2013)	Anita Raghavan	Nonfiction	United States	Female
March	*And the Mountains Echoed* (2013)	Khaled Hosseini	Fiction	Afghanistan / France / United States	Male
April	*How to Get Filthy Rich in Rising Asia* (2013)	Mohsin Hamid	Fiction	Fictional Country, Like Pakistan	Male
May	*The In-Between World of Vikram Lall* (2003)	M. G. Vassanji	Fiction	Kenya / Canada	Male
June	*The Great Tamasha: Cricket, Corruption, and the Turbulent Rise of Modern India* (2013)	James Astill	Nonfiction	India	Male

Month	Title	Author	Fiction / Nonfiction	Country of Setting	Gender of Author
July	*The Hundred-Foot Journey* (2011)	Richard Morais	Fiction	India, French Alps	Male
August	*Family Life* (2014)	Akhil Sharma	Fiction	India, United States	Male
September	*Calcutta: Two Years in the City* (2013)	Amit Chaudhuri	Nonfiction	India	Male
October	*The True American* (2014)	Anand Ghiridharadas	Nonfiction	United States	Male
November	*On Sal Mal Lane* (2013)	Ru Freeman	Fiction	Sri Lanka	Female
December	*The Last Taxi Ride*	A. X. Ahmad	Fiction	United States	Male
2013					
January	*Instant City: Life and Death in Karachi* (2012)	Steve Inskeep	Nonfiction	Pakistan	Male
February	*The World We Found* (2012)	Thrity Umrigar	Fiction	India	Female
March	*Passage to India* (1924)	E. M. Forster	Fiction	India	Male
April	*One World Schoolhouse* (2012)	Salman Khan	Nonfiction	United States	Male
May	*Family Matters* (2003)	Rohinton Mistry	Fiction	India	Male
June	*Gang Leader for a Day: A Rogue Sociologist Takes to the Streets* (2008)	Sudhir Venkatesh	Nonfiction	United States	Male
July	*The Folded Earth* (2011)	Anuradha Roy	Fiction	India	Female
August	*Joseph Anton* (2013)	Salman Rushdie	Nonfiction	India, England, United States	Male

Month	Title	Author	Fiction / Nonfiction	Country of Setting	Gender of Author
September	*English, August: An Indian Story* (1988)	Upamanyu Chatterjee	Fiction	India	Male
October	*Partitions* (2011)	Amit Majmudar	Fiction	India / Pakistan	Male
November	*Swami and Friends* (1935)	R. K. Narayan	Fiction	India	Male
December	*A Walk Across the Sun* (2012)	Corban Addison	Fiction	India	Male
2012					
January	*River of Smoke* (2011)	Amitav Ghosh	Fiction	India	Male
February	*American Veda* (2010)	Philip Goldberg	Nonfiction	United States	Male
March	*Letters from Burma* (1998)	Aung San Suu Kyi	Nonfiction	Burma	Female
April	*An Atlas of Impossible Longing* (2008)	Anuradha Roy	Fiction	India	Female
May	*Last Man in Tower* (2011)	Aravind Adiga	Fiction	India	Male
June	*Monsoon* (2010)	Robert Kaplan	Nonfiction	Indian Ocean	Male
July	*The Wandering Falcon* (2011)	Jamil Ahmad	Fiction	Afghan-Pakistan Border	Male
August	*The Home and the World* (1916)	Rabindranath Tagore	Fiction	India	Male
September	*Behind the Beautiful Forevers* (2012)	Katherine Boo	Nonfiction	India	Female
October	*The Guide* (1958)	R. K. Narayan	Fiction	India	Male
November	*Mumbai Fables: A History of an Enchanted City* (2010)	Gyan Prakash	Nonfiction	India	Male

Month	Title	Author	Fiction / Nonfiction	Country of Setting	Gender of Author
December	*The Man Who Knew Infinity* (1991)	Robert Kanigel	Nonfiction	India and England	Male
2011					
January	*Creating a World without Poverty* (2008)	Muhammad Yunus	Nonfiction	Bangladesh	Male
February	*Field Notes on Democracy* (2009)	Arundhati Roy	Nonfiction	India	Female
March	*The Mimic Men* (1967)	V. S. Naipaul	Fiction	India / Caribbean / London	Male
April	*The Great Partition* (2007)	Yasmin Khan	Nonfiction	India / Pakistan	Female
May	*Complications* (2003)	Atul Gawande	Nonfiction	United States	Male
June	*Stones into Schools* (2010)	Greg Mortenson	Nonfiction	Afghanistan	Male
July	*Luka and the Fire of Life* (2010)	Salman Rushdie	Fiction	Fictional Setting	Male
August	*India Calling* (2011)	Anand Giridharadas	Nonfiction	India	Male
September	*State of Wonder* (2011)	Ann Patchett	Fiction	Amazon	Female
October	*The Emperor of All Maladies* (2010)	Siddhartha Mukherje	Nonfiction	United States	Male
November	*The Good Muslim* (2011)	Tahmima Anam	Fiction	Bangladesh	Female
December	*Great Soul* (2011)	Joseph Lelyveld	Nonfiction	India	Male
2010					
January	*Cutting for Stone* (2009)	Abraham Verghese	Fiction	Ethiopia	Male

Month	Title	Author	Fiction / Nonfiction	Country of Setting	Gender of Author
February	*The Marriage Bureau for Rich People* (2010)	Farahad Zama	Fiction	India	Male
March	*The Hamilton Case* (2003)	Michele de Kretser	Fiction	Sri Lanka	Female
April	*Indian Summer* (2008)	Alex Von Tunzelmann	Nonfiction	India	Female
May	*AIDS Sutra* (2008)	Anthology	Nonfiction	India	Mixed
June	*Daughter of the Ganges* (2007)	Asha Miro	Nonfiction	India	Female
July	*Family Planning* (2008)	Karan Mahajan	Fiction	India	Male
August	*The Weight of Heaven* (2009)	Thrity Umrigar	Fiction	India	Female
September	*One Amazing Thing* (2010)	Chitra Divakaruni	Fiction	India	Female
October	*Imagining India* (2010)	Nandan Nilekani	Nonfiction	India	Male
November	*Nine Lives* (2010)	William Dalrymple	Nonfiction	India	Male
December	*The Calcutta Chromosome* (2001)	Amitav Chosh	Fiction	India	Male
2009					
January	*Sea of Poppies* (2009)	Amitav Ghosh	Fiction	India and Diaspora	Male
February	*The Enchantress of Florence* (2009)	Salman Rushdie	Fiction	India	Male
March	*Palace of Illusions* (2009)	Chitra Divakaruni	Fiction	India	Female
April	*Q&A* (2005)	Vikas Swarup	Fiction	India	Male
May	*Marrying Anita* (2009)	Anita Jain	Nonfiction	India / United States	Female

Month	Title	Author	Fiction / Nonfiction	Country of Setting	Gender of Author
June	*Evening Is the Whole Day* (2009)	Preeta Samarasan	Fiction	Malaysia	Female
July	*A Case of Exploding Mangoes* (2010)	Mohammed Hanif	Fiction	Pakistani	Male
August	*In Spite of the Gods* (2008)	Edward Luce	Nonfiction	India	Male
September	*Burnt Shadows* (2009)	Kamila Shamsie	Fiction	Japan and Pakistan	Female
October	*In Other Rooms, Other Wonders* (2009)	Daniyal Mueenuddin	Fiction	Pakistan	Male
November	*Three Cups of Tea* (2006)	Greg Mortenson	Nonfiction	Afghanistan	Male
December	*Delhi Noir* (2009)	Hirsh Sawney, Ed.	Fiction	India	Mixed authors
2008					
January	*The World Is Flat* (2007)	Thomas Friedman	Nonfiction	N/A	Male
February	*A Thousand Splendid Suns* (2008)	Khaled Hosseini	Fiction	Afghanistan	Male
March	*The Reluctant Fundamentalist* (2009)	Mohsin Hamid	Fiction	United States / Pakistan	Male
April	*The Perfect Man* (2006)	Naeem Murr	Fiction	United States	Male
May	*Gifted* (2008)	Nikita Lalwani	Fiction	United States / England	Female
June	*Unaccustomed Earth* (2008)	Jhumpa Lahiri	Fiction	United States and England	Female
July	*If Today Be Sweet* (2008)	Thrity Umrigar	Fiction	India and United States	Female
August	*A Good Indian Wife* (2008)	Anne Cherian	Fiction	India and United States	Female

Month	Title	Author	Fiction / Nonfiction	Country of Setting	Gender of Author
September	*A Golden Age* (2008)	Tahmima Anam	Fiction	Bangladesh	Female
October	*Animal's People* (2009)	Indra Sinha	Fiction	India	Male
November	*The Last Song of Dusk* (2006)	Siddarth Dhanvant Shanghvi	Fiction	India	Male
December	*The White Tiger* (2008)	Aravind Adiga	Fiction	India	Male
2007					
January	*Ramayan* (2004)	Ramesh Menon	Fiction	India	Male
February	*Nectar in a Sieve* (1954)	Kamala Markandya	Fiction	India	Female
March	*The Argumentative Indian* (2006)	Amartya Sen	Nonfiction	Indian culture	Male
April	*Storywallah* (2004)	Shyam Selvadurai	Fiction	Mix, short story collection	Male
May	*Saturday Morning Omelets* (2006)	Kavita Khanna	Fiction	India and United States	Female
June	*Under Her Skin* (2004)	Ed Pooka Makhijani	Nonfiction	United States	Female
July	*Sacred Games* (2007)	Vikram Chandra	Fiction	India	Male
August	*Husband of a Fanatic* (2005)	Amitava Kumar	Nonfiction	India, Pakistan, and United States	Male
September	*A Space Between Us* (2007)	Thrity Umrigar	Fiction	India	Female
October	*Climbing the Mango Tree: A Memoir of Childhood in India* (2007)	Madhur Jaffrey	Nonfiction	India	Female

Month	Title	Author	Fiction / Nonfiction	Country of Setting	Gender of Author
November	*Splendor of Silence* (2006)	Indu Sundaresan	Fiction	India	Female
December	*Ramayan* (2004)	Ramesh Menon	Fiction	India	Male
2006					
January	*Maximum City* (2005)	Suketu Mehta	Nonfiction	India	Male
February	*Shalimar the Clown* (2006)	Salman Rushdie	Fiction	India and the United States	Male
March	*The Kite Runner* (2004)	Khalid Hosseini	Fiction	Afghanistan	Male
April	*If You Are Afraid of Heights* (2005)	Raj Kamal Jha	Fiction	India	Male
May	*Feast of Roses* (2003)	Indu Sundaresan	Fiction	India	Female
June	*The Red Letters* (2004)	Ved Mehta	Nonfiction	India	Male
July	*Two Lives* (2005)	Vikram Seth	Nonfiction	India and Germany	Male
August	*The Rice Mother* (2004)	Rani Manicka	Fiction	Sri Lanka and Malaysia	Female
September	*The Red Carpet* (2006)	Lavanya Sankaran	Fiction	India	Female
October	*The Royal Ghosts* (2006)	Samrat Upadhyay	Fiction	Nepal	Male
November	*The Great Indian Novel* (1993)	Shashi Tharoor	Fiction	India	Male
December	*The Sari Shop* (2004)	Rupa Bajwa	Fiction	India	Female
2005					
January	*Brick Lane* (2003)	Monica Ali	Fiction	England, Bangladesh	Female
February	*Suburban Sahibs* (2003)	S. Mitra Kalita	Nonfiction	United States	Female

Month	Title	Author	Fiction / Nonfiction	Country of Setting	Gender of Author
March	*Where Are You From?* (2003)	Dhooleka Raj	Nonfiction	London	Female
April	*Freedom Song* (2000)	Amit Chaudhari	Fiction	India and England	Male
May	*Such a Long Journey* (1991)	Rohinton Mistry	Fiction	India and Bangladesh	Male
June	*Memories of Rain* (1994)	Sunetra Gupta	Fiction	India and London	Female
July	*Baumgartner's Bombay* (2000)	Anita Desai	Fiction	India and Germany	Female
August	*Sadhika's Way* (2004)	Hina Haq	Fiction	Pakistan and America	Female
September	*I Dream of Microwaves* (2004)	Imad Rahman	Fiction	Pakistan and America	Male
October	*Maps for Lost Lovers* (2005)	Nadeem Aslam	Fiction	Pakistan	Male
November	*Monsoon Diary* (2003)	Shobha Narayan	Nonfiction	India	Female
December	*Beneath a Marble Sky* (2006)	John Shors	Fiction	India	Male
2004					
January	*Born Confused* (2003)	Tanuja Hidier Desai	Fiction	United States	Female
February	*The Shadow Lines* (2005)	Amitav Ghosh	Fiction	India and England	Male
March	*White Teeth* (2000)	Zadie Smith	Fiction	Britain	Female
April	*The Autobiography of an Unknown Indian* (1951)	Nirad Chaudhuri	Nonfiction	Bangladesh	Male
May	*A House for Mr. Biswas* (1961)	V. S. Naipaul	Fiction	Trinidad	Male
June	*Untouchable* (1935)	Mulk Raj Anand	Fiction	Indian	Male

Month	Title	Author	Fiction / Nonfiction	Country of Setting	Gender of Author
July	*Shame* (1983)	Salman Rushdie	Fiction	Pakistan	Male
August	*Madras on Rainy Days* (2004)	Samina Ali	Fiction	India	Female
September	*The Twentieth Wife* (2002)	Indu Sundaresan	Fiction	India	Female
October	*The Holder of the World* (1993)	Bharati Mukherjee	Fiction	India and United States	Female
November	*Clive Avenue*	T. S. Tirumurti	Fiction	India	Male
December	*Hero's Walk* (2002)	Anita Rau Badami	Fiction	India	Female
2003					
January	*A Fine Balance* (1995)	Rohinton Mistry	Fiction	India	Male
February	*Darjeeling* (2002)	Bharti Kirchner	Fiction	India and United States	Female
March	*Train to Pakistan* (1956)	Khushwant Singh	Fiction	India and Pakistan	Male
April	*Heat and Dust* (1975)	Ruth Prawer Jhabvala	Fiction	India	Female
May	*The Unknown Errors of Our Lives* (2001)	Chitra Banerjee Divakaruni	Fiction	India and United States	Female
June	*The Impressionist* (2003)	Hari Kunzru	Fiction	India, England, Africa	Male
July	*Manhattan Music* (1996)	Meena Alexander	Fiction	India and United States	Female
August	*A Singular Hostage* (2002)	Thalassa Ali	Fiction	India	Female
September	*Life of Pi* (2001)	Yann Martel	Fiction	India and Canada	Male
October	*White Mughals* (2002)	William Dalrymple	Nonfiction	India	Male

Month	Title	Author	Fiction / Nonfiction	Country of Setting	Gender of Author
November	*The Namesake* (2003)	Jhumpa Lahiri	Fiction	United States	Female
December	*The Golden Gate* (1986)	Vikram Seth	Fiction	United States	Male
2002					
January	*A Suitable Boy* (1994)	Vikram Seth	Fiction	India	Male
February	*A Suitable Boy*: Part 2	Vikram Seth	Fiction		
March	*Difficult Daughters* (2009)	Manju Kapur	Fiction	India and Pakistan	Female
April	*Age of Kali* (1999)	William Dalrymple	Fiction	India	Male
May	*Salt and Saffron* (2002)	Kamila Shamsie	Fiction	Pakistan and United States	Female
June	*Anil's Ghost* (2000)	Michael Ondaatje	Fiction	Sri Lanka	Male
July	*Fasting Feasting* (2000)	Anita Desai	Fiction	India and United States	Female
August	*Riot* (2002)	Shashi Tharoor	Fiction	India	Male
September	*The Moor's Last Sigh* (1995)	Salman Rushdie	Fiction	India	Male
October	*Romantics* (1999)	Pankaj Mishra	Fiction	India	Male
November	*The House of Blue Mangoes* (2003)	David Davidar	Fiction	India	Male
December	*The Buddha of Suburbia* (1991)	Hanif Kureishi	Fiction	England	Male
2001					
January	*A Bend in the River* (1989)	V. S. Naipaul	Fiction	Africa	Male

Month	Title	Author	Fiction / Nonfiction	Country of Setting	Gender of Author
February	*Motiba's Tattoos* (2000)	Mira Kamdar	Nonfiction	India, Burma, United States	Female
March	*The Story of My Experiments with the Truth* (1957)	Mohandas K. Gandhi	Nonfiction	India	Male
April	*Curry Coast* (1999)	Binoo K. John	Nonfiction	India	Male
May	*Chakori* (1999)	Chandrasekhar Kambar	Fiction	Indian	Male
June	*Bolo! Bolo!* (2001)	Anthology	Mixed	Mixed	Mixed
July	*The Death of Vishnu* (2002)	Manil Suri	Fiction	India	Male
August	*Samsara* (2000)	Rajiv Vrudhula	Fiction	United States	Male
September	*Glass Palace* (2002)	Amitav Ghosh	Fiction	Burma	Male
October	*The Karma of Brown Folk* (2001)	Vijay Prashad	Nonfiction	United States	Male
November	*Moth Smoke* (2001)	Mohsin Hamid	Fiction	Pakistan	Male
December	*Malgudi Days* (1943)	R. K. Narayan	Fiction	India	Male
2000					
January	*Homework* (1999)	Suneeta Perez de Costa	Fiction	Australia	Female
February	*Reef* (1996)	Romesh Gunesekra	Fiction	Sri Lanka	Male
March	*In Light of India* (1998)	Octavio Paz	Fiction (Poetry)	India	Male
April	*Beach Boy* (1997)	Ardashir Vakil	Fiction	India	Male

Month	Title	Author	Fiction / Nonfiction	Country of Setting	Gender of Author
May	*The Snake Charmer* (1999)	Sanjay Nigam	Fiction	India	Male
June	*The Blue Bedspread* (1999)	Raj Kamal Jha	Fiction	India	Male
July	*My Own Country* (1994)	Abraham Verghese	Nonfiction	United States	Male
August	*Cinnamon Gardens* (1998)	Shyam Selvadurai	Fiction	Sri Lanka	Male
September	*Junglee Girl* (1995)	Ginu Kamani	Fiction	India	Female
October	*Meatless Days* (1991)	Sara Suleri	Nonfiction	Pakistan	Female
November	*Pilgrimage* (2000)	Pramila Jayapal	Nonfiction	India	Female
December	*Cracking India* (1991)	Bapsi Sidhwa	Fiction	Pakistan	Female
1999					
January	*Love and Longing in Bombay* (1998)	Vikram Chandra	Fiction	India (Bombay)	Male
February	*Arranged Marriages* (1995)	Chitra Bannerji Divakaruni	Fiction	United States and India	Female
March	*Midnight's Children* (1981)	Salman Rushdie	Fiction	India	Male
April	*Arrow of the Blue Skinned God* (2000)	Jonah Blank	Nonfiction	India	Male
May	*Midnight to the Millennium* (1998)	Shashi Tharoor	Nonfiction	India	Male
June	*May You Be the Mother of a Hundred Sons* (1991)	Elisabeth Bumiller	Nonfiction	India	Female

Month	Title	Author	Fiction / Nonfiction	Country of Setting	Gender of Author
July	*Shiva Dancing* (1999)	Bharti Kirchner	Fiction	India and United States	Female
August	*Hullabaloo in the Guava Orchard* (1999)	Kiran Desai	Fiction	India	Female
September	*The Invisibles* (1998)	Zia Jaffrey	Nonfiction	India	Female
October	*Snakes and Ladders* (1997)	Gita Mehta	Nonfiction	India	Female
November	*What the Body Remembers* (2001)	Shauna Singh Baldwin	Fiction	India and Pakistan	Female
December	*Interpreter of Maladies* (1999)	Jhumpa Lahiri	Fiction	India and United States	Female
1998					
October	*The God of Small Things* (1997)	Arundhati Roy	Fiction	India and United States	Female
November	*Tennis Partner* (1999)	Abraham Verghese	Nonfiction	United States	Male

APPENDIX 4

INTERVIEW QUESTIONS FOR NETSAP BOOK CLUB INTERVIEWEES

General Reading Practice

1. Would you describe yourself as an avid reader? If so, then why do you like reading? How does it enhance your life? If not, are there reasons why not? Are you too busy, are there other things you enjoy doing more?
2. What are your favorite genres to read? What kinds of books do you usually enjoy? Do you like fiction, Nonfiction, poetry, drama, newspapers, magazines?

Transnational South Asian Literature

3. Do you have a specific interest in transnational South Asian literature? What are some of the authors that you have read? Please list as many names as you can remember off the top of your head.
4. Who among those writers are your favorites? Can you tell me why?
5. Do you like to read lots of multiethnic literatures or is transnational South Asian writing your primary preference? What other kinds of multiethnic literatures interest you? Why? What is it that you enjoy about reading them?
6. What initially compelled your interest in transnational South Asian literature? Was there anything in particular you were hoping to learn or find out about yourself and/or your identity by reading this literature?
7. Are there any particular themes that you see repeated in this body of literature? If so, can you name a few of them? Can you tell me a few

of the books that you've seen those themes repeated in? Have you given any thought as to why these themes may repeat?

8. What do you think about those themes? Do you think that they are important and informative, and do you think they provide accurate representations of transnational South Asian culture? Can you give me some specific examples of where they might be accurate and where they might be a bit unfounded?
9. Do you think that transnational South Asian literature has an impact on the social or political lives of South Asians in the United States? If so, in what senses?
10. What is the benefit of describing a shared experience? If it is common to all of us, what is the use in reading about it?

Transnational South Asian Literature, Identity, and Reading Practices

11. Does transnational South Asian literature tell readers of South Asian descent anything valuable about their transnational identities? Has it helped you figure anything out about your identity? If so, what is it? If not, what does it leave out?
12. Do you think that people who aren't of South Asian descent would have any interest in transnational South Asian literature? If so why? Do you know people who are interested in the literature? What writers in particular seem to interest them?
13. What compels interest in transnational South Asian literature outside of the community of South Asian diasporics? Why do you think people of other races and ethnicities might be interested in reading this body of literature? Could they learn anything from it?
14. Do you think there is a difference between the transnational South Asian writers that people who are South Asian like and those who non-South Asians might like? Can you give me specific examples of which writers you're thinking of?

NetSAP Book Club

15. How long have you been involved in the NetSAP book club? How many meetings have you attended?
16. Why did you get involved in the NetSAP book club?
17. How do you decide which meetings to attend?
18. What have been some of your favorite meetings/discussions? Which books have those meetings centered on?
19. Have you ever been a part of any other book clubs?

20. Do you attend other NetSAP events?
21. Why do you think that this book club formed around South Asian identity? What do you think the purpose of forming book clubs around an ethnic identity might be?
22. What do you think of the conversations at the book club meetings? Do they generally meet your expectations?

NOTES

Introduction. Mad for Difference

1. Scholars such as Elizabeth Long who study reading and readership concur that reading, although often a practice associated with loneliness or a desire for solitude, has historically been a very social activity, supported institutionally and socially by familial relationships, classrooms, and universities (31, 11).

2. See, for example, Grewal, 35–79, Narayan, 1–11, and Srikanth, *World*, 1–48.

3. The term "South Asian" itself, much like any other panethnic formulation, brings together disparate traditions, cultures, and histories of the region, representing the nations of India, Pakistan, Nepal, Bhutan, Bangladesh, Sri Lanka, Myanmar, and Maldives as members of a subcontinental region.

4. Throughout this book I use the term "transnational" and "diasporic" to describe two different but interrelated elements of South Asian identity and culture in the United States. I use the term "diaspora" and "diasporic identity" to describe the experiences of South Asian subjects who have established communities outside of the national contexts of South Asia. Taking my cues from the book club, throughout this study I use the term "transnational" most often when describing the South Asian literature selected by NetSAP book club participants. In other words, "transnational" is a term I invoke to describe the cultural production of South Asian migrants across the globe. Unlike more specific terms such as "Indian American fiction," "South Asian immigrant fiction," or "South Asian postcolonial literature," the term "transnational" reflects the expansive swath of literature that NetSAP book clubs select—literature that deals in themes related to South Asia and its corresponding circulation among a variety of national contexts in the subcontinent, the United States, the UK, Canada, Africa, and the Caribbean. In this, I

employ the term "transnational" as Grewal defines it, to describe "the networks of knowledge and power [. . .] that traversed and rearticulated national boundaries" (3), in this case particularly through literature and practices of reading.

5. I borrow from Melamed's succinct definition of the term "neoliberal multiculturalism." Multiculturalism, she argues, took on the global reach and market-based ideologies of neoliberalism, thus coalescing in "neoliberal multiculturalism" as "a market ideology turned social philosophy" (138). Furthermore, as Pamela Thoma explains, these economic policies are reflected in accompanying social philosophies that advocate for "the withdrawal of the welfare state from social provision in favor of individual market behavior or 'freedom' and 'choice,' responsibility, and entrepreneurialism" (16).

6. Although the paradigm of the "American dream" may seem a salient theoretical omission from this book, I have found that the readers in the NetSAP book club never articulate their own subjectivity in relation to this paradigm, which I believe is in part because they or their families have already acquired economic and cultural capital.

7. See http://na.netip.org/partners. 14 June 2015.

8. The ongoing preoccupation in transnational South Asian communities and cultures, particularly in the middle and upper classes, with issues of representation emerges time and again as South Asian cultural production takes on increasing transnational and multicultural cache. In the United States, the prominence of South Asians in the media and popular culture has created a kind of testing ground for what kinds of representations are and are not acceptable.

9. All names of interviewees and book club participants are pseudonyms. Quotations have been edited for clarity.

10. While it is not an international best-seller, *The Hamilton Case* won the Tasmania Pacific Prize, the Encore Award (UK), and a regional Commonwealth Writer's prize in 2004 for Southeast Asia and the Pacific.

11. I aim to be as specific as possible whenever I can, but I also tend to use the term "South Asian" where applicable in order to defer to the usage preferred by readers in the NetSAP book club, who tend to use this term as a gesture toward intraethnic solidarity and community.

12. The terms "exotic" and "authentic" have come to mark South Asian difference in popular and literary cultures and are often dialectically connected. For the purposes of this study, I find that the first is often rendered subordinate to the second when readers are discussing these two terms, reflecting Salman Rushdie's characterization of the relationship between exoticism and authenticity in his landmark essay "Commonwealth Literature Does Not Exist." He argues that a desire for exoticism in South Asian literature often obscures a deeper, foundational desire for the authentic. Both terms derive from the commodification of homogenous, static notions of traditional culture—in Rushdie's words, "Authenticity is the respectable child of old-fashioned exoticism" (*Imaginary Homelands*, 67).

13. Throughout this book, I draw heavily in my use of the terms "ethnicity" and "race" on Michael Omi and Howard Winant's foundational work *Racial Formation in the United States* (1994). I refer to South Asian ethnic identity and ethnicity when I intend to disaggregate South Asians culturally from the larger racial paradigm of Asian America. Conversely, I invoke the terminology of race and racialization when I want to indicate South Asian American connections to the racial formation of Asian Americans. As Omi and Winant define it, the process of "racial formation" or "racialization" is "the sociohistorical process by which racial categories are created, inhabited, transformed, and destroyed" (55). They emphasize that "race is a matter of both social structure and cultural representation" (56). When I describe South Asian American identity as a race identity or a racialized group, I am speaking of how this group is recognized through state policy, political action, and public representation (22–23).

14. Gayatri's response can be seen as an example of Kandice Chuh's notion of the "subjectlessness" of Asian American identity formation (10).

15. Perhaps this duality in their reading is a function, at least in part, of the fact these primarily Indian readers are here analyzing a Sri Lankan (rather than Indian) text. However, situating this conversation among the broader ethnography of readership on which this book is based demonstrates that a desire for familiar and strange representations pervades NetSAP book club participants' practice of reading.

16. Stephen W. Foster captures the paradoxes of the exotic configured as the authentic when he describes the exotic as "what is assigned to the unfamiliar, derived from what is close at hand" (22).

17. As Monisha Das Gupta points out, it is a discourse that can be employed to build "alternative cultures," cultures that allow "survivors of domestic abuse, single mothers, divorced or single women, queers, domestic workers, and taxi drivers" to feel that "they too are South Asians and that their stories are also part of the immigrant story" (61).

18. Notions of ethnic authenticity can also authorize intraethnic exclusions that do not account for women who are oppressed, individuals with nonheteronormative sexualities, or working-class South Asians, thereby perpetuating South Asian marginalization in the United States by objectifying "difference" and fetishizing "origins" (Maira "Ideologies of Authenticity," 142).

19. The specter of essentialization has long plagued the reception of multiethnic literatures, ambivalently popularizing the work of particular minority writers as "authentic" and realistic while also confining them to narrow, representative positions (Karem 15).

20. For similar arguments, see Grewal and Palumbo-Liu, *Ethnic*.

21. The NetSAP book club in Washington, DC, is one of only two regional chartered chapters (the other is Boston) out of twenty-four total chapters that have chosen to replace the term "Indian" with the term "South Asian." Both of the

NetSAP DC book club leaders that I interviewed for this project emphasized that they were conscious of this deviation from NetIP norms and supported it. They explained that they felt the term "South Asian" attracted a broader base of book club participants and made the group more inclusive. Additionally, the South Asian construction of the group encouraged participants to select more diverse books. According to the organization's by-laws, each regional, chartered chapter is free to alter the name to express whichever affiliation its founding leaders deem appropriate (test.netip.org/aboutus/bylaws).

22. test.netip.org/aboutus/our-mission.

23. As I discuss in more detail in chapter 1, the DC-based book club constitutes and organizes a significant amount of NetSAP DC's cultural programming. Notably, only eight chapters—those in Philadelphia, DC, Chicago, Atlanta, Dallas, Seattle, Miami, and New York—currently have an active book club.

24. From 2000 through 2010 the DC metropolitan area had the third-largest South Asian population in the United States as reported in "A Demographic Snapshot of South Asians in the United States," published by South Asian Americans Leading Together and the Asian American Federation. http://saalt.org/wp-content/uploads/2012/09/Demographic-Snapshot-Asian-American-Foundation-2012.pdf.

25. www.si.edu/about.

26. The sociality of these groups is often based in shared values, tastes, locations, privilege, and a desire for community (see Radway, *Reading*, and Long).

27. The neutrality and privileges of whiteness that are often associated with book club culture render the class and racial aspects of book club formation unremarkable. Long (59–73) provides a detailed historical account of why book clubs in the United States are the purview of white, middle-class, women. In *Reading Up: Middle-Class Readers and the Culture of Success in the Early Twentieth Century United States* (2012), Amy Blair explores the formation of cultures of taste among mainly white, middle-class readers in the late nineteenth and early twentieth centuries. And finally, Janice Radway's *A Feeling for Books* focuses on the creation of white, middlebrow culture through the buying services and taste arbitration of the Book of the Month Club.

28. For example, when I was conducting my ethnography, readers chose Booker Prize–winning novel *The Inheritance of Loss* by Kiran Desai as well as *The Royal Ghosts*, a collection of short stories by Nepalese author Samrat Upadhyay.

29. The primary form of communication among book club members during the time I conducted my research was a Yahoo group Listserv. Calls for hosting and information about the book club were emailed to members via group Listserv. The group never really shifted to using Facebook in lieu of the Listserv. Notably, however, the nonprofit as a whole has a very large Facebook presence. NetSAP DC's Facebook page, for example, reports 3146 members as of October 2016, whereas only 68 people have "liked" the NetSAP DC book club Facebook page. NetSAP DC book club meetings are announced on the Facebook page, but

in order to attend one must have access to the information on the Yahoo Listserv so that one can RSVP to the host for that month and learn where the discussion is taking place.

30. I never took an official poll of the ethnic or religious constituency of the members attending a given book club meeting because I felt it would be disruptive, but readers would often reveal their national and diasporic affiliations during the course of conversation. See appendix 1 for more detail.

31. http://test.netip.org/partners.

32. In *A Feeling for Books* Radway elucidates the links between reading and social mobility through an analysis of the iconic mail order subscription service provided by the Book of the Month Club. The service was a cultural institution that created a community of readers for whom the practice of reading was inexorably bound to what Radway terms a kind of "social pedagogy" (15). Similarly, in *Reading Up* Blair traces how literature in the early twentieth century served "as a guide to middle-class life" (19). In both cases, the practice of reading takes on a pedagogic function. It initiates a class of middle-class professionals working in information and culture industries, along with individuals who aspired to partake of this professional status, into middlebrow culture.

33. And yet clearly this controversy was not solely about identifying the rightful arbiters of literary taste in the United States. Laura Miller argues that it shows how gender continues to divide American book culture and exemplifies the stronghold of submerged class anxieties in the American reading public. As she explains it, the debate gives voice to a pervasive divide in America's book culture: "One side sees itself as scorned by a snotty self-styled elite and the other sees itself as keepers of the literary flame, neglected by a vulgarian mainstream that would rather wallow in mediocrity and dreck" (2).

34. However, as Bishnupriya Ghosh points out in a gloss on Brennan's work, even Brennan concedes that cosmopolitan literary production is diverse and contradictory: it is commercial, multicultural, and exploitative of the third-world "other" but it also has the potential to launch a radical critique of these geopolitical power differentials (20).

35. See Robbins and Cheah 31, Ghosh 22, and Rajan and Sharma 18.

36. In *Distinction: A Social Critique of the Judgment of Taste* (1984), Bourdieu links his empirical studies of culture to a theorization of how individuals' judgments on elements of culture, such as art, museum-going, literature, language, décor, and entertainment is both an expression and consolidation of one's position in the social hierarchy. As he says, "Taste classifies, and it classifies the classifier. Social subjects, classified by their classifications, distinguish themselves by the distinctions they make, between the beautiful and the ugly, the distinguished and the vulgar, in which their position in the objective classifications is expressed or betrayed" (6). Bourdieu's theory of "habitus," which is crucial to this study, explains an individual's propensity to feel comfortable or uncomfortable in particular set-

tings. Habitus refers to one's place in the objective social order according to where an individual places on the various, interrelated scales of social, economic, and cultural hierarchy. In this system of stratification, economic and cultural privilege are deeply interdependent: the system of cultural stratification is as determinative in shaping people's lives as is their differential relationship to the economy and material wealth (169–225).

37. I use the term "coethnic" throughout this book to denote the ethnic kinship that NetSAP book club readers feel with one another—a sense of shared, origin despite being from various regions and nations in South Asia.

38. This is not to discount the several examples of scholarship in South Asian American studies that focus on progressive politics and resistance to racial subjection. See Prashad, M. Das Gupta, Maira, *Desis*, S. Shankar, and Sharma.

39. For further information on debates surrounding the term "South Asian" see Desai, *Beyond* 5–9, Srikanth and Shankar 2–3, Srikanth, *The World* 3, and Mani, *Aspiring* 1–16. The term "South Asian" emerging from Cold War politics, levels the diversity in the region it describes. Additionally, among older generations, the term has done little to displace the more dominant and recognizable term "Indian." As Sunaina Maira observes, it is more common for first generation immigrants to see themselves as Indian or Indian American while their children and subsequent generations may identify with broader coalitional identities ("Henna" 113). In a similar vein, Srikanth notes that regardless of whether they live in the region or abroad, South Asians often define themselves in national, linguistic, religious, and regional rather than in panethnic terms (2–3).

40. There is a third term that is popular largely within the South Asian community in the United States: "desi." "Desi" describes South Asians who have emigrated from the subcontinent, deriving from the Sanskrit word "desh," or "homeland." I do not employ this term in the book because it is not a term that NetSAP book club participants regularly use to describe their diasporic experiences.

41. For a summary of how the framework of resistance and accommodation has come to shape Asian American cultural politics, see Thoma 28–29.

42. See, for example, Chuh 10, Chow 13, Kang 20, and Nguyen 7.

43. For critiques of how this binary of the "good" and "bad" Asian American subject functions within the field of South Asian American studies, see Jain 240, Maira, "Ideologies" 360, and Mani, *Aspiring* 13.

44. See Dave et al.

45. While South Asia is not a former U.S. colony, there is much to study in terms of US imperial and military interest in the region (Maira, *Missing* 27–28).

46. Arguably, in general the trend is shifting toward devoting more attention to the cognitive, affective, and ethnographic affects of literary texts, to "acknowledge[ing] the different goals of various reading practices and the different kinds of subjectivity that they call into being" (Sweeney 17). For more information on empathetic or transformative modes of reading, see Felski 25,

Kaplan 13, and Long 145. In the field of Asian American studies see Palumbo-Liu, *Deliverance*.

47. Warner invokes a heuristic division between "uncritical" and "critical" practices of reading in order to subvert it, emphasizing that all reading practices "are embedded within and organized by ethical projects for cultivating one kind of person or another" ("Uncritical Reading"19). Felski argues that one way to understand the dubious binary opposition between the theological (the tendency to read as if literature is at its most transformative when it is read as unique and separate from the social world) and the ideological (the notion that the best literature is positioned "squarely in the social world") is through the persistent interpretive debate about whether responses to literature are best framed experientially or analytically; even though these two categories are not discrete, they are often treated as if they were, or as Felski explains, in literary criticism one mode of reading usually tends to dominate any given interpretation (5). DeFazio argues that celebrations of affective, and experiential modes of reading unwittingly reproduce the binaries of the economy and proposes as an alternative a "labor theory of reading" that emphasizes that reading is always influenced by the historical conditions in which those readings are produced (3). Kaplan explains that critical feminist reading necessitates identification and disidentification with "textual mirrors" (33).

Chapter 1. The Glue That Keeps Us Together

1. As Omi and Winant explain, racial identity, as opposed to ethnic identity, makes manifest how a group is recognized through a process of racialization that informs state policy, political action, and public representation (55). I use the term "ethnicity" here to deliberately separate the ethnic and cultural self-identification of South Asian Americans in the NetSAP book club from the broader racial experiences of Asian Americans (23).

2. See also Bonus and Vo 18.

3. My focus on difference within this seemingly homogenous group evokes Lisa Lowe's foundational theorization of heterogeneity as central to the construction of Asian American identity and extends this concept specifically to the South Asian American experience. The NetSAP book club demonstrates that the production of South Asian American culture is community-based process informed by South Asian traditions, family histories, cultural mores, colonial histories, and a relationship to the dominant culture rather than an inheritable legacy, or as a set of traditions passed from one generation to the next (Lowe 65).

4. Writing in 1998, Koshy suggests that the study of race and ethnic identification within this group is particularly pressing because of the coming-of-age of the second generation of South Asians in the United States, who may grapple more directly with the political stakes of racial identification. This ethnography of readership suggests that Koshy's argument still holds true and that affluent

South Asians in the United States continue to identify themselves in ethnic and cultural terms rather than in terms of politicized racial constructs.

5. In 2011 the festival's organization came primarily under the auspices of the Smithsonian's Homespun Indian American Heritage Project, an initiative that sought to showcase the Indian American experience and that culminated in the creation of the *Beyond Bollywood* exhibit, which was on display at Smithsonian's National Museum of Natural History from 27 February 2014–16 August 2015 and was curated by the Smithsonian's Asian Pacific American Center. While this programming has been growing, SALTAF has not been held since 2011.

6. www.bigtent.com/groups/indus.

7. See http://dc.netip.org/about. "Our members come to NetIP for one important reason: the Human Connection. People join NetIP to forge lasting relationships with others and their community." The NetSAP book club has been an integral element in promoting and achieving the goal of community awareness because it has been one of the most continuous and significant elements of the broader nonprofit of NetSAP DC's "cultural awareness and preservation" programming.

8. As of January 2013 the reading list was no longer published on the NetSAP DC website. In fact, the websites for the regional chapters seem to have been pared down and standardized, and greater emphasis is now placed on using social media to help promote events and programs. Just as when I was conducting this research, the book club meeting dates and the process of selection are managed and announced largely through the Yahoo Listserv. However, now book club events are further promoted on NetSAP DC's Facebook page and a newly formed (and therefore lesser known) NetSAP DC book club Facebook page. The full reading list is available both through the Yahoo group and NetSAP DC book club's Facebook.

9. Of course, the overrepresentation of Indians in the book club reflects their majority status among South Asians in the United States.

10. The call center industry is controversial for several reasons. First, outsourcing has been an economically vexed issue between India and the United States in the twenty-first century. Second, as Rajini Srikanth explains, the call center phenomenon starkly illustrates the economic and cultural hegemony of the United States in the global market. Call center workers are asked to take on American personas and an American name, to go through training to adopt an "American" accent, and to familiarize themselves with American popular culture (*The World* 32). And finally, call centers have incited controversy in India, as young men and women are asked to work around the clock together, an arrangement that conflicts with traditional notions of decorum and propriety.

11. I borrow this concept from critical discourse analysis; it is in these differences that the complexities of the reading process emerge. See Benwell 151.

Chapter 2. There's a Whole Other Class

1. The model minority paradigm is problematic for several reasons: it undermines Asian American connections other minority groups, and it obscures the 1965 Immigration Act legislation that favored Asians and South Asians with a mastery of English and other professional and social advantages. South Asian American achievement is coded as a success story made possible by the opportunities available in this benevolent, colorblind meritocracy when in fact it is the a result of the highly skilled labor force of English-speaking South Asian engineers, doctors, and computers scientists who benefited from this legislation. The central irony of the model minority paradigm is that the United States takes credit for achievements that are largely the result of South Asian Americans' education in their countries of origin. And finally, model minority discourse perpetuates a troubling legacy of class-based stereotypes for Asian Americans, advancing the idea (as does its opposite stereotype, the yellow peril) that "Asian achievements" are of an "inhuman" or even "species-different character" (Kibria 133).

2. Several sociological studies on this population observe that affluent South Asians in the United States celebrate their elite status and accept the narrative of the model minority that is frequently attached to their success (Bhatia 189; Prashad, *Karma* 6). The model minority myth produces two competing and prevalent views on South Asian American racial formation. On the one hand, as Susan Koshy argues, South Asian Americans, many of whom are part of the middle class, navigate the exigencies of U.S. multiculturalism by avoiding racialization and by asserting an ethnic difference made palatable by class and educational privilege. This approach has gained most traction with conservative Indian-American organizations and among those middle-class Indians who embrace the rhetoric of America as a colorblind meritocracy to explain their own success ("Category" 285). On the other hand, progressive South Asian scholars and activists see South Asian American acceptance of model minority stereotypes as an apolitical denial of minority solidarity that has ramifications beyond race (Prashad, *Karma* 6). Monisha Das Gupta, for example, explains that collusion with constructed narratives of South Asian American success impacts interracial coalition and props up heterosexual patriarchy in the name of culture and tradition (59).

3. According to Hindu doctrine, humanity is divided into four groups, each of which has different obligations and duties: Brahmins, the revered priest caste, Kshatriya, warriors and nobles, Vaishya, tradespeople and merchants, and Shudra, service workers and menial laborers. The "untouchables," as they were once called, were situated either at the bottom of the Shudra caste or outside of caste entirely. There are several subcastes associated with each of these castes based on identification with particular professions. Theorists of caste agree that adherence to the system varies across different regions and that its political importance is determined by other factors such as class, profession, educational status, and loca-

tion. Caste cannot be understood as a transhistorically stable social structure, as evidenced by recent movements among lower-caste groups seeking equality and governmental affirmative action policies seeking to redress caste hierarchies as well as by the self-renaming of "untouchables" as Dalits. See Searle-Chatterjee and Sharma 1–24.

4. These percentages come from a 2012 a report entitled "A Demographic Snapshot of South Asians in the United States" (http://saalt.org/wp-content/uploads/2012/09/Demographic-Snapshot-Asian-American-Foundation-2012.pdf) issued by the Asian American Federation (AAF) and South Asian Americans Leading Together (SAALT).

5. There are 3.4 million South Asians living in the United States. As the AAF and SAALT report indicates, "South Asian populations are often undercounted or overcounted in the Census [. . .] due to various factors, including non-Indian individuals needing to write-in their ethnicity on Census forms and fear among certain populations to participate in government surveys" (http://saalt.org/wp-content/uploads/2012/09/Demographic-Snapshot-Asian-American-Foundation-2012.pdf).

6. www.census.gov/content/dam/Census/library/publications/2014/acs/acsbr13-02.pdf.

7. The fact that their median income and professional status is higher than that of the national average is an immense source of pride for many members of the ethnic community (Bhatia 187). As with other privileged South Asians residing in the United States, even though they are marked as racial others, their affluence and education go a long way toward easing assimilation. While I argue that class enables the assimilation of elite South Asians in the United States, I note along with other scholars in the field that the events of September 11 have demonstrated that South Asians cannot entirely escape racialization or racial profiling via elite class status. See Ahmad 111 and Maira, "Missing" 4.

8. South Asian immigration to the United States, Great Britain, and Canada, not to mention other diasporic locations, has taken different forms and thus has resulted in different types of racial or ethnic coalitions. For example, immigrants to the United States and Canada from 1965 to the mid 1980s were generally skilled, professionals trained in information technology, engineering, medicine, and other scientific fields. More recently, immigrants to these countries have come from more varied economic backgrounds. South Asian immigrants to the UK, in contrast, have long come from the working class. See Brown 128 and Shukla 15.

9. See Das Gupta, *Unruly*, Maira, *Desis*, Koshy, "Category," and Prashad, *Karma*, for analyses of South Asian American racialization and class.

10. See, for example, Pawan Dhingra's *Life Behind the Lobby* for an in-depth study of how the model minority paradigm impacts South Asian motel owners in the United States.

11. Aihwa Ong makes the case that that privileged Asian American subjects are now accepted as "honorary whites" (*Buddha* 276).

12. As scholars of South Asian film in particular have observed, some of the most popular and even acclaimed representations of South Asians in transnational cinema, the most notorious example being *Slumdog Millionaire*, cast them as slum dwellers steeped in an inescapable cycle of poverty. See, for example, Desai, "Pulp Frictions" 72–73.

13. I cannot be sure how present this contrast was in book club participants' minds, given that to some degree the shared class composition of the group made these kinds of settings unremarkable.

14. In contrast to previous meetings that I attended, the NetSAP book club meeting on *Nectar in a Sieve* was perhaps most consciously affected by my research and attendance. While all the other novels and short story collections that we read prior to this meeting were chosen before I had started attending, *Nectar* was a novel that, at the prompting and request of the book club leader, I had nominated at the start of the year to be considered during the yearly voting process. I was surprised to find out that book club members had voted to read the novel and had chosen it as one of the first selections of the year. In general, reading selections tend to be more contemporary and thus the main reason I was interested in reading *Nectar* with the book club was to see how the members would respond to an older work of South Asian diasporic fiction. The meeting to discuss this novel was the last book club meeting I had planned to attend as a researcher and participant, and by that time I had become something of a regular at the meetings. Participants were aware that I was conducting research on South Asian diasporic literature but prior to the meeting did not know that I was writing on Kamala Markandaya. At the book club meeting, I felt some compulsion to "confess" my already developed interest in Markandaya's work because this was the only book of all the book selections I had read that I had studied as a scholar. As I had anticipated, once I had explained my academic interest in the novel, participants in the group asked me to talk about Markandaya's life and the reception history of the novel, periodically calling on me to give more about details of the novel's reception at the time of publication and to ask if it was popular in India as well. But as I had seen at other book club meetings, NetSAP book club participants' critical interpretations might be in dialogue with more "official" literary resources, but academic perspectives and popular review were never privileged in the group's discussion.

15. On the first, see Parmeswaran 66. On the second, see, for example, Afzal-Khan 103, who speculates that Markandaya's failure to use a hybrid form of Indian English is symptomatic of her desire for a Western audience—this charge in particular is probably the one that underlies much of the negative criticism surrounding her work. On the third, see Almeida 81.

16. Their primary criticism of the novel concerned the way that it is written. They felt that Markandaya makes poor use of Indian English. As Niha explained, Rukmani's use of standard English seems out of place: "With the little bit of education she's had, she wouldn't be speaking so formally even in her own language"

(NetSAP book club meeting, *Nectar in a Sieve*). They also said that they found Markandaya's incorporation of Indian words awkward and inconsistent. Vikram, a regular and vocal NetSAP book club participant, summarized this point: "The reason I asked about the English language is [. . .] because I found an inconsistency. Sometimes there'll be regional words like 'jupka.' She'll put it in the text with no italics, just in the sentence. But then to say 'old granny' [instead of using the Hindi words 'naani' or 'daadi'] just didn't seem consistent" (NetSAP book club meeting, *Nectar in a Sieve*). These objections resonate strongly with a critique advanced by Rochelle Almeida on the use of Hindi words in the novel. Almeida asserts that Rukmani's prose is alternately exoticizing and inauthentic (81).

17. Trained as an engineer in India, Zama, a native of Vizag and a proponent of arranged marriage, has lived all over the world and currently resides in South London with his family. He began writing as a secondary career: as he reports on his website, he writes on his commute and in his spare time. While the novel has won a few minor awards and has been translated into languages other than English, its circulation and popularity has been relatively limited. Almost all of the popular reviews on the novel mention stylistic shortcomings or narrative stretches, even as they celebrate Zama's inclusion of sensual, lush details of Indian customs and descriptions of Indian food—indeed the novel includes recipes for many of the Indian dishes that it mentions.

18. See Varatharajah.

Chapter 3. A Narrow View of the World

1. Their different responses are probably also impacted by the forum in which they were sharing them: that Priya was speaking one on one with me might have influenced what she chose to share about her affective reading experiences, just as the more impersonal forum of a blog might have inspire the more sardonic and distant commentary of the readers commenting on the infographic.

2. See Mannur for another analysis of this infographic. She notes the dissonance between its exoticized culinary tropes and the "radical critique of racialized assumptions" that the novel explores (110).

3. In this way, South Asian American literature exemplifies what Pamela Thoma terms the "feminizing genres" (10) of popular Asian American literature, such as "mother-daughter narrative, chick lit, detective fiction, and food writing" (4). These genres, Thoma points out, encode the gendered and racialized processes through which Asian American fiction engages discourses of citizenship and belonging (10).

4. See Chatterjee for an elucidation of the colonial construction of South Asian femininity as symbolic of traditional culture (121). See Das Gupta and Das Gupta for an explanation of how this symbolism translates to the United States (326–27).

5. The gendered effects of book cover art have been noted in popular culture but have been underanalyzed in scholarship. Using social media, author Maureen

Johnson recently initiated a project called "Coverflip" to illustrate that gendered book covers influence readers' perceptions of a book's value and worth. She asked her Twitter followers "to take a well-known book, then to imagine the author of that book was of the opposite gender, or was genderqueer, and imagine what that cover might look like."

6. Both Ween and Rahman refer to Foucault's influential essay "What Is an Author?" to elucidate the expectations that ethnic authorial personas will offer authentic narratives and supply cultural knowledge. Foucault's essay provides a crucial touchstone for understanding how the multiple meanings of a text can be restricted when a singular, stable authorial persona is called into being and conflated with his or her text.

7. For a critique of the idea that this boom in South Asian cultural production was a "renaissance," see Ghosh (4).

8. In saying this, Rushdie was using his platform as the venerable father of this transnational literary tradition to denigrate the literary production of South Asian writers living and writing on the subcontinent in a presumed effort to consolidate the ascendancy of Indian writing in English. Rushdie wrote that prose writing in English by Indian authors, is a "stronger and more important body of work than most of what has been produced in the 16 'official languages' of India" (*Mirrorwork* viii).

9. See Kumar, "Louder," in which he critiques the remove and elitism of South Asian diasporic writers while also acknowledging the global reach and influence of South Asian diasporic writers.

10. Ghosh offers an excellent summary of the tensions between resurgent nationalism and globalization during this period. She explains that the post-Emergency era galvanized the Indian left. In responding to criticism from the Hindu right, the left began engaging with Marxist philosophy and international socialism and became more radicalized. "India's trade liberalization and media privatization through the 1980s made globalism troubling in fresh ways," she explains, and exposed the "viciousness of the Hindu Right" (5). The manifestation of these tensions in the riots that followed the Babri Masjid destruction in 1992 "imparted an ethical charge to political dilemmas" that in turn spurred a number of discursive formations, such as subaltern studies and the politicized writing of South Asian diasporics, through which progressive South Asians writers, activists, and scholars engaged the conflict between national politics and globalization. See Ghosh 5.

11. See Arnove 69–70. In addition to the repeated comparisons with Rushdie, virtually all analyses of *The God of Small Things* include a requisite rundown of the extraordinary circumstances of her literary debut that invites a conflation of the author with her work. As the story goes, prior to completing the manuscript Roy was an architect, aerobics instructor, and screenwriter.

12. See, for example, Kumar 85.

13. According to Jason Cowley, "It is as if the older writer, who himself did so much in *Midnight's Children* to redefine the boundaries of the Anglo-Indian novel, is bestowing a special favour on the younger Roy, marking her out." In the photo, Anita Desai stands beside Roy and Rushdie, while other authors such as Romesh Gunesekera, the only Sri Lankan writer included, is partially obscured. As several scholars have noted, the photo is striking because it visually instantiates a cohesive body of modern South Asian literary culture. Fiction editor Bill Buford literally creates this imagined community of South Asian authors, whose meeting, he asserts, might have taken place anywhere "except India," despite the fact that many of them live in India. Citing Buford's comments, several scholars have emphasized the historical and constructed nature of this photo. The photo has inspired a good deal of analysis, with critics conjecturing that it ironically emblematizes the fiction of a unified, coherent body of transnational South Asian writers: the authors who seem most comfortable in the photo also occupy dominant national (Indian) and aesthetic (postmodern) positions within this body of literature. See Huggan 59–60 and Wachinger 71.

14. Of course, as Ghosh points out, this kind of association is a "periodizing gesture" that reflects the still-emergent qualities of this literary tradition and imparts literary credentials and respectability (6). As she notes, "Rushdie's many refracted images, as sound bites from the offending text, entered mass circulation. Rushdie became [. . .] the 'father' of a new kind of writing" (16). Even while Ghosh explains Rushdie's centrality in the field of transnational South Asian writing as the confluence of several factors, she employs the language of paternity—albeit ironically—that characterizes his literary preeminence in the field.

15. As Grewal explains, in South Asian diasporic literatures "cosmopolitan internationalism is gendered as a masculine articulation" (47).

16. Feminist scholars such as Jane Tompkins (xiv) and Nina Baym (124–25) discuss how the association of Anglo-American women's writing in both the nineteenth and twentieth centuries with popularity, sentimentality, domesticity, and romance contributed to its denigration.

17. As Jani explains, *Midnight's Children* earned a particularly iconic status within South Asian diasporic literatures after winning the commemorative "Booker of Bookers" in 1993, twelve years after its original publication, and the Best of the Booker award in 2008 (15). See also Huggan 69.

18. Cowley likewise observes that "Roy is diminutive, not much more than 5ft, and her legs scarcely touch the ground. As she talks her face is never still. A small diamond gleams in one nostril, catching the light."

19. Padmini Mongia notes that Roy was presented in these contexts as a "home-grown product but one who partook of a cosmopolitan moment. Both in India and the West, Roy was very proudly defined as the indigenous writer" (107).

20. The suit was filed by a Syrian Christian lawyer, Sabu Thomas. See Bumiller.

21. See Lodge 47 and Leah Cohen 11.

22. See, for example, Kaplan 12.

23. The only audiobook version of the novel is read by English actress Diana Quick.

24. See Ujala Sehgal's summary of these responses from Jennifer Egan, William Langley, and Jacki Lynden.

25. See also Shukla 134–35, 160–70.

26. As Nina Baym argues, in making meaning around literature, literary critics are not just commentators but are also "engaged in the act of *creating* literature" (139).

27. See L. Shankar 53 and Shankar and Srikanth, "South Asian " 380.

28. Much work has been done that not only accounts for South Asian marginalization in Asian America but that also underscores South Asian legacies of racialization, migration, and historical influence in the United States and remedies the omission of these histories from the record. Sunaina Maira, for example, has studied how the discrimination and the racialization of South Asians in the United States, particularly youth of Sikh and Islamic background in the aftermath of 9/11, is central to the broader history of U.S. imperialism (*Missing* 28–29). Projects such as the South Asian American Digital Archive, along with recent, rich historical scholarship, have sought to fill in salient gaps in South Asian American culture and politics. In *Bengali Harlem and the Lost Histories of South Asian America* Vivek Bald addresses the purported absence of South Asians in America from 1917 and 1965 by tracing the social and political lives of Bengali seamen residing in New York, Baltimore, New Orleans, and Detroit during this period. Seema Sohi, in *Echoes of Mutiny: Race, Surveillance, and Indian Anticolonialism in North America* counters the prevailing wisdom that there were virtually no South Asians in the United States during the early 1900s by attending to the interimperial collaboration between the U.S. and British empires that allowed the United States to borrow ideological tools from the British to repress anticolonial nationalists. In doing so, she demonstrates that political, military, and ideological connections between South Asia and the United States originated during the early twentieth century.

Chapter 4. Thinking and Feeling with Her

1. *Bookslut* has been named one of the fifty best websites by *Time* magazine and one of the best literature websites by the *New York Times* (http://www.bookslut.com/advertise.php).

2. While I do not analyze popular media reviews of the novel in this chapter, of the twenty-two reviews that I read, eighteen were positive.

3. The few negative reviews mainly took issue with Lahiri's style of writing and narrative pacing, lamenting the book's "incorrigible mildness," "excess of dispassionateness," "dry, synoptic style," and failure to live up to the promise of her previous work. See Metcalf, Munson 68, *Kirkus Reviews*, and *Publisher's Weekly*.

4. In fact, it serves as a quintessential example of Jim Collins's thesis in *Bring on the Books for Everyone: How Literary Culture Became Popular Culture* (2010) that in

contemporary American society, literary experiences are propagated and mediated through accompanying film and television adaptations of literary works (3–4).

5. www.neh.gov/about/awards/national-humanities-medals/jhumpa-lahiri.

6. Lahiri was also featured in the October 2009 issue of *Vogue India* in fashion spread called "You're the Inspiration."

7. With the recent publication and reception of *The Lowland* (2013), Lahiri has complicated but perhaps not cast off her association with the South Asian American milieu that she has previously written about.

8. See also Hai 205–6 and Mannur 162.

9. Dhingra admits that her thinking on Lahiri's commodification of Indian culture has changed and expanded from the time she published "Not Too Spicy." See Dhingra, "Feminizing" 141.

10. For background on the interplay between ethnic authenticity and gender in South Asian America, see S. Das Dasgupta and Maira, *Desis* 132–37.

11. The term "Indo-chic" describes the wave of neo-Orientalist interest in consuming various cultural artifacts of the East such as bindis, saris, yoga, and Eastern mysticism. The term is also self-orientalizing and can describe an affluent, South Asian consumer aesthetic. See Huggan 67.

12. See Caesar 103, Field 168, and Brada-Williams 453. As I discuss in chapter 1, ABCD is an acronym for "American-born confused desi" that refers to South Asian American bicultural confusion and displacement.

13. Gogol's first relationship in college is with a white woman named Ruth—it is a more minor relationship than the one he has with Maxine.

14. See also Maxey.

15. In "Minority Cosmopolitanism" Koshy advances the argument that the South Asian American male subject becomes an object of exoticization and consumption in the short story "Sexy." While I see the viability of that interpretation in "Sexy," it seems less applicable in the case of *The Namesake*, where the female romantic interests seem so subordinate to Gogol's quest to find his identity.

16. See also Koshy, "Category" 287.

17. See Ma 66–67.

18. The trope of failed marriage in *The Namesake* repeats a familiar paradigm in Asian American narratives in which the unsuccessful marriage plot symbolizes the protagonists' thwarted assimilation. See Chu 18–19.

19. Arguably, the narrative highlighting liberation that lay and academic readers find attractive and compelling invokes problematic paradigms of Eastern oppression and Western choice. See Grewal for an exposition of how these paradigms function more broadly in South Asian diasporic literature (65).

20. Mira Nair's film adaptation of *The Namesake*, released on 9 March 2007 to the broader public in the United States, foregrounds the first-generation experience of Ashoke and Ashima. Eighteen of my interviews (the entire first round) were conducted before the release of the film. While it is likely this foreground-

ing played a role in readers' focus on Ashima in the second round of interviews, when I was interviewing NetSAP book club participants they were always quite clearly describing their reactions to the novel rather than the film. Additionally, in keeping with Jim Collins's work on the intersections of popular and literary culture, I take the novel's filmic adaptation as evidence of the fact that modern literary experiences are frequently mediated through film representation and that this may add to but does not diminish the effects of the original text.

21. For a more detailed explanation of this theme in Asian American literature, see Chu 19.

Afterword. Beyond Ambivalence?

1. For two salient examples of how ambivalence has become a major theme of South Asian American literature, see Jain and Mani, *Aspiring*.

2. In 2013, for example, Jhumpa Lahiri's *The Lowland* was a finalist for the National Book Award, while in 2014, Akhil Sharma's *Family Life* was noted as one of the ten best books of the year by the *New York Times* and also won the UK-based Folio award in 2015. The Jaipur Literature Festival, which was founded in 2006, aims to promote the literary contributions of writers of South Asian origin across the world. It has gained international attention and popularity over the years, drawing celebrity participants like Oprah Winfrey, Salman Rushdie, and Chetan Bhagat. In 2012, Salman Rushdie was scheduled to read at the festival but had to cancel his appearance because of threats made on his life. In 2015, the festival expanded outside of its normal location in the Diggi Palace hotel in Rajasthan to locations in London's Southbank and Boulder, Colorado.

3. As Niharika Mandhana reports, 18,500 people, mainly of India descent, gathered at Madison Square Garden on 28 September 2014, to hear Prime Minister Modi speak. The presentation was filled with Bollywood dance routines and was met with much enthusiasm and fanfare by Indian Americans in the audience, who expected Modi, "to kick-start economic growth and modernize India by building much-needed infrastructure and removing bureaucratic hurdles to business."

4. On the decline of reading, see, for example, the NEA study that I discuss in the introduction. A May 2014 study by commonsensemedia.org shows that rates of reading have been declining mainly among teenagers. See www.commonsensemedia.org/research/children-teens-and-reading.

5. On the Winfrey culture wars, see Farr; on the denunciation of female readers of *Fifty Shades of Grey*, see Deller and Smith, "Reading." Both *Fifty Shades of Grey* and the *Twilight* series were very popular among a largely female audience. Both series were commercially successful, but they came under a considerable amount of attack for being poorly written, trashy, and antifeminist. In tracking the commentary on social media about these two series and their adaptation into films, it struck me that lay and professional criticism did not take

into account the gendered dismissal of these authors and the sexist infantalization of their readership. It seemed another instance of how women's practices of reading are publicly and unfairly scrutinized without any consideration as to the complicated ways in which readers use a variety of literatures to meet different needs. For a humorous and ironic commentary on the "whiteness" of the *New York Times* 2015 summer reading list, see "New York Times Summer Reading List Finally Achieves 100% Whiteness," http://review.gawker.com/nyt-summer-reading-list-finally-achieves-100-percent-wh-1706658703.

REFERENCES

Aarthi. Personal interview. 5 Dec. 2009.

Adair, Lara. "Lahiri Finds Writing Life No Easier after Pulitzer." Rev. of *Unaccustomed Earth,* by Jhumpa Lahiri. *San Francisco Chronicle* 7 Oct. 2003.

Afrah. Personal interview. 6 Mar. 2010.

Afzal-Khan, Fawzia. *Cultural Imperialism and the Indo-English Novel: Genre and Ideology in R. K. Narayan, Anita Desai, Kamala Markandaya, and Salman Rushdie.* University Park: Pennsylvania State UP, 1993.

Ahmad, Muneer. "Homeland Insecurities: Racial Violence the Day after September 11." *Social Text* 20.3 (2002): 101–15.

Ajay. Personal Interview. 12 Sept. 2006.

Almeida, Rochelle. *Originality and Imitation: Indianness in the Novels of Kamala Markandaya.* Jaipur: Rawat Publications, 2000.

Anderson, Benedict. *Imagined Communities.* Rev. ed. New York: Verso, 1991.

Andrew, Anthony "Arundhati Roy: Goddess of Big Ideas." *Guardian* 23 Nov. 2014. www.theguardian.com/books/2014/nov/23/arundhati-roy-interview-goddess-of-big-ideas.

Anil. Personal Interview. 12 Oct. 2006.

Arnove, Anthony. *An Ordinary Person's Guide to Empire.* New York: South End Press, 2004.

Arya. Personal Interview. 2 May 2010.

Bagashree, S. "Sankaran's Success Story." Rev. of *The Red Carpet: Bangalore Stories,* by Lavanya Sankaran. *Hindu* 5 Sept. 2005. www.thehindu.com/mp/2005/05/09/stories/2005050901540100.htm.

Bakrania, Falu. *Bhangra and Asian Underground: South Asian Music and the Politics of Belonging in Great Britain.* Durham, NC: Duke UP, 2013.

Bald, Vivek. *Bengali Harlem and the Lost Histories of South Asian America.* Cambridge, MA: Harvard UP, 2013.

Baym, Nina. "Melodramas of Beset Manhood: How Theories of American Fiction Exclude Women Authors." *American Quarterly* 33.2 (1981): 123–39.

Benwell, Bethan. "'Lucky This Is Anonymous': Ethnographies of Reception in Men's Magazines: A 'Textual Culture' Approach." *Discourse and Society* 16.2 (2005): 147–72.

Bhabha, Homi. *The Location of Culture.* New York: Routledge, 1994.

Bhatia, Sunil. *American Karma: Race, Culture, and Identity in the Indian Diaspora.* New York: New York UP, 2007.

Blair, Amy L. *Reading Up: Middle-Class Readers and the Culture of Success in the Early Twentieth Century United States.* Philadelphia: Temple UP, 2011.

Boehmer, Elleke. "East is East and South is South: The Cases of Sarojini Naidu and Arundhati Roy." *Women: A Cultural Review* 11.1–2 (2000): 37–41.

Bonus, Rick, and Linda Trinh Vo. *Contemporary Asian American Communities: Intersections and Divergences.* Philadelphia: Temple UP, 2002.

Bourdieu, Pierre. *Distinction: A Social Critique of the Judgment of Taste.* Trans. Richard Nice. Cambridge, MA: Harvard UP, 1984.

———. *The Inheritors: French Students and Their Relation to Culture.* Trans. Richard Nice. Chicago: U of Chicago P, 1979.

———. *The State Nobility: Elite Schools in the Field of Power.* Trans Lauretta C. Clough. Cambridge, UK: Polity Press, 1988.

Brada-Williams, Noelle. "Reading Jhumpa Lahiri's *Interpreter of Maladies* as a Short Story Cycle." *MELUS* 29.3–4 (2004): 451–64.

Brennan, Timothy. *At Home in the World: Cosmopolitanism Now.* Cambridge, MA: Harvard UP, 1997.

———. "The Cultural Politics of Rushdie Criticism: All or Nothing." *Critical Essays on Salman Rushdie.* Ed. M. Keith Booker. New York: Hall, 1999. 107–28.

Brown, Judith M. *Global South Asians: Introducing the Modern Diaspora.* Cambridge: Cambridge UP, 2006.

Buford, Bill. "Declarations of Independence: Why Are There So Many Indian Novelists?" *New Yorker* 30 June 1997: 7–8.

Bumiller, Elisabeth. "A Novelist Beginning with a Bang." Rev. of *The God of Small Things,* by Arundhati Roy. *New York Times* 29 Jul. 1997.

Caesar, Judith. "Gogol's Namesake: Identity and Relationships in Jhumpa Lahiri's *The Namesake.*" *Atenea* 27.1 (2007): 103–19.

Chatterjee, Partha. *The Nation and Its Fragments: Colonial and Postcolonial Histories.* Princeton, NJ: Princeton UP, 1993.

Cheung, Floyd, and Lavina Dhingra Shankar. "The Inheritance of Postcolonial Loss: Asian American Melancholia, and Strategies of Compensation in Jhumpa Lahiri's *The Namesake.*" *Naming Jhumpa Lahiri: Canons and Controversies.* Lanham, MD: Lexington Books, 2012. 27–50.

Choudry, Roohi. "Four Conversations about One Thing." *Bookslut* Jul. 2004.
Chow, Rey. *Writing Diaspora: Tactics of Intervention in Contemporary Cultural Studies.* Bloomington: Indiana UP, 1993.
Chu, Patricia P. *Assimilating Asians: Gendered Strategies of Authorship in Asian America.* Durham, NC: Duke UP, 2000.
Chuh, Kandice. *Imagine Otherwise: On Asian Americanist Critique.* Durham, NC: Duke UP, 2003.
Cohen, Leah Hager. "Life's Little Details Framed by Tenderness." Rev. of *The God of Small Things,* by Arundhati Roy." *Christian Science Monitor,* 24 Nov. 1997. http://www.csmonitor.com/1997/1124/112497.feat.books.1.html.
Cohen, Patricia. "A Rant of His Own: V. S. Naipaul Takes on Women Writers." *New York Times* 3 June 2011. http://artsbeat.blogs.nytimes.com/2011/06/03/a-rant-of-his-own-v-s-naipaul-takes-on-women-writers.
Collins, Jim. *Bring on the Books for Everybody: How Literary Culture Became Popular Culture.* Durham, NC: Duke UP, 2010.
Cowley, Jason. "The Goddess of Small Things." *Sunday Times* 18 Oct. 1997.
Craig, Amanda. Rev. of *The God of Small Things,* by Arundhati Roy. *New Statesmen* 27 June 1997.
Cullen, Jim. *The American Dream: A Short History of an Idea That Shaped a Nation.* New York: Oxford UP, 2003.
Das Gupta, Monisha. *Unruly Immigrants: Rights, Activism, and Transnational South Asian Politics in the United States.* Durham, NC: Duke UP, 2006.
DasGupta, Sayantani, and Shamita Das Dasgupta. "Women in Exile: Gender Relations in the Asian Indian Community in the United States." *Asian American Studies: A Reader.* Ed. Jean Yu-Wen Shen Wu and Min Song. New Brunswick: Rutgers UP, 2009. 324–37.
Dasgupta, Shamita Das. Introduction. *A Patchwork Shawl: Chronicles of South Asian Women in America.* New Brunswick: Rutgers UP, 1998. 1–20.
Dave, Shilpa. *Indian Accents: Brown Voice and Racial Performance in American Television and Film.* Urbana: U of Illinois P, 2013.
Dave, Shilpa, et al. "De-Privileging Positions: Indian Americans, South Asian Americans and the Politics of Asian American Studies." *Journal of Asian American Studies* 3.1 (2000): 67–100.
Deb, Siddhartha. "Arundhati Roy, the Not-So-Reluctant Renegade." *New York Times* 5 Mar. 2014. www.nytimes.com/2014/03/09/magazine/arundhati-roy-the-not-so-reluctant-renegade.html.
de Certeau, Michel. *The Practice of Everyday Life.* Trans. Steven Rendall. Berkeley: U of California P, 1988.
DeFazio, Kimberly. "Reading is the Other Name of Class." *The Red Critique: Marxist Theory and Critique of the Contemporary* (Winter–Spring 2006): n.p. www.redcritique.org/WinterSpring2006/readingistheothernameofclass.htm.
De Kretser, Michelle. *The Hamilton Case.* New York: Little Brown, 2003.

Deller, Ruth A., and Clarissa Smith. "Reading the BDSM Romance: Reader Responses to Fifty Shades." *Sexualities* 16.8 (2013): 932–50.

Del Rosario, Simone. "From White Castle to White House." *Washington Post Online* 4 Sept. 2012. www.washingtonpost.com/politics/kal-penn-from-white-castle-to-the-white-house/2012/09/04/4db74a0c-f6e8-11e1-8398-0327ab83ab91_story.html.

Desai, Jigna. *Beyond Bollywood: The Cultural Politics of South Asian Diasporic Film.* New York: Routledge, 2003.

———. "Pulp Frictions." *Re-Orientalism and South Asian Identity Politics: The Oriental Other Within.* Ed. Lisa Lau and Ana Christina Mendes. New York: Routledge, 2011. 72–88.

Dhingra, Pawan. *Life Behind the Lobby: Indian American Motel Owners and the American Dream.* Stanford, CA: Stanford UP, 2012.

Fallon, Amy. "V. S. Naipaul Finds No Woman Writer His Literary Match." *Guardian* 1 June 2011 www.guardian.co.uk/books/2011/jun/02/vs-naipaul-jane-austen-women-writers.

Farr, Celia Konchar. *Reading Oprah: How Oprah's Book Club Changed the Way America Reads.* Albany: State U of New York P, 2004.

Felski, Rita. *Uses of Literature.* Malden, MA: Blackwell, 2008.

Field, Robin E. "Writing the Second Generation: Negotiating Cultural Borderlands in Jhumpa Lahiri's *Interpreter of Maladies* and *The Namesake.*" *South Asian Review* 25.2 (2004): 165–77.

Fitzpatrick, Kathleen. *The Anxiety of Obsolescence: The American Novel in the Age of Television.* Nashville, TN: Vanderbilt UP, 2006.

Foster, Stephen W. "The Exotic as Symbolic System." *Dialectical Anthropology* 7.1 (1982): 21–30.

Foucault, Michel. "What Is an Author?" *The Foucault Reader.* Ed. Paul Rabinow. New York: Pantheon, 1984. 101–20.

Gayatri. Personal Interview. 28 Mar. 2010.

Genette, Gerard. *Paratexts: Thresholds of Interpretation.* Cambridge: Cambridge UP, 1997.

Ghosh, Bishnupriya. *When Borne Across: Literary Cosmopolitics in the Contemporary Indian Novel.* New Brunswick, NJ: Rutgers UP, 2004.

Gopinath, Gayatri. *Impossible Desires: Queer Diasporas and South Asian Public Cultures.* Durham, NC: Duke UP, 2005.

Gorra, Michael. *After Empire: Scott, Naipaul, Rushdie.* Chicago: U of Chicago P, 1997.

Grewal, Inderpal. *Transnational America: Feminisms, Diasporas, Neoliberalisms.* Durham, NC: Duke UP, 2005.

Hai, Ambreen. "Re-rooting Families: The Alter/Natal as the Central Dynamic of Jhumpa Lahiri's *Unaccustomed Earth.*" *Naming Jhumpa Lahiri: Canons and Controversies.* Lanham, MD: Lexington Books, 2012. 181–209.

Huggan, Graham. *The Postcolonial Exotic: Marketing the Margins.* New York: Routledge, 2001.

Islam, Naheed. "In the Belly of the Multicultural Beast." *Our Feet Walk the Sky: Women of the South Asian Diaspora.* Ed. Women of South Asian Descent Collective. San Francisco: Aunt Lute Books, 1993. 301–12.

Jain, Anupama. *How to Be South Asian in America: Narratives of Ambivalence and Belonging.* Philadelphia: Temple UP, 2011.

Jardine. Lisa. "The Brit Reaction to the Booker." Sawnet.org 14 Oct. 1997. www.sawne18t.org/news/news220.html.

Jha, Parmanad. "Home and Abroad: Jhumpa Lahiri's *Interpreter of Maladies.*" *Indian Journal of English Studies* 38 (2000–2001): 106–17.

Johnson, Maureen. "The Gender Cover-Up." *Huffingtonpost.com* 7 May 2013.

Joseph, Miranda. *Against the Romance of Community.* Minneapolis: U of Minnesota P, 2002.

Kachka, Boris. "The Confidence Artist." *New York Magazine* 27 Mar. 2008. http://nymag.com/arts/books/profiles/45571.

Kaipa, Summi, and Prageeta Sharma. "Not Your Mother's Diaspora: Voices of the Asian American Avant-Garde." *Women's Review of Books* Jul. 2002: 27–28.

Kang, Laura. *Compositional Subjects: Enfiguring Asian/American Women.* Durham, NC: Duke UP, 2002.

Kaplan, Carla. *The Erotics of Talk: Women's Writing and Feminist Paradigms.* New York: Oxford UP, 1996.

Kapur, Akash. Rev. of *The White Tiger,* by Aravind Adiga. *New York Times* 7 Nov. 2008.

Karem, Jeff. *The Romance of Authenticity: The Cultural Politics of Regional and Ethnic Literatures.* Charlottesville: U of Virginia P, 2004.

Kaur, Tejinder. "Cultural Dilemmas and Displacements of Immigrants in Jhumpa Lahiri's *The Namesake.*" *Journal of Indian Writing in English* 32.2 (2004): 34–44.

Kibria, Nazli. *Becoming Asian American: Second-Generation Chinese and Korean-American Identities.* Baltimore, MD: Johns Hopkins UP, 2002.

Kirkus Reviews. Rev. of *The Namesake,* by Jhumpa Lahiri. 1 June 2003: 773.

Koshy, Susan. "Category Crisis: South Asian Americans and Questions of Race and Ethnicity." *Diaspora* 7.3 (1998): 285–320.

———. Introduction. *Transnational South Asians: The Making of Neo-Diaspora.* Ed. Koshy and R. Radhakrishnan. New York: Oxford UP, 2008. 1–41.

———. "Minority Cosmopolitanism." *PMLA* 126.3 (2011): 592–609.

———. "Morphing Race into Ethnicity: Asian Americans and Critical Transformations of Whiteness." *boundary 2* 28.1 (2001): 153–94.

———. "Why the Humanities Matter for Race Studies Today." *PMLA* 123.5 (2008): 1252–59.

Kumar, Amitava "Louder Than Bombs." *Transition* 79 (1999): 80–101.

Kutty. Madhavan. "Comrade of Small Jokes." *Indian Express* 9 Nov. 1997.

Lahiri, Jhumpa. "My Two Lives." *Newsweek* 6 Mar. 2006: 43–44.

———. *The Namesake*. Boston: Houghton, 2003.

———. "Questions for Jhumpa Lahiri: Crossing Over." By John Glassie. *New York Times Magazine* 7 Sept. 2003: 19.

Lalita. Personal Interview. 13 Oct. 2006.

Langley, William. "V. S. Naipaul: Grand Old Man of Toxic Letters." *Telegraph* 4 June 2011. www.telegraph.co.uk/culture/culturenews/8557017/VS-Naipaul-Grand-old-man-of-toxic-letters.html.

Leonard, Karen Isaksen. *The South Asian Americans*. Westport, CT: Greenwood Press, 1997.

Lodge, Sally. Rev. of *The God of Small Things*, by Arundhati Roy. *Publisher's Weekly* 13 Jan. 1997: 47.

Long, Elizabeth. *Book Clubs: Women and the Uses of Reading in Everyday Life*. Chicago: U of Chicago P, 2003.

Lowe, Lisa. *Immigrant Acts: On Asian American Cultural Politics*. Durham, NC: Duke UP, 1996.

Ma, Sheng-mei. *Immigrant Subjectivities in Asian American and Asian Diaspora Literatures*. Albany: State U of New York P, 1998.

Maira, Sunaina Marr. *Desis in the House: Indian American Youth Culture in New York City*. Philadelphia: Temple UP, 2002.

———. "Henna and Hip Hop: The Politics of Cultural Production and the Work of Cultural Studies." *Journal for Asian American Studies* 3.3 (2000): 329–69.

———. "Ideologies of Authenticity: Youth, Politics, and Diaspora." *Amerasia Journal* 25.3 (1999–2000): 139–49.

———. *Missing: Youth, Citizenship, and Empire after 9/11*. Durham, NC: Duke UP, 2009.

Mandhana, Niharika. "Narendra Modi Taps Indian Diaspora in U.S." *Wall Street Journal Online* 28 Sept. 2014. www.wsj.com/articles/narendra-modi-taps-indian-diaspora-in-u-s-1411946161.

Mani, Bakirathi. *Aspiring to Home: South Asians in America*. Stanford, CA: Stanford UP, 2012.

———. "*Beyond Bollywood:* Exhibiting South Asian America." *Journal of Asian American Studies* 18.2 (2015): 193–211.

Mannur, Anita. *Culinary Fictions: Food in South Asian Diasporic Culture*. Philadelphia: Temple UP, 2010.

Markandaya, Kamala. *Nectar in a Sieve*. New York: J. Day, 1954.

Maya. Personal Interview. 18 Feb. 2010.

Maxey, Ruth. "'Who Wants Pale, Thin, Pink Flesh?' Bharati Mukherjee, Whiteness, and South Asian American Writing." *Textual Practice* 20.3 (2006): 529–47.

McGirk, Jan. "Indian Literary Star Faces Caste Sex Trial." *Sunday Times* 29 June 1997.

McHenry, Elizabeth. *Forgotten Readers: Recovering the Lost History of African-American Literary Societies.* Durham, NC: Duke UP, 2002.

Meena. Personal Interview. 1 May 2010.

Meera. Personal Interview. 15 Jul. 2006.

Melamed, Jodi. *Represent and Destroy: Rationalizing Violence in the New Racial Capitalism.* Minneapolis: U of Minnesota P, 2011.

Metcalf, Stephen. "Out of the Overcoat." *New York Times* 28 Sept. 2003: A11.

Miller, Laura. "Book Lovers' Quarrel." *Salon.com* 26 Oct. 2001.

Mohanraj, Mary Anne. "Red Sari: An Analysis of South Asian and Diaspora Book Covers." www.mamohanraj.com/redsari/red-sari-an-analysis-of-s-asian-and-diaspora-book-covers.html.

Moira. Personal Interview. 27. Oct. 2005.

Mongia, Padmini. "The Making and Marketing of Arundhati Roy." Ed. Alex Tickell. *Arundhati Roy's* The God of Small Things. New York: Routledge, 2007. 103–9.

Mullaney, Julie. "'Globalizing Dissent?' Arundhati Roy, Local and Postcolonial Feminisms in the Transnational Economy." *World Literature Written in English* 40.1 (2008) 56–70.

Munson, Sam. "*The Namesake* and *The Fortress of Solitude.*" *Commentary* 116.4 (2003): 68–71.

Narayan, Pavithra. *What Are You Reading? The World Market and Indian Literary Production.* New Delhi: Routledge, 2012.

National Endowment for the Arts. *Reading at Risk: A Survey of Literary Reading in America.* Washington, DC: National Endowment for the Arts, 2004.

———. *Reading on the Rise: A New Chapter in American Literacy.* Washington, DC: National Endowment for the Arts, 2008.

NetSAP book club meeting. Discussion of *Cutting for Stone,* by Abraham Verghese. 14 Jan. 2010. Transcript.

———. Discussion of *Delhi Noir,* ed. Hirsh Sawhney. 10 Dec. 2009. Transcript.

———. Discussion of *The Feast of Roses,* by Indu Sundaresan. 5 Nov. 2006.

———. Discussion of *Hamilton Case,* by Michele de Kretser. 11 Mar. 2010. Transcript.

———. Discussion of *The Inheritance of Loss,* by Kiran Desai. 9 Nov. 2006. Transcript.

———. Discussion of *In Other Rooms, Other Wonders,* by Daniyal Mueenuddin. 8 Oct. 2009. Transcript.

———. Discussion of *The Marriage Bureau for Rich People,* by Farahad Zama. 18 Feb. 2010. Transcript.

———. Discussion of *Nectar in a Sieve,* by Kamala Markandaya. 8 Feb. 2007. Transcript.

———. Discussion of *The Red Carpet: Bangalore Stories,* by Lavanya Sankaran. 14 Sept. 2006. Transcript.

———. Discussion of *The Red Letters,* by Ved Mehta. 8 June 2006. Transcript.
———. Discussion of *The Royal Ghosts,* by Samrat Upadhyay. 12 Oct. 2006. Transcript.
———. Discussion of *Three Cups of Tea,* by Greg Mortenson and David Oliver Relin. 12 Nov. 2009. Transcript.
———. Discussion of *Two Lives,* by Vikram Seth. 13 Jul. 2006. Transcript.
Ninh, erin Khue. *Ingratitude: The Debt Bound Daughter in Asian American Literature.* New York: New York UP, 2011.
Nishi. Personal Interview. 11 June 2006.
Nixon, Rob. *London Calling: V. S. Naipaul, Postcolonial Mandarin.* Oxford: Oxford UP, 1992.
Nguyen, Viet Thanh. *Race and Resistance: Literature and Politics in Asian America.* New York: Oxford UP, 2002.
Omi, Michael, and Howard Winant. *Racial Formation in the United States.* 2nd ed. New York: Routledge, 1994.
Ong, Aihwa. *Buddha Is Hiding: Refugees, Citizenship, the New America.* Berkeley: U of California P, 2003.
———. *Neoliberalism as Exception: Mutations in Citizenship and Sovereignty.* Durham, NC: Duke UP, 2006.
Padma. Personal Interview. 10 Sept. 2006.
Pais, Arthur. "In Quiet Light, Kamala Markandaya, 1924–2004." *India Abroad* 4 June 2004.
Palumbo-Liu, David. *The Ethnic Canon: Histories, Institutions, and Interventions.* Minneapolis: U of Minnesota P, 1995.
———. *The Deliverance of Others: Reading Literature in a Global Age.* Durham, NC: Duke UP, 2012.
Parameswaran, Uma. *Kamala Markandaya.* Jaipur: Rawat Publications, 2000.
Paranjape, Makarand R. "Inside and Outside the Whale." *The New Indian Novel in English: A Study of the 1980s.* Ed. Viney Kirpal. New Delhi: Allied Publishers, 1990. 213–26.
Pooja. Personal Interview. 10 Sept. 2006.
Prashad, Vijay. *The Karma of Brown Folk.* Minneapolis: U of Minnesota P, 2000.
Priya. Personal Interview. 14 Jul. 2006.
Priti. Personal Interview. 11 Sept. 2006.
Publisher's Weekly. Rev. of *The Namesake,* by Jhumpa Lahiri. 7 Jul. 2003: 48.
Purdue, Melissa M. "From Sarojini Naidu's Curved and Eloquent Little Mouth to Arundhati Roy's Mass of Untamed Curls and Smoldering Dark Eyes." *Atenea* 23.2 (2003): 87–103.
Purkayastha, Bandana. *Negotiating Ethnicity: Second-Generation South Asian Americans Traverse a Transnational World.* New Brunswick: Rutgers UP, 2005.

Radhakrishnan, R. *Diasporic Mediations: Between Home and Location.* Minneapolis: U of Minnesota P, 1996.

Radway, Janice A. *A Feeling for Books: The Book-of-the-Month Club, Literary Taste, and Middle-Class Desire.* Chapel Hill: U of North Carolina P, 1997.

———. *Reading the Romance: Women, Patriarchy, and Popular Literature.* 2nd ed. Chapel Hill: U of North Carolina P, 1991.

Rahman, Shazia. "Marketing the Mem: The Packaging and Selling of a First Novel." *Toronto Review of Contemporary Writing Abroad* 18.1 (1999): 86–99.

Raj. Personal Interview. 12 Jul. 2006, 12 Dec. 2009.

Rajan, Gita. "Ethical Responsibility in Intersubjective Spaces: Reading Jhumpa Lahiri's *Interpreter of Maladies* and 'A Temporary Matter.'" *Transnational Asian American Literature: Sites and Transits.* Ed. Shirley Geok-lin Lim et al. Philadelphia: Temple UP, 2006. 123–41.

Rajan, Gita, and Shailja Sharma. "New Cosmopolitanism: South Asians in the United States at the Turn of the Twenty-first Century." *New Cosmopolitanisms: South Asians in the U.S.* Ed. Rajan and Sharma. Stanford, CA: Stanford UP, 2006. 1–36.

Rakesh. Personal Interview. 27 Mar. 2010.

Reddy, Vanita. *Fashioning Diaspora: Beauty, Femininity, and South Asian American Culture.* Philadelphia: Temple UP, 2016.

Rinki. Personal Interview. 27 Nov. 2009.

Robbins, Bruce, and Pheng Cheah. *Cosmopolitics: Thinking and Feeling Beyond the Nation.* Minneapolis: U of Minnesota P, 1998.

Rose, Nikolas. "Governing 'Advanced' Liberal Democracies." *Foucault and Political Reason: Liberalism, Neo-liberalism, and Rationalities of Government.* Ed. Andrew Barry, Thomas Osborne, and Nikolas Rose. Chicago: U of Chicago P, 1996. 37–64.

Rothstein, Mervyn. "India's Post-Rushdie Generation; Young Writers Leave Magic Realism and Look at Reality." *New York Times* 3 Jul. 2000.

Rudrappa, Sharmila. *Ethnic Routes to Becoming American: Indian Immigrants and the Cultures of Citizenship.* New Brunswick, NJ: Rutgers UP, 2004.

Rushdie, Salman. *Imaginary Homelands: Essays and Criticism, 1981–1991.* New York: Penguin, 1991.

Rushdie, Salman, and Elizabeth West, eds. *Mirrorwork: 50 Years of Indian Writing in English 1947–1997.* New York: Henry Holt, 1997.

Sankaran, Lavanya. *The Red Carpet: Bangalore Stories.* New York: Dial Press, 2005.

Searle-Chatterjee, Mary, and Ursula Sharma. *Contextualizing Caste: Post-Dumontian Approaches.* Oxford, UK: Blackwell, 1994. 1–24.

Sedgwick, Eve Kosofsky. "Paranoid Reading and Reparative Reading; or, You're So Paranoid, You Probably Think This Introduction Is about You." *Novel Gazing: Queer Readings in Fiction.* Ed. Sedgwick. Durham, NC: Duke UP, 1997. 1–37.

Sehgal, Ujala. "Did V. S. Naipaul Get a Pass on Calling Women Writers Inferior?" *Atlantic Wire* 5 June 2011. www.theatlanticwire.com/entertainment/2011/06/vs-naipauls-declaring-them-inferior-men/38506.

Sen, Mandira. "Names and Nicknames." Rev. of *The Namesake,* by Jhumpa Lahiri. *Women's Review of Books* Mar. 2004: 9–10.

Shankar, Lavina Dihingra. "Feminizing Men? Moving Beyond Asian American Literary Gender Wars in Jhumpa Lahiri's Fiction." *Naming Jhumpa Lahiri: Canons and Controversies.* Ed. Shankar and Floyd Cheung. Lanham, MD: Lexington Books, 2012. 135–55.

———. "The Limits of (South Asian) Names and Labels: Postcolonial of Asian American?" *A Part, yet Apart: South Asians in Asian America.* Ed. Shankar and Rajini Srikanth. Philadelphia: Temple UP, 1998. 49–66.

———. "Not Too Spicy: Exotic Mistresses and Cultural Translation in the Fiction of Chitra Divakaruni and Jhumpa Lahiri." *Other Tongues: Rethinking the Language Debates in India.* Ed. Nalini Iyer and Bonnie Zare. Amsterdam, Netherlands: Rodopi, 2009. 23–52.

Shankar, Lavina Dhingra, and Floyd Cheung. "Introduction: Naming Jhumpa Lahiri: Bengali, Asian American, Postcolonial, Universal?" *Naming Jhumpa Lahiri: Canons and Controversies.* Ed. Shankar and Cheung. Lanham, MD: Lexington Books, 2012. vii–xxii.

Shankar, Lavina Dihingra, and Rajini Srikanth. "Introduction: Closing the Gap? South Asians Challenge Asian American Studies." *A Part, yet Apart: South Asians in Asian America.* Ed. Shankar and Srikanth. Philadelphia: Temple UP, 1998. 1–22.

———. "South Asian American Literature 'Off the Turnpike of America' of Asian America." *Postcolonial Theory and the United States: Race, Ethnicity, and Literature.* Ed. Amritjit Singh and Peter Schmidt. Jackson: U of Mississippi P, 2000. 370–87.

Shankar, Rajiv. "Forward: South Asian Identity in Asian America." *A Part, yet Apart: South Asians in Asian America.* Ed. Dhingra Shankar and Rajini Srikanth. Philadelphia: Temple UP, 1998. ix–xv.

Shankar, Shalini. *Desi Land: Teen Culture, Class, and Success in Silicon Valley.* Durham, NC: Duke UP, 2008.

Sharma, Nitasha Tamar. *Hip Hop Desis: South Asian Americans, Blackness, and Global Race Consciousness.* Durham, NC: Duke UP, 2010.

Shimer, Dorothy Blair. "Sociological Imagery in the Novels of Kamala Markandaya." *World Literature Written in English* 14.2 (1975): 357–70.

Shukla, Sandhya Rajendra. *India Abroad: Diasporic Cultures of Postwar America and England.* Princeton, NJ: Princeton UP, 2003.

Sohi, Seema. *Echoes of Mutiny: Race, Surveillance, and Indian Anticolonialism in North America.* New York: Oxford UP, 2014.

Song, Min Hyoung. *The Children of 1965: On Writing and Not Writing as an Asian American.* Durham, NC: Duke UP, 2013.

Spivak, Gayatri Chakravorty. "Can the Subaltern Speak?" *Marxism and the Interpretation of Culture.* Ed. Cary Nelson and Lawrence Grossberg. Urbana: U of Illinois P, 1988. 271–313.

Sri. Personal Interview. 8 Oct. 2009.

Srikanth, Rajini. "What Lies Beneath: Lahiri's Brand of Desirable Difference in *Unaccustomed Earth.*" *Naming Jhumpa Lahiri: Canons and Controversies.* Lanham, MD: Lexington Books, 2012. 51–71.

———. *The World Next Door: South Asian American Literature and the Idea of America.* Philadelphia: Temple UP, 2004.

Steinbery, Sybil S. Rev. of *The God of Small Things*, by Arundhati Roy. *Publisher's Weekly* 3 Mar. 1997: 62.

Sunil. Personal Interview. 10 June 2006.

Sweeney, Meg. *Reading Is My Window: Books and the Art of Reading in Women's Prisons.* Chapel Hill: U of North Carolina P, 2010.

Thoma, Pamela. *Asian American Women's Popular Literature: Feminizing Genres and Neoliberal Belonging.* Philadelphia: Temple UP, 2013.

Tickell, Alex, ed. *Arundhati Roy's* "The God of Small Things." New York: Routledge, 2007. 103–9.

Tompkins, Jane P. "Introduction: The Cultural Work of American Fiction." *Sensational Designs: The Cultural Work of American Fiction, 1790–1860.* New York: Oxford UP. 1985. xi–xix.

Uma. Personal Interview. 27 Mar. 2010.

United States Census Bureau. *Asian Population: 2010.* 1–23.

———. *Asian/Pacific Heritage Month: Facts and Figures May 2012.* 1–9.

Varatharajah, Sinthujan. "We Have Cleansed Our Eyes and Tongues: On Diasporic Denials and Revisionism." *Roundtable India* 26 Apr. 2014: n.p.

Vij, Manish. "Anatomy of a Genre." *Sepia Mutiny* 24 Jan. 2006. www.sepiamutiny.com/sepia/archives/002888.html.

Wachinger, Tobias. A. "Spicy Pleasures: Postcolonial India's Literary Celebrities and the Politics of Consumption." *Ariel: A Review of International English Literature* 34.2–3 (2003): 71–94.

Warner, Michael. "Uncritical Reading." *Polemic: Critical or Uncritical.* Ed. Jane Gallop. New York: Routledge, 1994. 13–38.

Ween, Lori. "This Is Your Book: Marketing America to Itself." *PMLA* 118.1 (2003): 90–102.

Williams, Laura Anh. "Foodways and Subjectivity in Jhumpa Lahiri's *The Interpreter of Maladies.*" *MELUS* 32.4 (2007): 69–79.

Wong, Sau-ling Cynthia. *Reading Asian American Literature: From Necessity to Extravagance.* Princeton, NJ: Princeton UP, 1993.

———. "'Sugar Sisterhood': Situating the Amy Tan Phenomenon." *The Ethnic Canon: Histories, Institutions, and Interventions.* Ed. David Palumbo-Liu. Minneapolis: U of Minnesota P, 1995. 174–210.

Wood, James. "An Indelicate Balance: The Noisy Pluralism of Indian Fiction." *New Republic* 29 Dec. 1997: 32–36.

Zama, Farahad. *The Marriage Bureau for Rich People.* New York: Amy Einhorn Books, 2009.

INDEX

TAMARA BHALLA is an assistant professor of American studies at the University of Maryland, Baltimore County.

THE ASIAN AMERICAN EXPERIENCE

The Hood River Issei: An Oral History of Japanese Settlers in Oregon's Hood River Valley *Linda Tamura*

Americanization, Acculturation, and Ethnic Identity: The Nisei Generation in Hawaii *Eileen H. Tamura*

Sui Sin Far/Edith Maude Eaton: A Literary Biography *Annette White-Parks*

Mrs. Spring Fragrance and Other Writings *Sui Sin Far; edited by Amy Ling and Annette White-Parks*

The Golden Mountain: The Autobiography of a Korean Immigrant, 1895–1960 *Easurk Emsen Charr; edited and with an introduction by Wayne Patterson*

Race and Politics: Asian Americans, Latinos, and Whites in a Los Angeles Suburb *Leland T. Saito*

Achieving the Impossible Dream: How Japanese Americans Obtained Redress *Mitchell T. Maki, Harry H. L. Kitano, and S. Megan Berthold*

If They Don't Bring Their Women Here: Chinese Female Immigration before Exclusion *George Anthony Peffer*

Growing Up Nisei: Race, Generation, and Culture among Japanese Americans of California, 1924–49 *David K. Yoo*

Chinese American Literature since the 1850s *Xiao-huang Yin*

Pacific Pioneers: Japanese Journeys to America and Hawaii, 1850–80 *John E. Van Sant*

Holding Up More Than Half the Sky: Chinese Women Garment Workers in New York City, 1948–92 *Xiaolan Bao*

Onoto Watanna: The Story of Winnifred Eaton *Diana Birchall*

Edith and Winnifred Eaton: Chinatown Missions and Japanese Romances *Dominika Ferens*

Being Chinese, Becoming Chinese American *Shehong Chen*

"A Half Caste" and Other Writings *Onoto Watanna; edited by Linda Trinh Moser and Elizabeth Rooney*

Chinese Immigrants, African Americans, and Racial Anxiety in the United States, 1848–82 *Najia Aarim-Heriot*

Not Just Victims: Conversations with Cambodian Community Leaders in the United States *Edited and with an introduction by Sucheng Chan; interviews conducted by Audrey U. Kim*

The Japanese in Latin America *Daniel M. Masterson with Sayaka Funada-Classen*

Survivors: Cambodian Refugees in the United States *Sucheng Chan*

From Concentration Camp to Campus: Japanese American Students and World War II *Allan W. Austin*

Japanese American Midwives: Culture, Community, and Health Politics *Susan L. Smith*

In Defense of Asian American Studies: The Politics of Teaching and Program Building *Sucheng Chan*

Lost and Found: Reclaiming the Japanese American Incarceration *Karen L. Ishizuka*

Religion and Spirituality in Korean America *Edited by David K. Yoo and Ruth H. Chung*

Moving Images: Photography and the Japanese American Incarceration *Jasmine Alinder*

Camp Harmony: Seattle's Japanese Americans and the Puyallup Assembly Center *Louis Fiset*

Chinese American Transnational Politics *Him Mark Lai, edited and with an introduction by Madeline Y. Hsu*

Issei Buddhism in the Americas *Edited by Duncan Ryûken Williams and Tomoe Moriya*

Hmong America: Reconstructing Community in Diaspora *Chia Youyee Vang*

In Pursuit of Gold: Chinese American Miners and Merchants in the American West *Sue Fawn Chung*

Pacific Citizens: Larry and Guyo Tajiri and Japanese American Journalism in the World War II Era *Edited by Greg Robinson*

Indian Accents: Brown Voice and Racial Performance in American Television and Film *Shilpa S. Davé*

Yellow Power, Yellow Soul: The Radical Art of Fred Ho *Edited by Roger N. Buckley and Tamara Roberts*

Fighting from a Distance: How Filipino Exiles Helped Topple a Dictator *Jose V. Fuentecilla*

In Defense of Justice: Joseph Kurihara and the Japanese American Struggle for Equality *Eileen H. Tamura*

Asian Americans in Dixie: Race and Migration in the South *Edited by Jigna Desai and Khyati Y. Joshi*

Undercover Asian: Multiracial Asian Americans in Visual Culture *Leilani Nishime*

Islanders in the Empire: Filipino and Puerto Rican Laborers in Hawai'i *JoAnna Poblete*

Virtual Homelands: Indian Immigrants and Online Cultures in the United States *Madhavi Mallapragada*

Building Filipino Hawai'i *Roderick N. Labrador*

Legitimizing Empire: Filipino American and U.S. Puerto Rican Cultural Critique *Faye Caronan*

Chinese in the Woods: Logging and Lumbering in the American West *Sue Fawn Chung*

The Minor Intimacies of Race: Asian Publics in North America *Christine Kim*

Reading Together, Reading Apart: Identity, Belonging, and South Asian American Community *Tamara Bhalla*

The University of Illinois Press
is a founding member of the
Association of American University Presses.

Composed in 10.5/13 Minion Pro
with Berthold Akzidenz Grotesk and Barberino RG display
by Kirsten Dennison
at the University of Illinois Press
Cover designed by Jennifer S. Holzner
Cover illustration: Nadia Janjua, *Flight by Letter*, 2012.
© nadiajart.com

University of Illinois Press
1325 South Oak Street
Champaign, IL 61820-6903
www.press.uillinois.edu